Managing Mothers

First published in 1991, *Managing Mothers* (now with a new preface by the authors) provides a detailed, authoritative inside story of the lives of parents, and particularly mothers, who return to work after the birth of a first child. It is based on a study of couples who have combined the transition to parenthood with two full-time jobs in the labour market. The authors provide extensive personal accounts from interviews and statistical data that shed light on the experience and significance of this growing social group. They reveal that mothers are the main managers of the dual-earner lifestyle; hence, they are the principal characters in this story as the authors explore women's occupational mobility, their social networks, social and emotional support, and psychological health.

The book exposes a variety of constraints upon women: the continuing power of unsupportive ideologies concerning breadwinning, marriage and family life; the failure of government to organize good quality childcare; the failure of employers to make provisions that would enable parents to fulfil their employment and domestic responsibilities; and the failure of husbands to take an equal share in household work. An understanding of these constraints is essential if the increased need for women in the labour market is to lead to better and more equal employment for women and the removal of the 'double burden' that weighs so heavily on many working mothers. This volume will be a beneficial read for students and researchers of sociology and psychology.

Managing Mothers

Dual Earner Households After Maternity Leave

Julia Brannen and Peter Moss

Routledge
Taylor & Francis Group

First published in 1991
by Unwin Hyman Ltd

This edition first published in 2024 by Routledge
4 Park Square, Milton Park, Abingdon, Oxon, OX14 4RN

and by Routledge
605 Third Avenue, New York, NY 10017

Routledge is an imprint of the Taylor & Francis Group, an informa business

Publisher's Note
The publisher has gone to great lengths to ensure the quality of this reprint but points
out that some imperfections in the original copies may be apparent.

Disclaimer
The publisher has made every effort to trace copyright holders and welcomes
correspondence from those they have been unable to contact.

A Library of Congress record exists under ISBN LCCN:

ISBN: 978-1-032-87490-6 (hbk)
ISBN: 978-1-003-53289-7 (ebk)
ISBN: 978-1-032-87492-0 (pbk)

Book DOI 10.4324/9781003532897

MANAGING MOTHERS

*Dual Earner Households
after Maternity Leave*

Julia Brannen and Peter Moss

London
UNWIN HYMAN
Boston   Sydney   Wellington

Published by the Academic Division of

Unwin Hyman Ltd
15/17 Broadwick Street, London W1V 1FP, UK

Unwin Hyman Inc.,
955 Massachusetts Avenue, Cambridge, MA 02139, USA

Allen & Unwin (Australia) Ltd,
8 Napier Street, North Sydney, NSW 2060, Australia

Allen & Unwin (New Zealand) Ltd in association with the
Port Nicholson Press Ltd,
Compusales Building, 75 Ghuznee Street, Wellington 1, New Zealand

First published in 1991

British Library Cataloguing in Publication Data

Brannen, Julia *1944–*
   Managing Mothers: dual earner households after
   maternity leave
   1. Great Britain. Working mothers. Social conditions
   I. Title   II. Moss, Peter *1945–*
   305.430941

   ISBN 0–04–301257–4
   ISBN 0–04–445898–3 pbk

Library of Congress Cataloging in Publication Data

Brannen, Julia, 1944–
   Managing Mothers: dual earner households after
   maternity leave / Julia Brannen, Peter Moss.
       p.   cm.
   Includes bibliographical references and index.
   ISBN 0–04–301257–4: $49.95 (U.S.).— ISBN 0–04–
   445898–3 (pbk.): $17.95 (US)
   1. Dual-career families–Great Britain. 2. Working
   mothers–Great Britain. 3. Work and family–Great
   Britain. I. Moss, Peter.
   II. Title
   HQ614.M687 1990
   306.87–dc20   90–12524

Typeset by Falcon Typographic Art Ltd and printed
in Great Britain by Billing & Sons Ltd, London and Worcester

Preface to the Reissue

Managing Mothers was first published thirty-five years ago based on longitudinal research proposed in 1980 and undertaken in the mid-1980s. It is, of course, very much of its time and the world has changed in many ways since then. Most relevant to the book, it was a period in which the majority of women gave up their jobs at the birth of their first child and the benefits for young children were assumed to lie with having a full-time mother—with some part-time employment to be taken up in due course, often fitted into evenings, weekends or school hours.

Our focus was on 'dual earner households after maternity leave', in which first-time mothers resumed employment only a few months after giving birth. So it was only with great difficulty that we identified women taking up maternity leave rights; statutory maternity leave had just made it into law, before the Thatcher years, very late in the day by European standards, and no more concessions were then on offer.

Harder still to find were mothers using the various types of childcare we wanted to include; readers today may find it hard to imagine that London then had only a few dozen day nurseries for infants. Moreover, almost 40 per cent of those women in our study who did return to full-time work after maternity leave did not stay in their full-time jobs by the time of their child's third birthday, the reasons for which included childcare arrangements breaking down, downward occupational mobility and job loss. This percentage excluded women taking a second period of maternity leave and is likely to have been higher had we been able to identify more women returners in manual employment.

But it is also the context in which the research was conceived and carried out that has changed beyond all recognition. The policy context was the end of the post-war Keynesian regime described as an era of 'state-managed capitalism of the class compromise' (Streeck, 2022: 9), based on assumptions of 'social progress'—though the welfare reforms of that regime, based on the war-time Beveridge report, assumed that mothers stayed at home with their young children. However, the research itself was undertaken in the early years of the neoliberal order, personified by the political dominance in the 1980s of Prime Minister Margaret Thatcher. At that stage the state's ideological response to questions of parental employment was shifting from a general hostility towards 'mothers work' to a laissez-faire stance that deemed a 'parent's' employment to be a matter of 'individual choice', and none of the state's business to interfere; any 'parent' (in practice any 'mother') who wanted to work must therefore make their own arrangements, including finding 'childcare' in a still embryonic 'childcare market'.

The cultural context still bore the mark of the post-war reaction to women's employment—by contrast, in wartime it had been not only accepted but positively encouraged. At the time of the study, fathers were still regarded as the 'main breadwinners', with full-time motherhood considered the ideal form of care for children and equalitarianism inscribed in modern marriages/partnerships. From a theoretical point of view this was one of the more significant contributions of the study, namely its examination of how parenthood and paid work were socially constructed in a particular time, place, and social conditions. Through recourse to the concept of 'ideology' the book showed how the moral authority of dominant agencies and institutions such as professionals and the state underpinned and sustained the status quo of full-time motherhood and afforded it enduring appeal.

In this context, mothers who returned to work after childbirth disrupted dominant assumptions about the 'proper' way of conducting family life and the 'natural' way of caring for children. *Managing Mothers* drew attention to the contradictions faced by women as they negotiated the return to work and managed their internalised assumptions about what constituted being a 'good mother'. As we wrote, 'the dual earner lifestyle "gives the lie" to the notion of normal family life' (p.11).

Much has changed in the last thirty years. In retrospect, we can see that the study was situated on the cusp of rapid change in employment among women with young children; in a subsequent publication, based on analysis of employment trends between 1984 and 1994, we described an 'increasing integration of women with children, particularly with young children, into the labour market', the product of growing demand for their labour and a growing desire on their part to continue in employment (driven in part by increased educational qualifications). In time, and especially from 1997 and the advent of the 'New Labour' administration, governments too moved from indifference to positive support, introducing a range of policy measures to positively encourage women's retention in or return to the labour market (Brannen and Moss, 1998). Leave policies were extended; a growing market in private childcare provision was officially encouraged; and parents were offered some financial support to enable them to access this market.

The cultural context is also much altered. The ideology of full-time motherhood is replaced by the new normative model of the 'dual earner household'. Mothers who do not conform to this household type are penalized through loss of state benefits if they lack earners in the household. Non-employed lone parents are *obliged* to seek full-time paid work (from 2023 to 30 hours per week) or face loss of benefits.[1] Given the precarity of the labour market and the low pay of many jobs, and cuts to welfare benefits in the name of 'austerity', nearly one third of children in the UK are now living in poverty, that is 3.9 m children; 38 per cent of working age lone parents and 20 per cent of working age two parent households are in poverty with signs of deepening poverty (Joseph Rowntree Foundation, 2024).

Parenthood is also ideologically constructed as a non-gendered enterprise that increasingly highlights the new care-giving model of fatherhood. Today, maternity leave is accompanied by paternity leave and parental leave. Such a study as ours, if conducted now, would most likely include fathers as research participants—rather than relying on women's reports on their partners. One of the more significant changes since the book was written concerns the expansion of 'parenting', fuelled by 'a multi-million-pound industry of 'advice' and 'support' (Lee et al., 2014) and 'early intervention' in deprived communities (e.g. Gillies, Edwards and Horsley, 2017), part of a vast industry of advice and support. But as Faircloth (2014) among others has shown, the rise in intensive expectations of

---

[1] The new work requirements, introduced by the Government last October, require lead carers of 3–12-year-olds to be available for work for up to 30 hours a week, up from 16 hours a week for parents of 3–4-year-olds and up from 25 hours for parents of 5–12-year-olds. Childcare of 30 hours per week is provided by government in theory but childcare often not available ....

motherhood has coincided with the wholesale entry into the workforce.

What, too, has changed is the research climate. The research on which this book is based took the form of a longitudinal and mixed-methods study of 255 women and their young children (as well as of the childcare arrangements made for these children). It spanned five years of repeat visits, and on a subject that was then of little policy interest. Yet it was funded by a government department, as part of its long-term support for a dedicated research centre—the Thomas Coram Research Unit, at the Institute of Education in London. As recent accounts of the Unit document (Cameron, Koslowski, Lamont and Moss, 2024; Brannen, Moss, Owen and Phoenix, 2022), that support was subsequently to wither and end. No similar research of such ambition and magnitude into an emergent policy issue is conceivable today.

So, is *Managing Mothers* to be treated in 2024 solely as a work of social history—a study of its time? We would argue not. For it seems to us that it touches on and indeed illuminates contemporary issues, in particular concerning how women and men manage the dual earner lifestyle. Recent qualitative work, for example by Faircloth (2014) and Twamley (2019) and long-term time diary analysis by Gershuny and Sullivan (2019), shows many continuities with *Managing Mothers,* the ideological discourse of equal partnership coming too readily undone when couples are confronted with negotiating household work. This poses considerable challenges for parents when both subscribe to the new intensive parenting ideologies and equalitarian relationships, requiring ways of resolving the uncomfortable contradictions that arise. Those with the financial resources can outsource the domestic help they need; but those lacking such resources must make more difficult compromises.

So, while the rhetoric of equal partnership may be louder today, its practice on the ground continues to lag. What we wrote in the book's concluding chapter still holds: 'the dual earner lifestyle continues to rely mainly on the hard work, organisational skills and sacrifices of women' (p.256), while the 'traditional masculine model of employment continue[s] to be the norm' (p.260). There may be more government support available to employed parents, but that support continues to sustain a maternalist approach to children's upbringing, with a 12-month period of maternity leave at its core.

There has undoubtedly been change since we wrote *Managing Mothers*—but change is limited and incremental and not radical and transformatory. The challenge confronting dual earner households after maternity leave has yet to be surmounted, and still requires

> a change in cultural goals with respect to gender roles in the workplace and in that most conservative of spheres – "family life". Only when society attaches importance to women being able to provide adequately for themselves and for their children throughout the course of their working lives, and only when husbands and fathers internalise a sense of day to day responsibility for children, will mothers, living with or without partners, no longer be forced into an inequitable position, trading motherhood against employment (p.262).

References

Brannen, J. and Moss, P. (1998) 'The polarisation and intensification of parental employment in Britain: consequences for children, families and the community', *Community, Work & Family*, 1 (3), 229–247,

Brannen, J., Moss, P., Owen, C. and Phoenix, A. (2022) Thomas Coram: the life and times of a research unit at the Institute of Education (London) *London Review of Education* 20 (1), 37. DOI: https://doi.org/10.14324/LRE.20.1.37.

Cameron, C. Koslowski, A. Lamont, A. and Moss, P. (2024) *Social research for our times*, London: UCL Press.

Faircloth, C. (2014) 'Intensive parenting and the expansion of parenting'. In E. Lee, J. Bristow, C. Faircloth and J. Macvarish (eds) *Parenting Culture Studies*. Basingstoke and New York: Palgrave Macmillan, 25–51.

Gershuny, J. and Sullivan, O. (2019) *What We Really Do All Day: Insights from the Centre for Time Use Research* London: Penguin.

Gillies, V., Edwards, R. and Horsley, N. (2017) *Challenging the Politics of Early Intervention: Who's saving children and why?* Bristol: Policy Press.

Joseph Rowntree Foundation (2024) *UK Poverty 2024*. York: Joseph Rowntree Foundation https://www.jrf.org.uk/uk-poverty-2024-the-essential-guide-to-understanding-poverty-in-the-uk (accessed 29 April 2024).

Lee, E., Bristow, J., Faircloth, C. and Macvarish, J. (2014) *Parenting Culture Studies*. Basingstoke and New York: Palgrave Macmillan.

Streeck, W. (2022) 'In the superstate'. *London Review of Books*, 44 (2), 9–12.

Twamley, K. (2019) "Cold intimacies" in parents' negotiations of work-family practices and parental leave? *The Sociological Review* 67 (5), 1137–1153.

Contents

Acknowledgements

This book draws on the experience of over 250 households after the birth of the first child. We are especially grateful to the mothers who participated in the five year research programme, which was conducted at the Thomas Coram Research Unit. They gave up a great deal of their precious time to be interviewed, not once but on several occasions. We would like to thank them for their cooperation in, and their enthusiasm for, the whole enterprise.

Thanks are also due to the research team, especially Mary Baginsky, Gill Bolland, Judy Cook, Ruth Foxman, Eva Lloyd, Sue Martin and Ann Mooney, who took part in the interviewing, and Heidi Mirza, who contributed to the analysis. Grateful recognition must also go to Jane Williams who co-ordinated the project and kept in touch with the sample; thanks also for her many insightful comments. We wish to thank Charlie Owen for all his work in the computing of the data. Other members of the team and the Thomas Coram Research Unit helped in various ways: in particular Ted Melhuish, Ian Plewis and Barbara Tizard. Thanks also to Gordon Smith at Unwin Hyman for his interest and helpfulness throughout the work. Julia wishes to record her thanks to Ann Oakley who supervised her Ph.D. which drew upon the data analysis and ideas which Julia contributed to the book.

The study was funded by the Department of Health. We appreciate their help and prescience in supporting research into a lifestyle which is likely to become increasingly significant in the 1990s. In particular we would like to acknowledge the assistance of Carolyn Davies, our liaison officer in the Department.

1

Introduction

This book is principally concerned with the experience of becoming and being a mother in full-time paid employment. It deals with two overlapping transitions: the transition to parenthood, since it focuses on women having a first child; and the transition back to employment, since it also focuses on women who resume work after taking maternity leave. To a lesser extent, it is also a study of dual earner households, since it is about mothers in two-parent households, nearly all with partners in full-time employment.

The book is based on a longitudinal study of dual earner households during the early years of parenthood. This study was conducted at the Thomas Coram Research Unit, and is described in more detail in the next chapter. The data were collected during the mid-1980s, at a time when few women resumed full-time employment after maternity leave and levels of full-time employment among women with children under 3 were low. Since then a combination of economic growth (especially in the south-east of England, where the study was undertaken) and a rapid fall in the number of young people (the number of people under 25 in the labour market is projected to fall by 1.2 million between 1987 and 1995) have created a substantially increased demand for women's employment; over 80% of the increase in the labour force up to 1995 will be accounted for by women (Department of Employment, 1988). This will have major implications for employment among women with pre-school children, who have had the lowest levels of labour force participation among the female population.

A substantial increase in full-time employment among mothers with young children and, consequently, in dual earner lifestyles has major implications for social policy. The group of full-time employed mothers in dual earner households is also of considerable sociological interest, in constituting a new variant form of family life. Where women resume employment after childbirth, they are faced with issues concerning the household allocation of responsibility for children, housework and the management of the dual earner lifestyle. The question then arises as to the consequences of this lifestyle for the ways in which parenting and employment are constructed.

These constructions can be examined and described in material and behavioural terms. But there is another important dimension – the ideological. As other studies of households which do not conform to the conventional model have shown, such households tend to present themselves to the world 'as if' they were 'normal' nuclear families; for example, parents of handicapped children draw upon the construction of 'normal' parenting (Voysey, 1975), while reconstituted families present themselves as first-time married couples (Burgoyne and Clark, 1984). The effects of powerful ideologies concerning 'normal family life' need therefore to be explored for their impact on dual earner households with young children. 'Family life' may be changing in significant ways, but in an ideological sense it may not be lived and represented as such. As others have argued, in the face of change, ideologies of family life are notable for their emphasis on stability and continuity (Morgan, 1975, 1985).

BACKGROUND THEORETICAL DEBATES

The Working Mothers Debate

There have been a number of theoretical approaches to the study of dual earner households with young children. The most influential and persistent has been the debate conducted largely within the psychology of child development – an approach which is often termed the 'working mothers debate'. As a consequence of attachment theory – the notion that the emotional development of the child depends in large part on a relationship with one person, the mother – the psychological study of childrearing has focused almost exclusively on the importance of stable, full-time mothering (Bowlby, 1951, 1958; Ainsworth, 1962). Shared childrearing is discussed in the context of maladjustment – typically whether daycare leads to insecure attachment in children (McCartney and Phillips, 1988). The approach has been to presume that the employment of the mother is disruptive of the family and damaging to the child (Bronfenbrenner and Crouter, 1982).

2

Even though a greal deal of research has found that maternal employment *per se* does not adversely affect children (Clarke-Stewart, 1982; Hoffman, 1989), the myth that employment is damaging to 'family life' has persisted. As psychologists themselves have noted, this is due to normative assumptions concerning the conduct of family relationships (Hoffman, 1987). Mothers who 'go out to work' are considered to be deviant. Although the specific representations of mothers may have changed over time (McCartney and Phillips, 1988), the image of working mothers has been generally negative with the exception of wartime. Moreover, since maternal responsibilities for children and childcare are treated as unproblematic givens which derive from the fact that it is women not men who give birth, the issue continues to be framed in terms of whether and to what extent children suffer from lack of full-time mothering, rather than the extent to which children (and their mothers) thrive when the care of children is shared with others. In the weaker forms of the argument the concern is to examine the conditions under which mothers may undertake employment without completely disturbing their maternal responsibility. The emphasis here is on the ways in which mothers 'balance' work and childcare, the typical solution being to work part-time (Hoffman, 1987, p. 380; Hoffman and Nye, 1974, p. 228).

Some psychological studies have been concerned simply to explore whether mothers' employment *per se* damages children. Other studies have postulated and tested more sophisticated hypotheses, in particular the effect of mediating factors; recent research has paid 'increased attention to the intervening processes rather than the simple examination of child outcomes' (Hoffman, 1989, p. 284). A typical factor presumed to mediate between employment and mothering effects and child outcomes is the extent to which employment provides mothers with a sense of achievement and satisfaction (Hoffman, 1961; Kliger, 1954; Gold and Andres, 1978a, 1978b, 1978c; Kessler and McRae, 1981). It is, however, not always clear how far such factors reflect attitudes to employment as opposed to domestic factors.

The majority of the studies within this paradigm ignore the historical, social and ideological contexts in which motherhood is located. This is highly problematic for the frequently advocated longitudinal studies of the effects of maternal employment on children. Mothers who work when the pattern is rare are likely to differ from those who work when it is common; we may learn a great deal about a pattern that no longer exists and very little about the pattern that does (Hoffman, 1984, p. 105). Similarly, the

3

effects on the child are likely to be different under different social conditions (for examples of how childcare services differ between societies, and the origins and consequences of these differences, see Melhuish and Moss, 1990).

Such studies are equally unspecific about the type of employment undertaken by working mothers. Employment tends to be treated as an undifferentiated whole; type of occupation, employment conditions and labour market situation are rarely explored or are ignored altogether. Their focus is limited to whether or not mothers are employed and for how many hours (see for example Hoffman, 1961; Kliger, 1954; Kappel and Lambert, 1972). Similarly, such studies rarely consider mothers' employment within the framework of the household. With some exceptions, studies in this paradigm have refrained from examining fathers' and mothers' employment simultaneously, particularly in relation to children's socialization experiences.

The theoretical framework underpinning these studies is defined in a highly deterministic way – in terms of the effects of maternal employment upon the individual mother and her child. There is no allowance in the approach for the ways in which mothers create the experience of motherhood and the relationship with the child. Mothers are conceptualized as passive objects rather than as active subjects who have some power to determine their own lives (for a contrasting framework see Gerson, 1987; Gilligan, 1982).

The Dual Roles and
Separate Spheres Approaches

The second theoretical approach to the study of dual earner households with young children is sociological, and has been largely conducted within the sociology of the family, rather than the sociology of employment. The relevant debates have been conducted either in terms of women's 'dual roles' or in terms of the 'separate spheres' model of home versus family life. These theoretical approaches have been applied in the substantive field known as 'married women's work', a rhetoric current in the 1960s and 1970s which today sounds somewhat dated (Jephcott, 1962; Myrdal and Klein, 1970; Yudkin and Holme, 1963).

The separate spheres approach, which followed on from the dual roles approach, is underscored by an implied functionalism. The process of industrialization is said to require the separation of the family from the workplace with the two spheres linked through the male breadwinner. The workplace is perceived as the productive world, associated with men, and is differentiated from the world of non-production, the home, which is associated with women. Within this framework women's labour in the home is rendered invisible and only the affective and socialization aspects of their endeavours – notably childrearing – receive sociological recognition. In so far as women enter the world of employment – signified by 'proper' work – they are still regarded as belonging in the non-productive world of the family in which it is assumed they will continue to bear the major responsibility for childrearing. Employment outside the home is presumed to be the lesser of women's two roles and subsidiary in importance to the role of the (male) breadwinner (Finch, 1983).

As Finch (1983) points out, in a succinct analysis, there have been two versions of the functionalist analysis of the separate spheres debate: the Marxist and the non-Marxist. Within the non-Marxist debate, the association of men with the world of work and women with home and childcare is seen as some-how 'natural', albeit deriving from the processes of socialization. Women's domestic contribution is seen as functional for the family and as complementing the activities of the male worker (Parsons and Bales, 1956). Although within the Marxist version women's domestic role was viewed as work (an improvement on the first analysis), women's labour in the home was seen simply to be functional for capital. Gender differences were thereby reduced to the effects of capitalism. Both analyses reinforce rather than question the status quo, emphasizing the ways in which gender roles and gender inequality are perpetuated rather than changed. They also deny the ideological dimension: in the second analysis, actors' definitions of their situations are reduced to their economic determinants.

Beechey (1987) argues that the re-entry of women into the world of work has been analysed according to the 'reformulated func-tionalist thesis': the effects of the increased demand for women's labour led to their performing dual roles associated with work and the family. One of the problems with this approach is that either no adequate explanation of these changes is offered or, in so far as explanations are offered, they are normative ones associated with industrialization, affluence and democracy – in short with the idea of the long march of social progress. A result of this has been an absence of analysis on the specific ways in which women's labour contributes to employment and domestic work.

The dual roles and separate spheres debates ignore the linkages and shifts of activities between the two (see, for example, Moss and Fonda, 1980). We refer here not simply to the ways in which they may be interdependent in material terms but also to the ideologically constructed separation of the two spheres. The analytical distinction between employment and family leaves sociologists bereft of conceptual and explanatory tools, preventing them from explaining the way in which activities common to both spheres, notably work, are treated differently on account of ideological constructions based on gender (Stacey, 1981).

Stacey (1981) and Beechey (1987) have begun to create theoretical links between women's waged labour and home life, which integrate public and private spheres. In their work, the structured 'accommodation' between the labour market and domestic gender roles is seen to originate in both the labour market and the domestic sphere. Patriarchal ideology percolates through to the labour market as well as the household, creating particular kinds of job as well as employment conditions which are designed to attract women's labour and specific groups of women such as mothers. Gender identities are not merely transported into the workplace, but are created there in definitions of masculinity and femininity which in turn feed back into the meaning of gender (Barrett and McIntosh, 1982).

This recent work affects ways of looking at conflict and contradiction. The separate spheres and dual roles approaches typically analyse tensions between women's dual roles at the level of individual conflict of roles. Each sphere – home and the workplace – is conceptualized as a set of constraints which are somehow external to the actor (see Morgan, 1985). Individuals, characteristically women, are caught between two sets of external constraints which act upon them, creating personal conflict. Beechey (1987) however interprets such individual conflict in terms of structural tensions between the labour process, occupational and industrial concentrations of women employees and the sexual division of labour.

THE APPROACH OF THE BOOK

The book draws on the second, sociological approach. In this study, both motherhood and employment have been conceptualized as work. Women's labour is central, in material terms, to both spheres; women are full-time wage earners, like their husbands, and they are carers of young children and workers in the home. Where women embark on maternity and continue to be full-time employees the question arises as to the distribution of domestic and

6

childcare responsibilities both within the household and outside it. A second question concerns the nature of women's employment and the way it is regarded vis-à-vis that of men. These questions bear on an issue at the heart of the book – the extent to which mothers' full-time employment challenges female dependency in material and ideological terms.

The book deals with the constraints upon women of combining employment and motherhood. But it also draws on a social constructivist / symbolic interactionist perspective – in other words, the ways in which actors continually interpret the world and the ways in which interpretations shape their actions (Brodersen, 1964; Blumer, 1969). Women are portrayed in an active, rather than passive, light. We examine how they themselves construct, in gendered terms, employment and motherhood and the roles which go with them.

Finally, the general approach of the book endeavours to locate women's definitions of their situations within wider ideological debates concerning 'family life' and the workplace. We shall consider the reciprocal inter-penetration of ideology and practice – the ways in which structure reaches into and shapes individual experience. Explanations for gender inequalities can therefore be sited within both employment and domestic spheres. Furthermore, through an analysis of women's accounts of motherhood, childcare and employment, we explore the mechanisms by which women reproduce and integrate contradictory elements of their beliefs, actions and the situations in which they find themselves. We are not, therefore, simply concerned with the way in which individuals manage the individual experience of tension, conflict and overload arising from their 'dual roles'. Rather we are interested in the way women knit together in their accounts seemingly contradictory elements of their beliefs and practices which they may or may not experience or represent as conflictual. These beliefs and practices are part and parcel of larger ideological debates concerning gender roles and the practice of everyday life.

THE FOCUS OF THE BOOK

The main focus of the book is the process of becoming a mother in paid full-time employment at a particular moment of the life course – namely, in the first three years after the birth of the first child. More specifically, the book focuses on three themes. The first theme – the active construction of the experience of working

7

motherhood – refers to the choices and decisions women make
as they construct their experiences of becoming a mother in the
context of their resumption of full-time employment. Adopting the
social constructivist approach discussed above, women are treated
as creative actors who make a variety of choices and decisions concerning their careers as mothers, employees, wives, and members
of social networks. We consider the way women manage employment and occupational experiences after childbirth, the meanings
they attribute to employment in the context of the household and
their own individual attachment to the labour market. Similarly,
with respect to motherhood, marriage and social networks, we
consider women's perspectives of motherhood, the ways in which
they define and respond to their partners' contributions to the dual
earner lifestyle and the support they receive, or fail to receive, from
their social networks.

The second theme concerns the structural constraints – material,
ideological and institutional – which impinge upon women as they
construct their lives and define their situations. These include the
constraints of the labour market which shape women's opportunities on their return to work – promotion opportunities and
employment provisions including childcare provision, employment rights and concessions granted by employers and by the
state. Also important are the availability of informal sources of
attitudinal, practical and emotional support for the dual earner
lifestyle from partners and social networks; and the ideological
constraints of marriage, motherhood and employment – in terms of
the dominant social meanings available to women as they conduct
their lives as mothers in full-time paid work.

The last theme involves the consequences over time of being a
mother in paid work. Three sets of consequences are explored.
First, the repercussions of becoming a mother for women's subsequent employment – the course of their employment histories
and careers and the effects on occupational mobility. Second, the
implications of being a paid worker for women's experiences of and
feelings about motherhood. And finally, the impact of employment
on women's physical and psychological well-being.

Although the book focuses mainly on mothers, it also pays
attention to their partners, in particular to the involvement by
fathers of young children in employment and the domestic
sphere. More broadly, therefore, it provides a study of dual
earner households, covering a broader range of themes than
most other studies of such households which mainly focus on
just one or two, most often the intra-household division of labour

and the way in which the heavy burden incurred by this lifestyle is managed (Rapoport and Rapoport, 1971, 1976; Hertz, 1986). Our study differs from most others on dual earner households in a number of other ways. They tend to focus on households at an established, rather than at a transitional, point in relation to parenthood and the adoption of lifestyle. Not all studies specify whether there are children in the family (for example, Pendleton, Paloma and Garland, 1982); others group children up to the age of 18 (for example, Bryson, Bryson and Johnson, 1978). Much of the research concentrates on professional, middle-class dual career couples, and rarely considers in any detail the wider contextual issues of the labour market and informal support. Finally, most of the recent research about dual earner households is American; with the exception of the work of the Rapoports, most British interest in the area has been focused on employed mothers (Moss and Fonda, 1980; Sharpe, 1984).

THE
CONCEPT OF RESOURCES

Most of the concepts used in the book (for example, history, career and social network) are discussed and defined in the particular chapters where they occur. In this introduction, we consider one concept which recurs throughout the book – resources, and in particular the resources of ideology, time, space and social and material support. Resources ought not to be seen as inert materials possessed by individuals (or not); they are part of social relations and intimately connected with power (Giddens, 1979, p. 91). Resources are vehicles of power; failure to enact them, at the micro-social level, assists in the understanding of the way in which individuals are subject to social constraint. Conversely, the enactment of resources may facilitate choices so that individuals become mistresses of their own destinies. In this conceptualization constraints are not considered to be macro-structural phenomena which somehow act upon women as external social forces. Rather, they and choices are an outcome of deploying or not deploying resources.

Ideology

There is a tendency for 'ideology' to be conceptualized as an external structural force. It is typically theorized to act at the macro-social level, exerting power from a great distance over the individual.

It can, however, also be conceptualized as a resource upon which actors draw in defining and redefining reality. Where there are a number of competing or alternative ideologies within a social arena, then ideology may provide people with choices, indicating to them a variety of courses of action or role models.

But where there is a dominant ideology in a social arena it is likely to act as a highly constraining force. One of the main arguments of this book is that there are a number of powerful linked ideologies – ideas about male breadwinning, full-time motherhood and equalitarianism in marriage – which permeate different areas of women's lives. It was these ideologies, discussed in more detail later in the book, upon which women in the study drew in their accounts of their lives as employed mothers – and in doing so illustrated the process whereby ideologies of family life are reproduced even where the practices of family members (for example, women combining motherhood with full-time employment) appear to contradict important components of those ideologies.

We have drawn on the concept of ideology, in preference to 'dominant norms', 'social rhetoric' or even 'discourse', for several reasons. First, ideology conveys the idea of moral authority, drawing attention to the agencies and institutions which are its source; for example the church, the state, and professional practitioners are a major influence upon ideologies of 'family life'. Second, ideology also conveys the staying power and enduring appeal of particular beliefs and assumptions. Third, it has the function 'of relativising the absolute, bringing out into the open what was previously thought not to exist' (Morgan,' 1975, p. 211). It is, therefore, peculiarly appropriate to the study of 'family life' which is frequently portrayed as a 'natural' or given state.

There are of course disadvantages to its usage. It tends to be used in the singular form, thereby implying an internally consistent set of beliefs; it is preferable therefore to use the term in the plural. The concept is somewhat deterministic and overarching, lacking the sensitivity needed to capture the complexity and subtlety of women's accounts of their lives – though this is less of a problem if it is conceptualized as a resource. Most problematically, it has connotations of false consciousness. This is the stance taken by critics who, in rejecting 'family life' as bourgeois ideology, then go on to 'debunk' such ideology in order to reveal the 'true' nature of household and kin relationships (see Miller's critique (1988, p. 4) of Barrett and McIntosh, 1982).

In this study we consider ideologies as ways of naming, speaking and thinking about social action and social relationships. In this sense ideology is inseparable from social actions and relationships; neither can exist independently of ideology since it is not possible to grasp the world without naming it. Moreover, in attempting to rid ourselves of particular persistent ideologies we should explore them carefully and recognize that it is necessary to replace them with alternatives.

In making sense of employed mothers' accounts of their lives we will therefore be concerned with revealing discrepancies between and within ideologies and action – the way women talk about employment, motherhood and childcare, the way these accounts are internally contradictory and the way they conflict with their actions. We shall endeavour to discern some of the mechanisms and processes whereby discrepant elements in their accounts of their lives are knit together into some kind of whole. To anticipate the conclusions, the concept of ideology will be used to explore how far the dual earner lifestyle 'gives the lie' to the notion of 'normal' family life and the ways in which, where this is the case, actors achieve some kind of integration between and within their ideological statements and their practices.

Time

Time is a resource to which employed mothers are likely to have limited access. These women may exert considerable ingenuity in their use of time, adopting a variety of strategies to maximize this material commodity (Brannen and Moss, 1988), and should not be considered victims of the lack of it. Yet its shortage inevitably sets limits upon them – lack of time for children, time for themselves, time for their husbands, the housework, their friends and kin.

Time is also likely to have an ideological and symbolic significance for these mothers. The giving of time to children can in itself be one of the defining features of a 'proper' mother; in Britain, for example, there has been a strong presumption that the rearing of young children requires full-time care by mothers (discussed further in Chapters 3 and 7). Time has two meanings in this context: undirected time – simply being with the child; and directed time – time spent with the child in order to develop it to its full developmental potential (Hallden, 1988). Although employed mothers are unlikely to be able to comply with demands upon their time, they may still see their role in these terms. One strategy, reported in the literature, is the creation by employed mothers of 'quality time' with their children, to compensate for not devoting all their time to them (Hoffman, 1980). This strategy has a symbolic as well as a material significance, determined as it is by the ideology of motherhood as much as by practical constraints.

Space

Although space was not an explicit focus of the study it is none the less an important resource which affects the choices of and the constraints upon employed mothers (Tivers, 1985). Partly associated with other resources – time and money for example – it is also important in its own right. The parenting and care of young children involves being tied in physical ways to their needs, and the quality of space matters a great deal, both inside the home and in the external physical environment. Moreover, space is a resource which is rarely subject to individual manipulation since it relates to material resources, including major environmental features of a society, which are usually outside the control of the individual – the nature and siting of workplaces, childcare provision, the type, quality and accessibility of transportation and so on. That it figures so little in women's accounts in this study is in part a reflection of the study's failure to address these issues directly. But it may also reflect a tendency for mothers to take spatial factors for granted because they have so little control over many of them.

In this respect it is important to remember that the study was conducted in Greater London with all the inconveniences which working and travelling in a metropolis entails – overcrowded roads and overcrowded, unreliable public transport, workplaces sited in the city centre and homes and childcare facilities located in distant suburbs.

Social Network Support

Social networks refer to the immediate circle of significant social ties surrounding the individual; their conceptualization is discussed in detail in Chapter 12. They constitute a resource in two ways. They provide an ideological resource which may constrain or facilitate the dual earner lifestyle. As ideological resources social networks comprise the normative beliefs of significant others concerning maternal employment when children are small. Network composition and structure are likely to affect the way in which the beliefs of significant others act upon the individual. However, as national surveys have shown, hostility towards maternal employment when children are young appears to be widespread and relatively invariable according to age, sex and parental status (Bell, McKee and Priestley, 1983; Martin and Roberts, 1984; Ashford, 1987).

12

Social networks also constitute a resource upon which mothers may draw for support of different kinds – financial help, material goods, services, especially childcare, and moral and emotional support. Given the lack of institutional support for working parents and their children, especially the absence of a widespread service of good quality childcare, mothers are often forced to rely on informal care. There are some paradoxes here, however. The first is that the event of maternity, together with a return to full-time employment, is likely to leave mothers with little time or energy with which to build up and maintain their social networks at a period when they may be of considerable use. The second paradox concerns women's definitions of the dual earner lifestyle. In so far as women regard it as a matter of 'individual choice' to return to work they are likely to believe in the virtues of autonomy, self-reliance and provision of services through state or market forces. They are also likely to be in a weak position to reciprocate services rendered.

There are, therefore, a number of contradictions surrounding the notion of social networks as a positive resource. These suggest that networks are likely to act as constraints as well as enabling resources upon the experience of maternal employment.

Material Support

Social networks may provide material support to dual earner households. However, the most significant sources of material support in these households are the mother's and father's earnings; these enable the purchase of goods and services – such as childcare, help with other domestic work, second cars, 'convenience' foods – which facilitate the dual earner lifestyle. Mothers in dual earner households experience less of a shortage of money than of some other resources, though this, and the ability to purchase such commodities, is likely to be affected by the status of the jobs of both partners.

In conceptualizing the significance of material support in these households we place considerable emphasis upon women's definitions of the importance of their own and their husbands' earnings. Thus we return to the notion of ideology as a resource. Women are likely to make employment decisions in accordance with the meaning and value they attribute to their employment and earnings rather than their absolute monetary value. In conceptualizing material resources within the household it is therefore important not only to examine who the contributors to income are, what the contributions are spent on and how the money is managed (Pahl,

1980). If we are to understand its significance by taking into account the processes of power and control over household resources it is also important to examine the ways in which each contribution to the household is defined and valued.

THE REST OF THE BOOK

The next chapter describes in more detail the study on which this book is based, in particular the sample and the methods used, and Chapter 3 considers some of the salient features of the broader social context in which the households in our study were situated. The rest of the book falls into three sections. The first (Chapters 4 – 6) focuses on the women in the study and covers their employment, experience of motherhood and well-being. The second (Chapters 7 – 11) introduces the fathers in the households, covering their employment but also the management of the dual earner lifestyle by parents with young children and related aspects of the marriage, especially women's satisfaction or lack of it with their partner's contribution to this management task. In the final section (Chapters 12 – 13), we move outside the household to consider social networks and their ability to provide support.

2

The Study

The research whose findings form the main part of this book was proposed in 1980. The project was to be a longitudinal study of mothers who resumed full-time employment within 9 months of having a first child and of their children. A priority in the study was to be the impact of different types of caregiving environment on the children, and to this end the initial design envisaged three sub-groups, each of 60 women and children, based on the type of non-parental care initially used: relatives, childminders and nurseries. A fourth sub-group, for purposes of comparison, would consist of households where the mother did not resume employment of any kind, at least until her child was 9 months old.

It was intended that each of the sub-groups should include women who, before giving birth, had been employed in a range of occupations, with roughly equal numbers of women from professional and managerial jobs (Registrar-General's Classification I and II) – referred to below as 'higher status' jobs – and from sales, clerical and manual jobs (Registrar-General's classification III, IV and V) – referred to below as 'lower status' jobs. Apart from the criteria of employment status and non-parental care, three other criteria were to be applied in selecting the sample: that the child was the mother's first; that both parents lived together at the start of the study; and that the mother was born in the UK or the Republic of Ireland.

Mothers and children were to be followed up for the first 3 years after birth through four contacts – at 4–5 months after the birth, which it was hoped would be just before mothers resumed employment, then at 10–11, 18 and 36 months (these are referred to below as Contacts 1, 2, 3 and 4). Mothers would be seen on all four occasions, children on all except Contact 2 at 10–11 months, while non-parental caregivers would be seen on the last two occasions.

The broad aims of the study were to describe the histories and experiences of the mothers and children; to assess their welfare and development; and to examine some of the factors that might affect that welfare and development, including the type and stability of non-parental childcare. To these ends a variety of methods were to be used, including interviews, observations and developmental assessments. The study began in 1982, with fieldwork on the main sample running from February 1983 until April 1987.

The study has produced a wide range of material, on children, mothers and households. This book focuses primarily on mothers and households. The results of the work on children's development and their experience in non-parental childcare are primarily reported elsewhere (see Melhuish, 1990).

WHAT HAPPENED IN
PRACTICE – THE EVOLUTION
OF A PROJECT

Each research project has its own history which rarely conforms to the original proposal. The larger and more complex the proposed project, and the longer its execution, the more scope exists for changes and development. This may be forced on researchers because of practical problems in implementing a design; or it may be the result of changes in researchers' perspectives and thinking. In practice the two may interact. Practical problems may reflect the real world intruding on unrealistic and poorly grounded assumptions, leading the researcher to re-evaluate what she or he is doing.

In some important respects our research project followed the original design closely. The various contact points for mothers, children and caregivers were followed, and at each contact a variety of methods was applied. The overall sample size was achieved and rather exceeded with an initial recruitment of 255 mothers and children. Attrition of the sample was very low; there were only 12 losses during the study. Throughout, the women in the sample showed a high level of interest in the study and were extremely co-operative. Many found the subject matter of immediate and considerable interest and relevance, and the research visits often provided a welcome opportunity to reflect on and review experiences and feelings; in this respect, for many women, the research provided a valuable source of support, especially given the uneven availability and responsiveness of other sources of support.

But a number of important changes did occur. Some of these come under the heading of changed perspectives, and they affected the theoretical approach to a number of topics being studied and some of the fieldwork and analysis methods adopted. These changes occurred for several reasons – external developments in research and society in general; the influence of researchers with new disciplines joining the research team and the Thomas Coram Research Unit; and the theoretical, methodological and value orientations of individual researchers. Three areas of change were particularly important.

Dual Earner Households

The study was originally conceptualized in terms of maternal employment and its consequences; it arose from and addressed the 'working mothers debate'. Over time, however, our approach has shifted in ways which were discussed in the previous chapter. In particular, we have become more aware of the need to analyse women's experience in ideological, material and social context and to examine the way that women, as active actors, construct their experiences of combining motherhood and employment. We have also become more conscious of situating employed mothers as members of dual earner households and of the need to consider the position of fathers in these households. This implies both a value position that women with children ought to have the same rights to employment as men, who in turn ought to have equal responsibility for children and their upbringing, but also the view that the appropriate unit for study is the household, rather than mother and child.

Motherhood, Employment and Income

We also became increasingly aware of the consequences and significance of employment during early parenthood for long-term employment and earnings prospects for women, and for household resources and their allocation. These emphasise the important linkages between motherhood and childcare on the one hand, and employment, the labour market, household income and equality issues on the other. An important background influence has been the national data on women's employment provided by

17

the Department of Employment's 'Women and Employment' survey; the results of analyses of these data were published from 1984 onwards.

It was not possible to reflect these changed perspectives fully in the project. For example, the original research design and the resources for its implementation simply could not accommodate paying equal attention to fathers and mothers. As a consequence there were no direct interviews with fathers, and observations in the home predominantly involved mothers and children. In some cases, though, for example occupational mobility and managing the dual earner lifestyle, it was possible to a considerable extent to extend data collection, analysis and interpretation to reflect new perspectives.

Fieldwork Methods

The shift in approach to the subject of the study was associated with, indeed required, a shift of methodology. The original proposal assumed that the project would be entirely oriented to a quantitative approach with statistical methods of analysis. Over time, however, a qualitative approach was also developed. This was reflected in the method of interviewing used with mothers, and subsequently in the processes of data analysis and the writing–up of the material.

Mothers were interviewed at each of the four contacts. At the first two contacts – when children were 4–5 months old and 10–11 months old – all mothers were given long interviews (average length $2^1/2$ and $2^1/4$ hours, respectively). They included both structured questions which were coded, and open-ended questions which offered possibilities for probing. All interviews were tape-recorded and most parts were subsequently transcribed.

For the last two contacts, all mothers had shorter, structured interviews. Contact 4, however, included an additional interviewing component. Since the study had become increasingly interested in dual earner lifestyles, and women's experience of them, the decision was taken to pay additional attention to those women who had been continuously employed full-time since their initial return from maternity leave. Two thirds of this group, a total of 66 women, received a long, semi-structured interview (average length $2^1/2$ hours), in addition to the short, structured interview; this long interview was tape recorded and fully transcribed. In these, and the earlier semi-structured interviews at Contacts 1 and 2, women were encouraged to talk freely and the interviewer to probe extensively. Interviewers were allowed to be flexible in the ordering and wording of most questions, to permit respondents maximum freedom and spontaneity in talking about experiences and feelings, addressing issues of significance to them in a context of their own choosing.

Analysis

These methods of interviewing left us with two sets of data. The long interviews at the first two contacts and the short interviews at the last two contacts were coded on the basis of work done during the pilot stage of the project. The quantitative data so collected were used for statistical analysis. In addition we had a large amount of transcribed material – from Contacts 1, 2 and 4 – which required the development of a qualitative approach to its analysis. For the first two contacts we decided to concentrate on the material from the 70 women interviewed on both occasions by the two of us, and which had been fully transcribed. However, in some cases for particular analyses, other interviews were also considered.

The two data sets had different uses. The quantitative data proved particularly useful to establish patterns of behaviour, both cross-sectionally and over time – for example, occupational mobility, the sharing of domestic work and social network contact. In general the data analysed qualitatively proved useful in the identification of conceptual issues; the qualitative analysis fleshed out the coded responses, elaborating the meanings already encapsulated in the codes or adding new meanings. For example, examination of the way in which women described decisions concerning the return to employment led to an understanding that those who did not intend to return did not regard it as a decision at all, while those who intended a return saw it as an individual rather than a household decision. If the issue had simply been addressed quantitatively, relying only on codes derived from structured questions, such insights would have been lost.

There was a second way in which the two approaches to analysis proved valuable, complementing each other. When multiple methods are used, a major issue concerns consistency between different data sets (Hammersley and Atkinson, 1983; Fielding and Fielding, 1986; Bryman, 1988). A rationale for the use of different methods within the quantitative paradigm is to increase the validity of data; within this paradigm the aim is to integrate different sets of data to create a coherent whole. By contrast, within the qualitative paradigm as applied in the interpretative theoretical tradition (Halfpenny, 1979) data derived from a variety of sources do not add up to some 'objective essence' (Cain and Finch, 1981). Apparent contradictions between different data are addressed in terms of the linkages between theory and data – in particular the specific conceptualization of the research problem which leads to a particular choice of method (Brannen, forthcoming).

In this study, there were instances where quantitative and qualitative data were at odds. For example, the coded data on women's satisfaction with their partners' role in the dual earner lifestyle indicated relatively low levels of dissatisfaction – even though their partners mostly did not take an equal share of work and responsibility and in spite of the fact that women subscribed to the belief that they ought to be shared equally. Examination of the qualitative analysis of women's comments suggested a more complex conclusion. In many cases a good deal of criticism or ambivalence was expressed, especially when women recounted particular incidents. Critical comments, however, were often retracted or qualified in response to direct global questions concerning satisfaction with husbands' participation. Faced by these different sets of data, the strategy adopted was to examine the contexts in which women's responses were located, together with a content analysis of responses. In this way the contradictions were confronted, and the processes identified by which dissatisfaction was played down and explained away.

Contradictions and inconsistency do not only arise from combining approaches. A qualitative approach tends to throw up contradictions within respondents' accounts through its penetration of the fragmented and multifaceted nature of human consciousness, the different elements of which are rarely in total consonance with one another. Not only does this approach reveal contradictions, it also demands interpretations of them. For example, we have sought to make sense of much of the contradiction and inconsistency in women's accounts in the study in terms of the disjunction between, on the one hand, dominant ideologies governing employment and motherhood and, on the other, women's actual practices in combining motherhood with full-time paid work.

While the analytic procedures for quantitative data are clearly laid down, the guidelines governing the analysis of qualitative data are not so transparent and are rarely described in detail in reports of research. In this study, the qualitative analysis followed several stages. First, a number of conceptual themes were identified, some during the development phase of the project, others during the pilot work and yet others during the main fieldwork and analysis phases.

20

Next, each interview was searched for comments relating to each theme, which were then extracted. At the third stage, these interview extracts were scrutinized and, if appropriate, grouped into further categories and the categories counted. In this last respect the analytic procedure was also a quantitative one. In addition, particular attention was given to deviant or negative cases, especially in terms of their implications for the reformulation of conceptual themes (Denzin, 1970).

The Presentation of the Data

Basically, there are three ways of combining qualitative and quantitative material in empirical research (Bryman, 1988). All three have been used in this book. Qualitative material has been used to exemplify results derived from quantitative analysis, perhaps the most traditional presentational use of such material. Equally, if not more, significant is the second way of treating and presenting data sets – quantitative material facilitating the qualitative data. An example of this approach has already been mentioned concerning women's satisfaction with their partner's participation in domestic work and responsibility. The method of starting with a qualitative analysis ensured that the quantitative material was not misinterpreted and therefore was not presented simply at its face value.

In the third approach, both types of data are given equal weight; qualitative and quantitative analyses proceed in parallel as separate exercises, but each complements the other. In general, the two types of data are used together to address different but associated questions. To take as an example women's individual attachment to employment, respondents' coded assessments of the degree of importance they placed upon their work have been juxtaposed with what they said about its qualitative importance.

Finally, we have presented cases in most of the following chapters. In general, these cases are not used as exemplars of findings or as representative in a statistical sense, but as indicators of logical processes – the ways in which the key factors identified in the rest of the analysis come together in an individual case and in a particular set of social circumstances (Platt, 1988). The cases mainly appear in pairs, and have been selected to contrast with one another according to factors identified as being important. What we have not done is present cases as explanations, which would have required that we apply procedures such as analytic induction and that we test out, on a case by case basis, the necessary and sufficient conditions under which these factors are related together (see, for example, Lindesmith, 1968).

THE SAMPLE

The 'Women and Employment' survey showed clearly that only a small proportion of women in Britain in the late 1970s resumed full-time employment during the first year after having a baby – 8% of those having a first birth between 1975 and 1979 had done so within 6 months, and only 25% had returned to any type of employment (full-time or part-time) within 12 months. There was no reason to believe the situation would be greatly changed when we began seeking our sample in 1983. Adding our other sample criteria (that the child was the mother's first, that both parents lived together at the start of the study, that the mother was born in the UK or the Republic of Ireland and that the child would initially be cared for in one of three types of provision) ensured that finding our sample would be even harder and more time-consuming.

We used three main sources to find our sample. Forty-seven large-scale employers of women in the London area were asked to pass on names of women on maternity leave. Regular 'rounds' were done of the maternity wards of seven large London hospitals. First-time mothers identified in this way were then telephoned or written to 10 weeks after giving birth, to ask about their employment intentions and, if planning to resume full-time jobs, what type of childcare they intended to use.

The third source of 'referrals' was nurseries. At the time of the study, not only did few women resume full-time employment after having a first child, but only a very small proportion of this group used nursery care for their infants. A national survey in 1979 found that such care was used for less than 5% of children under 1 with mothers in full-time jobs, or well under 1% of all children (Daniel, 1980). The only practical way therefore to find a 'nursery' sub-group was directly via nurseries themselves. Local authority nurseries were excluded because they do not cater for children from dual earner households who need care because both parents are employed. After a careful search throughout the Greater London area, we located just 33 non-local authority nurseries which took very young children – that is, 12 months or less; 21 of these nurseries were attached to places of work, mainly hospitals and educational establishments. For 18 months we asked these nurseries to refer to us admissions of very young children.

These various sources produced some 4,100 'referrals'. The great majority of these women were not intending to resume full-time work, while many of the rest did not fit all of our other criteria. This left 295 women who were approached to participate in the study, 255 of whom were interviewed at Contact 1, an initial response rate of 86%. In the sample, 75% of women resumed full-time employment within 9 months of birth, 3% resumed part-time employment and the remainder did not resume employment at all in this period.

While this was approximately the balance originally intended between 'returners' and 'non-returners', it proved impossible to get the intended balance between the three different types of non-parental childcare within the returner group. Despite the co-operation of virtually all non-local authority nurseries in Greater London which took children under 9 months of age, and 18 months allotted to the task, this source produced only 98 referrals. Most of these referrals did not meet our other criteria, so that our nursery sub-group consisted of only 36 children rather than an intended 60.

Despite failing to reach our target for nursery children, this sub-group was still far larger than would have occurred in a random sample, on account of our deliberate policy of seeking these children. However, the fact that children initially cared for by childminders ended up over target and were the largest sub-group (N=91, compared with N=63 for children initially cared for by relatives) was not the result of a deliberate policy on our part, and was a reversal of the situation nationally, where care by relatives was more common at the time (Daniel, 1980; Martin and Roberts, 1984). Most mothers referred to us who intended to use childminders or relatives were approached to take part. The final balance between these two types of care therefore reflects the referrals we got, which under-represented manual workers (discussed below) and excluded lone mothers, the two groups most likely to use relatives.

We also found it impossible to get an occupational balance among mothers whose children received different types of non-parental care. The group initially using nurseries contained 83% of mothers in 'higher status' jobs (mostly health and education workers), compared with only 25% of the group who used relatives. While there was a better balance for the childminder group, 64% of mothers had 'higher status' jobs. Finally, in the non-returner sub-group, mothers with 'low status' occupations before having their children were in a slight majority (59%).

Table 2.1 *Employment status of sample at Contacts 2, 3 and 4*

Employment Status	Contact		
	2	3	4
	%	%	%
Not employed	26	25	28
Maternity Leave	–	2	7
Employed Part-time – less than 8 hours a week	2	4	4
Employed Part-time – 8–29 hours a week	5	12	17
Employed Full-time (30 hours and over)	67	57	44
N =	248	246	243

Our best intentions to create a neat sample, with balanced sub-groups, were defeated by what we found when we moved from the drawing-board into the real world. Moreover, the situation got messier (from the perspective of the original design) as time went on. Table 2.1 shows the distribution of employment statuses in the sample at Contacts 2, 3 and 4, and how these distributions changed over time. However, these cross-sectional 'snap-shots' underestimate the amount of change that took place during the whole period of the study. As we shall see later (Chapter 4), the employment status of many women changed at least once over the course of the study. A large minority (39%) of women who had resumed full-time employment before their child was 9 months did not remain in full-time employment right through until their child's third birthday, but had periods of working part-time or of not being employed at all (this does not include a further 16% who had a second period of maternity leave).

Childcare arrangements also changed. Nearly half the children (45%) had two or more childcare arrangements while their mothers were in full-time employment – in other words had at least one change of placement. Some changes were between the same type of care – for instance, from one childminder to another. But a quarter of the children experienced at least one change in type of care – for instance, from a relative to a childminder.

By the end of the study therefore, when children were aged 3, not only were fewer women in full-time employment – 107 compared with 184 who resumed full-time jobs before their child was 9 months – but the distribution of children between different types of care had changed. The proportion with relatives and childminders had fallen (from 29% and 50% to 16% and 47%), while those at nurseries and with 'others' (mainly nannies) had risen (from 16% and 5% to 23% and 15%).

Some Characteristics of
the Initial Sample

The design of the study did not require a representative sample. The main intention was to build up a sample on the basis of type of non-parental childcare and mother's occupational status, taking account also of several selection criteria which excluded certain groups. Our sample also was drawn only from employers, hospitals and nurseries in the Greater London area.

It is however possible and useful to compare our sample, on the basis of the occupation before birth of the mothers, with a nationally representative sample surveyed 4 years earlier, in the 1979 Policy Studies Institute study of maternity rights (Daniel, 1980). In both studies (referred to as TCRU and PSI), the proportion of women in clerical, secretarial and sales jobs (that is, III non-manual using the Registrar-General's Classification) was similar, both among women returning full-time soon after birth (35% TCRU, 34% PSI) and those who did not return (53% and 58%). This broad occupational grouping accounted for the largest number of women workers having first children; but women in this occupational grouping were least likely to resume full-time employment soon after giving birth.

Compared with the national sample, however, our sample over-represented women in managerial and professional jobs, both for returners (56% TCRU; 34% PSI) and non-returners (40% TCRU; 19% PSI). The corollary of this was an under-representation of women in manual jobs, again both among returners (7% TCRU; 28% PSI) and non-returners (7% TCRU; 23% PSI). It is important to emphasize, therefore, that our study focuses on women in non-manual jobs, who form a substantial majority in the total female workforce, and it includes few women manual workers. It should also be emphasized that a large proportion of fathers in our sample (41%) were manual workers, though few were in semi-skilled or unskilled occupations. (A fuller description of the occupations of the women in the sample, and their partners, is given in Chapters 4 and 9.)

Most women (85%) who initially resumed full-time employment were 25 or over (average age 29), two thirds had qualifications at GCE 'A' level or higher and most (60%) had been living with their partners for 4 years or over at the time of birth. The great majority of households (85%) were owner-occupiers.

When originally selected, all households had both parents living together. Over the course of the study, 18 separations occurred (7% of the 243 women seen at all four contacts), all but one in households where the mother initially resumed full-time employment. Women who resumed employment early after birth were, therefore, significantly more likely to experience a separation. (We use the term 'significant' throughout to indicate where a relationship is statistically significant at the 5% level or less).

Women who resumed full-time employment within 9 months of their first child were also less likely to have had a second child during the course of the study, the difference again being statistically significant. A number of those women who did have a second child had stopped full-time employment during this period. As a consequence, most women in full-time employment by Contact 4 at the end of the study only had one child (80%), while most women who were not employed had two (69%).

3

Parental Employment and Childcare in Britain in the 1980s

We begin by situating the households in our study in a broader context. The defining feature of the main part of our sample was that they were following a very specific course – mothers resuming full-time employment after the birth of a first child, so that both parents worked full-time. We consider how this compared with the general pattern of behaviour among 'new' parents in Britain in the mid-1980s (the fieldwork period of the study, from 1983 to 1987). We also consider the availability of social support for dual earner households with young children at that time – not at the level of social networks, which is examined in detail later, but at the level of employers and government.

Since the time of the study there have been significant changes, arising in large measure from the impact of the so-called 'demographic timebomb' and the consequent increased demand for women, especially with children, in the labour market. These developments since the mid-1980s raise the question of the relevance of the findings from our study – are they primarily of historical interest, having been overtaken by events? Or are they still of current interest, indeed becoming more relevant as increasing numbers of women with young children enter employment? We consider this issue, and recent developments, in the concluding chapter.

PATTERNS OF EMPLOYMENT

The great majority of women in mid-1980s Britain still left the workforce after the birth of their first child. Among women having their first child at the end of the 1970s, only 17% had returned to employment within 6 months of the birth (8% to full-time employment, 9% to part-time) and only 25% had returned within 12 months; overall, a mere 3% resumed employment within 6

27

months of each birth, hence effectively remaining in employment throughout their childbearing years (Martin and Roberts, 1984). Working on the same data set, Joshi (1984) calculated that, as a result of childbearing, women in Britain lost, on average, between 4 and 9 years of employment, depending on how many children they had and the spacing of these children.

Some changes had been occurring over time, albeit slowly. The proportion of women returning to employment within 12 months of a first child nearly doubled from 13% in the early 1950s to 25% in the late 1970s. By the mid-1980s, women increasingly tended to return to work between births and to return to work sooner after childbearing was finished (Martin and Roberts, 1984.). Even so, by 1986 only a third of women with a child under 5 (33%) were employed at any one time (OPCS 1989, Table 9.11).

These increases in employment, however, were mainly due to an increased supply of part-time jobs, which in turn had been created in large part to tap the reservoir of unused wage labour represented by women with dependent children. Between 1971 and 1986, the number of part-time jobs increased by 49%, while full-time jobs decreased by 12%; by 1986 83% of part-time jobs were held by women and 44% of women were employed part-time. Part-time employment was not, however, evenly distributed. It was most common among women with dependent children, two thirds of whom had part-time jobs; women with dependent children accounted for 50% of all part-time work done by women, but only 18% of all full-time jobs (Central Statistical Office, 1989; Table 4.7). Among women with dependent children, part-time work was most common and hours of work were shortest for women with young children. In the 'Women and Employment' survey, for example, 52% of part-time employed women with a youngest child under 5 worked under 16 hours a week, compared with 43% with a youngest child of primary school age and 29% with a youngest child aged 11–15 (Martin and Roberts 1984, Table 2.18).

By the mid-1980s, patterns of male employment showed little sign of change. Parenthood only impinged to the extent that, by the 1980s, most men were taking a week or two off work at the time when their children were born. The predominant pattern remained a working lifetime of full-time employment, unbroken except for involuntary unemployment. The overwhelming proportion (98%) of employed fathers in 1986 (as in 1946) had full-time jobs and spent more time at work than the relatively few mothers in full-time employment (see Chapter 9). The difference in hours in paid work was even greater if comparison was made between

28

all employed fathers and all employed mothers, because of the high level of part-time working amongst the latter; the median hours of paid work for employed women with a child under 5 was 10–19 in 1986, compared with 40–49 for fathers. Moreover, among fathers, a large proportion – 25% – were normally working over 50 hours a week. Not only was this the highest proportion for any country in the European Community, but the average hours worked by employed mothers was the lowest (Moss, 1988).

GOVERNMENT POLICY

Policies which might provide some support for employed mothers or fathers have met a mixture of indifference and hostility from successive post-war governments. The tone was set in 1945. During the War, faced by a chronic labour shortage, rapid expansion of nurseries took place to encourage mothers into the labour force, where their work was desperately needed. Immediately the War ended, government urged women with young children to stay at home and began a rapid reduction in nursery provision. In 1986, there were only 29,000 places in public day nurseries, slightly less than 1 place for every 100 children under 5 – in 1945 there had been 62,780 places. Moreover, the limited places that have been available in these publicly funded childcare services have become essentially a social work resource, for the use of families with major problems, rather than a service for the general run of employed parents (Moss, 1990). The only other intervention on childcare services for employed parents by government was similarly negative: between 1984 and 1990, government has taxed most parents using nurseries which are subsidized by their employer.

The one measure of support to be introduced by a post-war government has been maternity leave. Even this one policy has been reluctantly and only partially conceded. The measure, introduced in 1976, is not really leave as such. In a proper maternity leave scheme, women maintain their status as employees while absent from work due to pregnancy and childbirth. Instead, under British legislation women have their contracts terminated with a guarantee of reinstatement in similar work, though not necessarily in their previous job, and are not entitled to non-statutory benefits, such as bonuses, during their absence. Moreover, the qualifying conditions imposed are so restrictive – women having to have worked for at least 2 years for the same employer – that many pregnant employed

29

women, nearly a half according to one study (Daniel, 1980), are not eligible. Benefit payments are only available for 18 of the 40 weeks 'leave' period, and for two thirds of this time only at a low flat-rate level.

The measure was limited from its inception, and since then it has been made if anything more restrictive, rather than being improved. No further leave entitlements for employed parents have been introduced. Indeed, the present UK Government has opposed a draft Directive, put forward by the European Commission in 1983, that would have required all Member States of the Community to provide parental leave and leave for family reasons and set minimum standards for these two types of leave.

Government policy, or lack of it, since 1945 has been justified by several arguments. The post-war rundown of nurseries was heralded by a Ministry of Health Circular (221/45) which articulated an ideology about motherhood and childcare that has been dominant in the post-war period (and which we discuss further in Chapter 7):

> The Ministers concerned accept the view of medical and other authority that, in the interests of the health and development of the child no less than for the benefit of the mother, the proper place for a child under two is at home with his mother. They are also of the opinion that under normal peacetime conditions, the right policy to pursue would be positively to discourage mothers of children under two from going out to work.

Over 20 years later, another Government Circular (on 'Day Care for Children under 5'; Ministry of Health 37/68) reiterated the view 'that wherever possible the younger pre-school child should be at home with the mother . . . because early and prolonged separation from the mother is detrimental to the child'.

More recently, another line of argument has been used to justify non-intervention. Government, it is argued, has no direct role to play in making provision to support employed parents and their children; if parents wish to go out to work, then they must deal with the consequences, either by themselves or in co-operation with their employers. This argument (with others) was being used in the mid-1980s to justify blocking the European Commission's proposal on Parental Leave, and for not providing public funds for childcare services.

The Government considers that the most appropriate way of dealing with the issues covered by the draft [European Commission] Directive [on Parental Leave] is through voluntary negotiations between employers and employees. (Select Committee of the European Communities, 1985, p. 2)

Day care will continue to be primarily a matter of private arrangement between parents and private and voluntary resources except where there are special needs. (John Patten, Parliamentary Under-Secretary of State at the DHSS, Hansard, 18.2.1985, col. 397)

This policy stance reflects a number of themes in the thinking of the post-1979 Conservative Government – reducing, rather than increasing, 'dependency' on the state; reducing legislative demands and constraints imposed on employers, and not adding new ones, as a means of improving economic competitiveness and performance; and viewing children and childcare as in general private issues, except in certain areas with long-established social involvement (compulsory schooling and health services) and in cases of extreme need (dire poverty, abuse).

Government policy in the mid-1980s was based not on an explicit objection to mothers with young children being employed, but on the view that 'parents' were free to choose whether they went out to work, and that if they did it was up to parents and employers to cope with the consequences. Provisions for working parents should be left to the operation of market forces, either through parents' paying for private childcare services, or through employers' providing childcare (either directly or indirectly through financial support) and other types of support for employees with children (for example, through employment adaptations) where labour shortages and similar considerations made it in the employer's interests to do so. Government therefore 'recognis(ed) that there is a range of measures which can be of help in reconciling career and family responsibilities', but limited its role to 'commending to employers the advice on these matters contained in the Equal Opportunities Commission's Code of Practice' (Central Office of Information, 1987, p. 3).

EMPLOYER SUPPORT FOR
EMPLOYED PARENTS

There were no reliable statistics in the mid-1980s on the extent or nature of employer support for employed parents, either in the form of help with childcare or through employment adaptations, such as leave entitlements, flexible hours or part-time work opportunities. Such evidence as there is, however, suggests that such support was not widespread at that time. At the end of 1985, for example, the 'number of women covered by maternity agreements which give significant improvements on the statutory provisions (was) very substantial' – but only in the public sector; with the exception of certain specialized areas of employment, 'women in most companies and industries got no more than the statutory provisions' (IDS, 1985). The same review noted that 'paid paternity leave is still the exception, not the norm'. There are no official statistics on childcare provision made by employers, but the proportion of employers making such provision was so small as to be insignificant.

The most widespread forms of employment practice which might benefit employed parents were flexitime and part-time employment. By 1987, flexitime was widespread among white-collar employees and particularly well established in the public sector (Cohen, 1988), though there was no information about the actual proportion of employed parents covered by flexitime schemes. Part-time employment, as already noted, had increased rapidly, especially among women with children.

> For many women with young children, the lack of facilities for the care and education of their children and their assumed domestic responsibilities leave them with little choice but to opt for part-time working . . . [while] employers have not been slow to recognise the financial advantages of tapping into such a cheap, well-educated and flexible labour reserve. (Elias, 1988, p. 102)

So, by the mid-1980s, an increasing supply of flexible, part-time jobs had been provided by employers intended, either implicitly or explicitly, to attract women with children. At the same time, the benefits of these developments were offset by substantial costs for women, which we consider below.

SOME CONSEQUENCES
OF GOVERNMENT AND
EMPLOYER POLICY

Employment

In the mid-1980s, parents in Sweden were entitled to a period
of 12 months post-natal leave which could be taken as full-time,
half-time or quarter-time leave. These parents could decide how
to divide the leave period between them; how to take the leave
(they could for instance take 9 months full-time leave, followed
by 6 months half-time leave); and when to take it, since the leave
could be taken at any time during a child's first four years, in one
block or several.

By contrast, at the same time in the UK many women were not
entitled to maternity leave and those who were entitled only had
the right to resume employment on an immediate full-time basis.
Once maternity leave was ended, there were no further employment rights for women (or men) with children. The situation in
the UK was very rigid, giving mothers little choice or control
at a period when they had just entered parenthood for the first
time. A mother wanting to resume employment after a period of
maternity leave, but finding immediate resumption of a full-time
job unsatisfactory for whatever reason, had three options: she
could negotiate with her employer in the hope he would offer a
part-time job; or leave her job and look for part-time employment
elsewhere; or leave employment altogether for a period, before
seeking a new part-time job. Our sample includes examples of
women who followed each of these courses, and these and other
employment histories are discussed further in the next chapter.

As already noted, employed mothers with young children
mostly had part-time jobs and mostly for less than 16 hours a
week. Part-time employment was, however, closely associated
with two related sets of negative consequences: occupational
downward mobility and poor pay, conditions and prospects.
We shall return to look at these consequences at a micro-level
when we examine the employment histories of the women in
our sample. At a macro-level, however, the results from several
large-scale studies are clear:

> These studies indicate that there is a clear relationship between
> family formation, part-time working and downward occupa-
> tional mobility. British women who have children are likely
> to return to part-time employment. In doing so, a substantial

33

proportion will experience a major downward shift relative to their previous occupational status and earnings. For those who have professional qualifications, many will be working in jobs in which they will not be able to utilise these qualifications . . . Part-time jobs are concentrated within a narrow range of occupations, principally in the area of low-skill personal service work. Where part-time jobs occur in other occupational groups, they are generally at the lowest hierarchical level within the vertical structure of an occupation group and carry a relatively less attractive set of fringe benefits. (Elias, 1988, p. 88)

For a number of reasons, including the dominant ideologies around motherhood and lack of support both within the household and without, many mothers may prefer part-time to full-time employment, especially when children are very young; a substantial proportion of the mothers in our sample, both not employed and employed full-time, expressed such a preference (Chapter 8). For most, though, the material consequences of working part-time are major losses in occupational status, pay and employment conditions, which endure through the rest of their working lives and into retirement (Joshi, 1987).

Childcare

In the early 1960s, a deliberate decision was made by the Danish Government to develop publicly-funded childcare services in response to the growing number of women entering employment. Denmark now has the highest level of publicly funded childcare services in Western Europe: a majority of children under 3 with employed parents are cared for in publicly funded childcare services, some with salaried childminders, others in nurseries or in centres which provide for pre-school children and after-school care for primary school children. This is a reflection of the availability of these services, though a contributory factor may be reduced availability of other forms of care, for instance by relatives, as employment rates for women of all ages have risen rapidly to come close to those for men.

At the other extreme, the United Kingdom makes virtually no publicly funded provision for children with employed parents, while certainly up to the end of our study period, very few parents had any support for childcare from their employers. In these circumstances, employed mothers – for it is mothers who mostly make childcare arrangements (Chapter 10) – relied for childcare on members of their social networks or on the private market, and in many cases tailored their working hours to fit in with the care that was available to them. Surveys in the early 1980s showed that a high proportion of part-time employed women with children under 5 depended on their partners to provide care while they were at work (Daniel, 1980; Martin and Roberts, 1984); and that nearly half did this work either in the evening or at night – 44% compared with under 15% for other women in part-time jobs (Martin and Roberts, 1984) – when their partners were most likely to be available to provide childcare. The same surveys showed that among full-time employed women with young children, the most common childcare arrangement continued to be care by relatives, followed a long way behind by childminders. Very few children, less than 5% of those under 2, were cared for in nurseries or by nannies (Daniel, 1980; Martin and Roberts, 1984).

Parents' choice in childcare was very restricted in the mid-1980s. Not only was there essentially no choice between public and private sector, but group care, for instance in a nursery, was available to very few parents. At the time of the study, we found very few nurseries which took children under 12 months and most of those which did were attached to specific workplaces and therefore were not generally available. At Contact 1, when discussing the return to employment, only half the mothers in our study perceived themselves to have a choice between types of childcare, for example between a relative and a minder or a minder and a nursery. Women who expected to use relatives or nurseries were far more likely to feel they had such a choice than those expecting to use childminders; usually, women using either relatives or nurseries did see childminding as an option. In a second dimension of choice – perceived choice within the same type of care, for instance between two or more nurseries – the position was reversed. At Contact 1, 40% of women expecting to use a relative and just 15% of the nursery sub-group thought they had a choice between two or more relatives or nurseries. In the childminder group, however, 84% felt they had a choice between childminders (Moss, 1986).

One consequence of the general lack of choice was that many mothers – 53% – felt, at least initially, that the childcare arrangements they were making were not what they would have ideally preferred. In a few cases, mothers said they wanted the same type of care as they had actually arranged – but a different placement. Mostly, though, mothers said they would have preferred a different type of care, with the highest level of dissatisfaction – 66% – expressed by mothers who were expecting to use childminders. Nurseries and nannies were popular preferred options.

At subsequent contacts, the proportion of mothers wanting a different type of provision fell somewhat – from 43% at Contact 1 to 26% at Contact 2 for instance (Moss, 1986). This may in part reflect positive experience of childcare in practice; but there may also be an element of coming to terms with what is available. The figures cannot be assumed to show what mothers would actually use if confronted with real choice. What they do indicate is a situation where real choice was not generally available.

Local authorities in the mid-1980s had a duty to regulate and supervise childminders and nurseries, but how rigorously this was done varied considerably from area to area, and even the most conscientious could only deal with the most basic standards (Moss, 1990). There was no system for defining and systematically monitoring quality, so no current and comprehensive information was available on quality. The only available evidence was from a few research studies, mostly of childminding, and usually small scale, local and done in the late 1970s. These studies did however suggest that 'the care received by at least some children at childminders falls well below what would be acceptable to most people and is a cause for concern . . . and there is a considerable variation in quality of care' (Moss, 1987).

There has been little research on variations in quality and in particular to identify who receives better or worse quality care. The operation of a mainly private market in childcare for parents with no access to relatives able or willing to provide childcare, should involve some relationship between parental resources, financial and otherwise, and the quality of childcare. The one UK study which has examined the subject provides some evidence of such a relationship: children of mothers born abroad and mothers in lower occupational groups received the poorest service from childminders (Mayall and Petrie, 1983).

More specifically, there is evidence of high turnover among childminders (Moss, 1987), while others have commented on high turnover among nannies and nursery workers (Cohen, 1988). High turnover contributes to substantial instability in childcare arrangements. In our sample, only half the children were in the same placement throughout the period their mother was in full-time employment. Nursery placements – the form of provision least available in the UK – were less likely than placements in other types of care to end in a move (though children in a nursery could experience changes in caregivers over time because of staff turnover). Under a quarter of nursery placements (23%) ended in a move, significantly fewer than for relatives (42%), childminders

(43%) and others, including nannies (42%). For both relatives and childminders, two fifths of moves were either because the caregiver felt she could not cope or because her circumstances changed (for instance, she got another job or moved home).

Support from Health and Welfare
Agencies

Health and welfare agencies and their workers figured little in women's accounts of their experiences and as sources of support. Social workers did not appear at all, except in a few cases as members of the sample, and after the early months, health visitors and welfare clinics were rarely seen, except for routine check-ups. Women did not expect health and welfare workers to be interested in their decisions to return to work, and they were the least frequently mentioned source of support in connection with this decision. Services played a more significant role in the initial search for childcare; around half the mothers contacted health or welfare services at some stage during this process, though nearly all of this group also employed their own social networks. The remaining mothers depended entirely on informal sources to find childcare. There was a high level of dissatisfaction with the support provided by Social Services and other agencies.

We consider the support provided by these formal agencies, and women's satisfaction with it, in more detail in Chapter 13.

Support at the Workplace

Because few women with very young children were in full-time employment at the time of our study, women in our sample often found themselves the only woman employee where they worked with a full-time job and a very young child. As a consequence, they often lacked contact with other women in the same situation, to act as role models and to share and exchange experiences and feelings (Chapter 12).

As already noted, employer provisions and policies to support employed parents – mothers or fathers – were uncommon in Britain at the time of our study. Our sample was more favoured in this respect. It included women working for several local authorities which had recently begun to introduce measures to help employees with children, as part of equal opportunities policies; and the search for a group of children going to nurseries produced far more women with access to nurseries provided by their employers than would have been the case in a random sample. Even so, only 28%

37

of women in full-time employment at Contact 2 reported that their employers made any allowances or special provisions for working mothers. The main provision mentioned – by 18% – was childcare provision; as already mentioned, this reflected the way we selected our sample. Excluding this provision, only 18% mentioned any 'special provisions', including 9% who were entitled to some time off to care for sick children and 5% who were entitled to changes in working hours (for example, a number of women worked for a local authority which did allow women resuming work after maternity leave to work part-time).

Whatever the formal policies and provision, how supportive the workplace is perceived to be will depend to a considerable extent on the behaviour and attitudes of work colleagues. At Contact 2, half of the mothers in the sample portrayed their bosses as helpful and supportive, usually because they were regarded as understanding and sympathetic, attitudes which might produce practical support through the exercise of discretion, for example in granting time off when children were ill or needed to be taken to medical appointments. A third of the mothers described their other colleagues at work as supportive. At the other extreme, a fifth described their bosses, and over a half at least some if not all of their other colleagues, as actively unhelpful.

For women seeking to continue full-time employment after having a child, Britain in the mid-1980s was not a supportive society. Neither government nor employers offered much. Dominant ideologies, especially about motherhood, were constraining, an issue we discuss in Chapter 7. The experiences of the women in our study, who did attempt to follow this still very uncommon course, can only be understood in this light.

4

Women's Employment Histories and Careers after Childbirth

In this chapter, we examine the main features of women's employment prior to giving birth; how the women who returned to full-time work after maternity leave (referred to below as the 'returners') differed in terms of past employment behaviour from those who did not return ('non-returners'); and the consequences of returning (or not returning) to employment for women's employment patterns during the three years following the birth of their first child. In the second half of the chapter, we examine the ways in which women constructed their employment trajectories – in terms of the decisions they made concerning returning (or not returning) to employment, giving up employment, and changing their jobs and hours to part-time work.

In the first part of the chapter, we draw on the concept of 'employment history' in describing women's employment patterns before and after the birth. Following traditional historical practice, history may be described as a process of reconstructing the past from the vantage point of the historian. The historian makes sense of the past by focusing on a series of events for which she or he supplies documentary evidence. In a similar way, the researcher concerned with the study of employment histories puts together a series of consecutive changes in employment status, using factual behavioural information – a series of job changes, hours of work changes and periods out of the labour market. An employment history is the summation of these concrete facts, but in practice the approach relies upon the collection of information from actors' accounts. These are seen by researchers to be affected by memory recall and by the interpretations that actors choose to place upon them; attempts are made to minimize these risks by careful interviewing. The concept of employment histories, therefore, is only seen as problematic in terms of the accuracy of respondents' accounts; the subjective and creative elements in respondents' accounts are usually ignored.

In the second part of the chapter, we draw on the concept of 'employment career' which by contrast to the concept of 'employment history' is more complex and problematic, since it includes subjective, interpretative elements as data. The term 'career' is not used here in the normative, masculinist sense of a life-long commitment to employment which, in the case of the male white-collar worker, means moving progressively up the organizational ladder. Instead the term is used here to refer to the construction by an actor of a pathway for a particular social role or area of social activity (Becker, 1963). Each career line is located in relation to other careers – for example, employment career in relation to motherhood career – and to the careers of other selected persons. An individual's set of careers intersect with one another, typically at the point where he or she embarks on or leaves a career; thus the decisions women make about resuming their employment careers take place in the context of a transition to the new career of motherhood. The intersection with other persons' careers occurs at the level of the household, for example where a husband's employment career typically has implications for the housing or employment career of the wife. The term 'career' also tackles the *strategic* nature of employment behaviour; the actor formulates a plan or intention which in turn affects the course of the employment career via a succession of decisions, events and stages.

EMPLOYMENT BEHAVIOUR
BEFORE THE BIRTH

There is little evidence in the study to suggest that returners differed in their employment history prior to birth compared with non-returners. Two thirds of both groups had worked for 8 or more years before the birth; less than 11% had been employed for under 5 years. The average number of employment years – between 9 and 10 – was the same in both groups. Returners were no less likely than non-returners to have changed jobs or to have experienced unemployment.

In terms of qualifications and training, there were some statistically significant differences between returners and non-returners, but only within the low status group. Low status returners were more likely to have 'O' Levels or higher qualifications (73%) compared with low status non-returners (44%). They were similarly more likely to have acquired training from their employers. It is therefore possible that low status returners had more of an incentive than low status non-returners to remain in the labour market. Returners earned on average 8% more than non-returners before going on maternity leave, but this difference was not statistically significant.

The occupational breakdown of women in the study at the end of pregnancy, according to their employment intentions, is shown in Table 4.1; this uses the reclassified version of the Registrar-General's Classification, developed for the 'Women and Employment' survey (Martin and Roberts, 1984), and referred to subsequently as the 'WES classification of occupations'. The table also shows the occupational distribution for all women in full-time employment nationally, taken from the 1981 Labour Force Survey (LFS). As already described in Chapter 2, because of the various aims of the study, the study sample was not randomly drawn and was not therefore representative; in particular, it under-represented manual workers and over-represented professional and managerial workers. Within the sample, intending returners were more likely to be in professional and managerial jobs and less likely to be in sales or clerical jobs (similar to differences found in the national PSI study in 1979 (Daniel, 1980)), although within the total sample of intending returners, clerical workers were the largest single sub-group (35%). Among intending returners within the broad 'professional and managerial group', teachers were the largest sub-group, making up nearly 1 in 4 of the total sample, followed by roughly equal numbers of women in health and welfare professions and management positions. The under-representation of manual workers in the study sample was accounted for by semi-skilled and unskilled workers; the small proportion of women in skilled manual jobs was similar to the national PSI and LFS samples.

EMPLOYMENT HISTORIES
AFTER THE BIRTH

As already noted in Chapter 2, more than a third of the women who resumed full-time employment within 9 months of birth did not remain in continuous full-time employment until their child's third birthday (this excludes women who only left full-time employment for a second period of maternity leave). By the end of the study, at Contact 4, only 44% of women in the total sample were still working full-time, with another 7% on second maternity leave, compared with 75% who had resumed full-time employment

41

Table 4.1 *Occupational distribution of mothers before birth by employment intentions after birth; and of full-time women workers in UK*

| | Occupational group | | | | | | | | |
| | Professional/Managerial | | | | Clerical/Secretarial/Sales | | Manual | | |
	1	2	3	4	5	6	7	8/9	10/11
Group A (N = 185) (%)	4	23	13	16	35	1	6	2	–
Group B (N = 70) (%)	1	14	4	21	47	3	9	–	–
A + B (N = 255) (%)	3	21	11	18	38	2	7	2	–
1981 Labour Force Survey: all women in full-time jobs in UK (%)	7	8	8	8	39	7	10	16	5

Key: Group A = women who intended to resume full-time employment within 9 months of birth; Group B = other women

Occupational groups

1 = Professional	4 = Other intermediate non-manual
2 = Teaching	5 = Clerical
3 = Health/Welfare	6 = Sales
	7 = Skilled manual
	8/9 = Semi-skilled
	10/11 = Unskilled

within 9 months of birth. A further 18% had part-time jobs of over 8 hours a week by this stage, compared with only 3% who had resumed part-time employment within 9 months of birth. This left 31% who were not employed or only worked very short hours (3%, mostly working less than 5 hours a week), compared with 22% who had not resumed employment initially.

Overall then, there was a high rate of attrition from full-time employment during a relatively short period of early motherhood (about 30 months, since the 'average' mother resumed employment 5 months after giving birth). This was part of an even higher rate of movement between the three main employment statuses (unemployment, part-time and full-time employment).

An examination of changes in individuals' employment over the course of the study suggests six types of employment history. This typology was arrived at by a reworking of the raw data on women's occupations, hours of work and periods of non-employment at the analysis stage, applying qualitative methods to data originally intended for purely quantitative analysis. Twelve women were not included in this analysis because of incomplete data or because they were 'lost' during the course of the study. It is also important to note that taking maternity leave was not counted as leaving work so long as women returned or at Contact 4 said they intended to return to employment.

Employment History Groups

1. *Group 1 – Continuous returners – full-time*
    Women who took maternity leave, returned to the *same* jobs and employers on a full-time basis and continued in full-time employment (42%, *n*=101).
2. *Group 2 – Continuous returners – part-time*
    Women who took maternity leave, returned to the *same* jobs and employers on a full-time basis but subsequently reduced their hours, usually to longer part-time hours of over 20 hours a week (9%, *n*=21).
3. *Group 3 – Returners who changed to new jobs*
    Women who took maternity leave, returned to the same jobs but subsequently resigned and found *new* jobs with different employers (18%, *n*=44).
4. *Group 4 – Non-returners who found new jobs*
    Women who resigned during maternity leave (or did not take it) and subsequently found *new* mainly part-time jobs with different employers (14%, *n*=35).

43

5.   *Group 5 – Non-returners who remained unemployed*
     Women who resigned during or before maternity leave and
     did not work again (9%, *n*=22).
6.   *Group 6 – Returners who resigned*
     Women who took maternity leave and returned to their
     former jobs for a while and then resigned and did not work
     again (8%, *n*=20).

Although the samples are not comparable, these six types of
employment history are in accord with, or complementary to,
the ideal-typical histories identified by Dex (1984) in her re-analysis
of the 'Women and Employment' survey. Her histories include the
'domestic career' in which women do not return after childbirth
(similar to our Group 5); the 'phased' work history in which
women work part-time between births (elaborated upon by our
Groups 3 and 4); and the 'continuous career' (which overlaps with
our Groups 1 and 2). Dex's other categories of 'restricted' and
'unexpected' histories are evaluative rather than descriptive but may
overlap with the careers, as opposed to histories, of some women
in the study. The only group for which there is no equivalent in
Dex's typology is 'returners who resigned' (Group 6).

   The work history groups differ significantly from one another on a
number of variables. On antecedent variables, the continuous returners (Groups 1 and 2) were older than the other groups. Average ages
were 29 and 30 years for Groups 1 and 2 respectively, compared with
27 for Groups 3 and 4, and 28 for Group 5. Women in Groups 1 and
2 were more likely to have higher qualifications ('A' level and above)
and less likely to have few or no qualifications – that is, compared
with those not working or who had changed jobs. They were also
more likely to have worked in higher status occupations prior to the
birth and to have earned more. Compared with the other groups
they were also more likely to have been with their employers for
longer periods of time before the birth (11.2 years compared with
a range of 9.0 to 10.7 for the other groups). In all these instances,
the differences were statistically significant, with the exception of the
earning differential between Groups 1 and 2, on the one hand, and
Group 3 on the other. There were however no significant differences
on other pre-birth labour market variables, such as labour market
segregation, amount of training and number of promotions.

   In Groups 3 to 6, where women did not return to employment
after maternity leave or where they did but subsequently resigned
from their original job, the length of non-employment varied
significantly with work history. Not surprisingly, women with

most time out were in work history Group 5 – non-returners who did not work during their child's first 3 years. Next came women in Group 6 – the returners who resigned – with an average of 13 months out of work; then non-returners who found new jobs (Group 4) with 12.4 months out; and lastly returners who took new jobs (Group 3) with 8.2 months out.

Women's employment histories were related to whether or not women had had a second child by Contact 4. Women continuously employed in full-time work (Group 1) were statistically less likely to have had a second child, compared with all other groups (25% compared with a range of 45%–95% in the other groups). Among the 70 women who had had a second child at least 7 months prior to Contact 4 (and whose maternity leave would have come to an end), 64% of those who had not been working when their first child was 12 months old were also not working at Contact 4. By contrast, 42% of those who had been working full-time when their first child was 12 months were not working at Contact 4, and those who were working in this group were more likely to have full-time jobs. Since numbers and differences are small (and not significant statistically) only a tentative conclusion can be drawn, suggesting the possibility of some relationship between employment patterns after first and second births, but not a very strong one.

EMPLOYMENT CAREERS

We turn now to the ways in which women constructed their experience of becoming a mother in paid employment, considering some of the key decisions women made with respect to their employment behaviour in the three years following their first birth. These include the decision whether or not to resume employment after the birth of the first child; for those who initially returned after maternity leave to their former full-time jobs, the decision to stop or stay in work, especially in the context of a second birth; and the decision to change to part-time hours or to a part-time job. These decisions were not mutually exclusive; some women made all three, while others only made one or two of them in the course of the study.

Resuming Employment
after the First Birth

Although the regulations governing maternity leave allow women a period of time after the birth to make up their minds about whether or not to return to work, the majority – 61% of returners and 65% of non-returners – said they had made up their minds *before* the pregnancy. An analysis of the qualitative data suggests that for the non-returners the decision to return was not really a decision at all. They simply took it for granted that they would resign their jobs and look after their children in their early years. Questions aimed at investigating the decision not to return were not productive; in general, women treated them as meaningless and irrelevant.

By contrast, women who intended to return were clear they were taking a decision. This was underlined by the fact that their proposed course of action went against the status quo, contravening the pervasive British culture of full-time motherhood when children are young. They described the decision in two ways. First, they saw it as a *personal* decision, one which they took as individuals rather than as a couple. Thus although Pahl (1984) suggests that such decisions should be conceptualized as a household strategy, women's accounts indicate they did not define them in these terms. Even in those cases where husbands had clearly urged their wives to return to work for financial reasons, women never talked in terms of 'a joint decision'. Second, they described their decision in terms of 'choice', albeit elsewhere in the interviews many said they felt constrained to return to work for financial reasons. Indeed over half of those who saw it as their 'choice' to return to work also said they felt financially constrained to return.

Not only was the decision to return to work regarded as a personal choice, but others (husbands, relatives, friends and professionals) played a minor role in influencing women's decisions. This is discussed further in the context of marriage and social networks, in Chapters 11 and 13, but women's experience can be easily summarized. Most husbands were said to 'sit on the fence' or to have left the decision to their wives – attitudes with which women were not necessarily happy. Relatives, friends and professionals were either regarded as hostile to the decision or had very little help to offer, either in terms of information or experience. For many women it was a lonely experience requiring considerable courage.

I think it takes great courage for a woman to go back to work. Even if she has gone back by choice, even if she wants to do it, it still takes great courage. I think women shouldn't be made to feel guilty . . . There's always this view 'You stay at home'. In the end it was my final decision that I made on my own, regretfully. I would have preferred someone to have forced me into it – no, I wouldn't. But it was a hard decision. (Cook; Contact 1)

Although returners felt they had made the decision to return themselves, the major beneficiary of the decision was seen to be the household, especially household resources. Taking *all* reasons mentioned for resuming their jobs, 63% of women in high status jobs and 72% in low status jobs mentioned housing or financial pressures. Asked for their *main* reasons, again housing costs and other financial reasons were most frequently mentioned, though for women in low status jobs the proportion was much higher (73%) than it was for women in high status jobs (44%).

The significance of 'money' is a complicated matter. At one level 'going back for the money' is a socially acceptable or legitimate response which is likely to provoke no further questions. Since almost every individual in our society is subject in one way or another to financial pressures, there are shared understandings of the problem, at least at a superficial level. The accepted social norm that it is impolite to pry too much into such 'private matters' is at odds with the requirements upon researchers to do just this. Certainly on many occasions some of the interviewers were reluctant to probe financial reasons.

Where they did probe, financial reasons took on several meanings. First, the decision to go back to work emerged as a possible way of avoiding marital conflicts over money. In continuing their employment after childbirth some women suggested that they would not have to budget as tightly as they would or had done on only one income. Moreover, because of the strong *belief* in marriage as a shared and equal partnership, women did not appear to want to calculate whether each partner was receiving fair and equal shares of household resources, especially since women so rarely do (Wilson, 1987). This mother is able to talk about money in a relaxed way because she has made the decision to return to work.

We don't have a lot of control over our money. If we've got it we spend it. We're not good at saving . . . If one of us needs money we'll give it to the other. It's just our money . . . It wasn't a conscious decision to do it this way. I've never wanted us to be divided about money. And I never wanted to get into a situation of thinking 'It's my money' or 'his money'. (Telephonist; Contact 2)

By contrast, many women (73% of returners and 42% of non-returners) looking back to maternity leave at Contact 2 described the experience of being financially dependent upon their husbands as highly distasteful.

A second meaning attached to 'returning to work for the money' was to provide for the needs of the household and the child. In practice returners contributed a large part of total net household income and their earnings went on routine household expenditure. Yet despite this very considerable contribution and the fact that in most cases they had been contributing to household income for many years, women did not usually see themselves as 'main breadwinners'; most saw their earnings as supplementary income. By implication, husbands' earnings were treated differently – as core rather than supplementary income – just as their employment was assumed to be a stable and continuous feature of everyday life (these issues are discussed in more detail in Chapter 6).

In this context, in emphasizing the importance of their return to work for the consumption career of the household, women dwelt on their contribution to short- or medium-term needs. According to the qualitative data, they described their money as 'helping' the household through the initial heavy expenditure incurred in starting a family and, in some cases, setting up house. Specific items included large one-off purchases for the household (often to improve the house), repaying loans or debts which had accumulated as a consequence of living on one income during maternity leave, or 'stopgaps' until their partners were able to earn more. A key concern of these households at this point in the life course was a suitable environment for children, which meant in practice 'a house and a garden of one's own'; 85% of households were buying their own homes and two thirds of women contributed towards the mortgage or rent.

While housing and financial factors were most frequently mentioned by women to justify their decisions to return, a substantial number referred to job satisfaction. This factor was most important among high status returners, 54% of whom mentioned job satisfaction compared with 27% of women in low status jobs. Yet, despite the priority given to these intrinsic factors, few high status workers took a 'careerist' or long-term view of their employment prospects: no-one referred to the long-term material benefits of staying in their jobs, retaining pension rights or of being self-sufficient in the event of a husband's departure by death or divorce. Instead their accounts dwelt on the immediate or short-term material and psychological advantages of being employed. Typically, they contrasted their employment status favourably with the negative experience of being at home full-time; women talked about the importance of being able to 'get out of the house' and the complementary importance of employment as a source of 'mental stimulation' and 'social contact'.

In taking the decision to resume full-time employment after childbirth women constructed the ongoing nature of their employment careers. However, the defining feature of these careers, viewed at this point, was the absence of a sense of 'career', either in terms of time or in terms of long-term rewards, monetary or otherwise (a similar finding is reported in a recent study of the careers of primary school headmistresses with childcare responsibilities (Evetts, 1988)).

After the Initial Return – Whether to go on Working

Only a relatively small number (*n*=16) resigned soon after returning to work (by Contact 2); unlike those who did not return after maternity leave, women who resigned shortly after resuming work felt they had to justify their decisions. Usually women resigned for multiple reasons. Some women felt hassled and exhausted in trying to combine full-time employment with looking after a small baby. Others felt torn and guilty in leaving the child in someone else's care. A few had specific problems with the childcare placement, though the existence of such problems did not necessarily lead women to give up. Some had only intended to return temporarily – that is, for a sufficient period of time to allow them to keep their employer's supplementary maternity pay (a condition imposed by most employers who provided maternity pay over and above the statutory minimum). A few mentioned stresses in the workplace.

A 22 year old clerical worker who lived in a tower block experienced a number of competing stresses. Married to a self-employed builder, she and her husband had hoped to save enough money to buy their own place. However, after four weeks she resigned.

> I couldn't cope with the journey, travelling, doing my work properly, coming home here and keeping the house in order. It was all too much. It was alright for the first couple of weeks . . . but after that I was getting very run down. I felt I had no time. Also I found people at work – their attitude . . . If the Inland Revenue had allowed me to change to a local office I would have carried on. It was a big relief to give up . . . If I'd had a shorter journey and a better childminder then perhaps it would have been different. I never felt on top of it, never felt I was doing anything properly. (Contact 2)

49

Not surprisingly, women who were weighed down by such stresses did not consider the long-term implications of their resignations for their future employment careers. There was a notable absence of regret.

The arrival of the second child was a time when many women began to review their employment decisions. One option considered by some women was to give up work for a time; another was to change to part-time hours or to a part-time job. In considering whether to work at all after the second birth childcare was a principal consideration, particularly its cost. Since women considered childcare arrangements to be largely their financial, as well as their practical, responsibility, the calculation of the cost of two children in care led them in some cases to doubt whether it was 'worth their while' working at all.

The prospect of their children starting at school, either nursery or primary, or even in some cases at playgroup, provided a second point at which women typically reviewed their employment decisions. For some women the prospect seemed to be one of added childcare complications – coping with school hours and holidays, getting children to and from school or having to move children from existing placements so they could attend their local school. In these cases mothers began to have serious doubts about their employment commitments. Giving up their current full-time occupation and getting a part-time job nearer home was thought by some to be the answer.

> I see myself stopping work or at least going part-time or job sharing when he starts school. Taking him to school and fetching him just wouldn't fit in . . . It would be impossible for me to do that . . . Hopefully if we have another child I'd like to leave altogether . . . maybe until the second one goes to school, then part-time. (Civil service clerk; Contact 4)

If returners were also unhappy in their current employment situations, this was an added impetus to thinking about giving up their full-time employment. This might be due to very specific circumstances, or to more general problems of dissatisfaction and demoralization in certain jobs; teachers for instance were affected by low morale and a protracted industrial relations dispute.

Some women talked about giving up work altogether once their children had started school. In such cases women were perhaps expressing a desire for freedom *from* constraints – both childcare and the feeling of 'having' to work – rather than a freedom *to*

50

do anything in particular. In effect they wanted some space for themselves.

> I've always said I'd give up work when she starts school. I feel then I could do more of the things then that I want to do . . . just potter around without being disturbed. *Do you think you will give up?* I can't see us paying like a week's money to take her to school and pick her up. And then of course there's the summer holidays . . . I don't need a job that much – always providing we have enough money. (Airline ground stewardess; Contact 4)

This mother's construction of her future employment career was shaped not only by a desire to have some time for herself, but also by the practical constraints of school hours and the assumption that the costs of childcare were a charge on her own earnings.

Although 42% of children at Contact 4 were going to some pre-school provision, the great majority were attending playgroup; few children were going to nursery class even on a part-time basis. The issue of regular school attendance was therefore very largely prospective. While many women saw school as a considerable hurdle, which might require a change in employment status, the study ended before the actual response to the reality of schooling could be observed.

The Decision to be a Part-time Worker

A preference for part-time work was a recurrent theme; throughout the study, between 50% and 60% of all women said that, ideally, they would prefer to be part-time workers (see Chapter 8 for more details). While the meaning of this is difficult to interpret, given the prevailing ideology about motherhood and employment and the social unacceptability of full-time work for women with young children, there was a movement towards part-time working during the course of the study. This movement followed two different paths – returners who stayed in their former jobs but reduced their hours; and returners and non-returners who had to find new jobs to reduce their hours.

Whatever their preferences, women resuming work after maternity leave have no legal entitlement to part-time hours and few women in our sample said that their employers provided returners from maternity leave with the option of job shares or part-time hours, especially those on supervisory or senior grades. Apart from the few employers who did provide this option, other

51

women negotiated changes in hours either on return or later. Many employers however were unhelpful, while in other cases women did not even ask, assuming that doing their job on a part-time basis would be unacceptable or impractical.

> But the job doesn't lend itself to part-time. And I've had the feeling for the past couple of years that I'd like a three day weekend. It is quite tiring. But I didn't pursue it . . . They'd have to employ someone else – no precedent for job sharing. People are so against it. The job market is so difficult. There are plenty of people for every post. (Nursing officer; Contact 4)

By Contact 4, only 21 of the 122 women who had remained continuously with the same employer had reduced their hours. The more common path to part-time work involved changing job. Some returners moved from full-time to part-time work, while women who did not initially resume employment, but returned to the labour market during the study, usually went back to part-time as opposed to full-time work. As we describe in the next chapter, these new part-time jobs often involved reduced pay, conditions and status; women who sought part-time employment were in a poor bargaining situation in labour market terms. This was not, however, a consideration women regarded as important at this point in the life course, and most sought and welcomed their new part-time jobs for a number of reasons. For women resuming work, they helped to *boost* household income, if only by a small amount; most importantly the short hours and convenient location (part-time jobs were often closer to home) enabled women to be the main carers of their children, which they saw as their over-riding priority at this time. For women who had been in full-time jobs, part-time work offered a way of reducing some of the stress and anxiety associated with combining motherhood and full-time employment.

The following case indicates the way in which a woman defined her move into part-time and lower level work. Becoming a mother at 31 years of age, after working for 9 years as a senior administrative assistant in a local authority, the woman did not return to work after the first birth – 'All things being well it is best to stay at home' (Contact 1). After a year at home she did 'miss seeing people and I get the feeling of being tied and not having anything to talk about. I think it's taken me a lot longer to get used to than I thought'. At this point (Contact 3) she was thinking about taking a part-time job 'not because I'm depressed but because we're thinking of having an extension to the house. So that would be the reason – moving towards that.' Eventually, when her child was two she took a casual job as a waitress on Saturday nights while her husband looked after the child. She also organized parties selling books, which averaged three hours a week. At Contact 4, she gave finances as a reason for working and was pleased with the money, even though she only earned £35 a month (as compared with £470 in her previous full-time job). She also mentioned the importance of having 'a diversion from children and home'. She did not expect to return to work in local government and took for granted the loss of the three promotions she had gained during her time with the local authority.

Women who took on, usually uncomplainingly, these low level poorly paid part-time jobs did so because they 'fitted in' with what they saw to be their central role as mothers and carers of their children. Even if they returned to work after childbirth and then left their full-time job for a new part-time one, they did not compare their new jobs unfavourably with their former jobs; rather they calculated that a less well paid and less demanding job would be offset by the benefits of lower financial costs (for example, travel to work and childcare) and more time, which they would devote to their children. At the most they would gain some satisfaction, at the least peace of mind.

As already noted, the period of the study saw a steady movement out of full-time employment into part-time work and periods of non-employment. Decisions were made by women in the context of an ideology hostile to women who have young children and work full-time, and which defined women's work and earnings as of secondary importance to men's (Chapters 6 and 7). Many saw their initial decision to resume full-time work after maternity leave as a temporary measure for a set of short-term and particular circumstances. Employment decisions had to be constantly reconsidered in the light of impending changes, notably to do with children and childcare. In some cases, problems in the workplace affected decisions, especially in certain public sector jobs. Perhaps most significant of all were the tensions engendered by coping with motherhood and employment – the feeling of being on a constant treadmill imposed by the double burden of these two tasks, and in some cases an unbearable sense of guilt and anxiety.

Not surprisingly, therefore, women considered all three decisions – going back to work, staying at work, going part-time – from a short rather than a long-term perspective, despite their past history of continuous full-time employment. Their view of the future was not especially marked by employment issues. Rather they envisaged their lives as punctuated by developments in their children's lives and in their own contingent lives as mothers. They looked forward to the birth of their second or third child, to their children starting nursery, primary or even secondary school. More immediately they sought a break from the unremitting grind of the double burden.

5

Childbirth and Occupational Mobility

In the previous chapter, we explored the consequences of returning to full-time employment after maternity leave in terms of subsequent employment patterns. For the first 3 years following the birth of the first child six employment histories were identified. In this chapter, we examine the consequences of these different histories for women's occupational mobility – the extent to which women were upwardly and downwardly mobile between and within occupational statuses – and the ways in which women define changes in occupational status as they construct their employment careers (Brannen, 1989).

Discontinuity of employment has major negative consequences for occupational mobility. In a study of the work histories of the long-term unemployed, White (1983) found substantial occupational downgrading (38% for women and 39% for men) among all age groups when comparing the longest job held before unemployment with the first job held after unemployment. Interruption of employment because of childbirth has a similar impact. Evidence from the 'Women and Employment' survey (WES) suggests that 37% of all women returning to employment within 10 or more years of having a first child are downwardly mobile (Martin and Roberts, 1984). Secondary analysis of the data from WES shows that though occupational downgrading occurs at all stages of women's employment histories, childbirth is the biggest single cause: 40–45% occurred after childbirth, with 25% occurring between the last job before childbirth and the first job after the first return (Dex, 1987). A second, smaller scale study also found that much of the downward occupational mobility took place over the period of the first break in employment due to childbirth (Chaney, 1981). The risk of downward mobility at this time is increased if women return to part-time jobs, and if they return to work after a longer

55

break; rates of downward mobility for those returning within a year of first birth are lower.

The WES data also shows that, by contrast, 80% of upward mobility occurs in the initial work phase before childbirth or in the final work phase after child rearing has ended. Much of this movement downwards and upwards cancels itself out, so that 'to some extent the loss of occupational status is balanced by upward mobility, and in these cases the downward move is not permanent' (Dex, 1987, p. 88). However, for a 'significant number the downward move is permanent', while the most many women can hope to achieve is to make up lost ground.

As estimates of occupational mobility, previous studies have major limitations. In particular, they use a restricted number of occupational categories. Even though WES expanded the Registrar General's classification to eleven categories, this WES version still uses relatively few categories and thus may considerably underestimate the extent of mobility. This is compounded because studies have not taken account of changed positions *within* occupations, and consequently overlook a whole important area of mobility involving downgradings and upgradings. In estimating occupational mobility for our sample, we have included regradings *within* the same occupation; but in comparing changes *between* occupational categories we have used the WES classification of occupations, with its restricted range classification system.

EMPLOYMENT HISTORIES
AND
OCCUPATIONAL MOBILITY

By the last contact, a quarter of the women who had been employed at some stage during the three years since childbirth (24%) were in lower status jobs (either at Contact 4 or, if not employed then, in their last job before Contact 4) compared with pre-childbirth jobs; two thirds (67%) of this downward mobility was due to changes *between* occupations, and a third (33%) due to changes of job *within* the same occupation. A further 17% of all women employed at some point after childbirth were upwardly mobile – mostly (78%) as a result of changes within, rather than between, occupations. The remainder, just over half (59%), stayed at the same level, though not necessarily in the same job. The corresponding experience of fathers is described in detail in Chapter 9; in sum, though, upward mobility was

Table 5.1 *Employment history groups by occupational mobility after childbirth*

Employment history groups		Downward mobility	Upward mobility	No change
Continuous returners (FT + PT) (*Groups 1, 2*) (N = 122)	(%)	7	20	73
Returners who change employers (*Group 3*) (N = 44)	(%)	45	23	32
Non-returners who change employers (*Group 4*) (N = 35)	(%)	60	–	40

NB: Employment history groups 5 + 6 are excluded because women in these groups were not employed or only for a short period.

slightly greater and downward mobility substantially less among these men.

Women with two types of employment history were particularly 'at risk' of downward mobility: women who resigned from the labour market at childbirth and who then found new jobs (Group 4; see Chapter 4), and those who resigned after returning from maternity leave and then took new jobs (Group 3) (Table 5.1). Together they accounted for 41 of the 49 cases of downward mobility; 60% of women in Group 4 and 45% in Group 3 were downwardly mobile. By contrast, only 7% of those women who were continuously employed with the same employer after maternity leave (Groups 1 and 2) were downwardly mobile.

Overall 20% of women in these two groups (1 and 2) were upwardly mobile; in other words they were more likely to move up than down. Although a similar proportion (23%) of women in Group 3 were also upwardly mobile, an even greater proportion moved down. While among the initial non-returners who later resumed employment (Group 4) there were no cases of upward mobility to offset the majority who moved down.

DOWNWARD MOBILITY

Between Occupations

Most downward mobility was of this type (33 of the 49 cases) (Table 5.2). The majority of changes – 20 – involved movement out of one of the 4 professional and managerial job categories into clerical, sales or manual work. In these cases women's educational qualifications and training were largely irrelevant to their new jobs. Women who had previously been in the 'intermediate non-manual' category (managers and administrators) were more likely to be downwardly mobile between occupations than women in one of the three professional categories, who were mainly teachers (14/33 v. 6/33); these findings are similar to those from other studies (Dex, 1987; Dale, 1987) and may be because professional occupations offered greater possibilities for part-time employment (Elias and Main, 1982). Downwardly mobile women from intermediate non-manual jobs may recover their lost status at a later date although WES data suggest that this group has the least chance of returning to the same occupation after the end of childbearing (Dex, 1987).

The following case – of a woman returner previously in the intermediate non-manual category who changed to a lower status job after childbirth – demonstrates the way in which a downwardly mobile occupational career is defined and managed. Aged 28 at the birth of her first child, this woman had worked as an Executive Officer in a government department for 9 years. She resumed her job at the end of the maternity leave period. Her mother had agreed to look after the baby but was taken ill shortly before the return to work, then decided she could not cope with the baby. The woman felt she could not cope with the thought of someone else looking after the child at this stage and resigned two days after her return. Her mother and her husband shared the child's care while she worked out her month's notice.

Two months later the woman took up childminding on a temporary basis as a favour for a friend. Despite the drop in status (childminding is categorized as 'semi-skilled manual work') she regarded childminding as important work:

> I do put quite a bit of importance on it . . . I agreed that if I took it on I would treat it as work. It's worthwhile . . . and it brings in a small amount of money.

When the childminding job came to an end she took a job as a part-time receptionist in a health centre but left because she found the journey too long. Next she became a support visitor for the National Childminders' Association but found 30 hours a week 'too much' and started looking for a job with shorter hours. At first she used her father-in-law as a carer, then found a childminder. However, she became concerned about spending too much time away from her child and changed her job yet again. She became an organizer of a 'drop in' centre for ten hours a week, mainly because she was able to take her daughter with her. This she described as a 'considerable step down career-wise' but one which she did not regret because she found it so 'convenient'.

Downward mobility between occupations was as common among non-returners who found new jobs (Group 4) (Table 5.2). A second case taken from this group provides another illustration of a downwardly mobile occupational career, this time from one of the nine women who moved out of clerical work into sales or manual work. The woman had previously been a bank clerk, but gave up her job at the birth of her first child (when aged 30). At the first interview it was clear that, like most non-returners in the study, she had always expected to care for her child at home and had never seriously considered returning, except in the unlikely event that she could choose her own hours. When her child was nearly $2^{1/2}$ she found casual work in a factory, doing 9 hours a week – as she said she needed 'the break' and 'the money'. But she found the work too exhausting and did not like being away from her child for so long. After a month she got a job as a cleaner for 4 hours a week while her mother-in-law looked after the child on an unpaid basis. She also did 'the books' for her husband's business for which she was not paid. At Contact 4, this mother made no reference to her downward mobility and was happy with her 'little job' because it 'fits in'.

In many cases women who were downwardly mobile between occupations spent some months out of the labour market. Non-returners resigned *in order* to become full-time carers of their children and when they found new lower status jobs they expected to continue to do most of the caring. Only one woman was downwardly mobile between occupations without changing employers or without a break in her employment career. Before the birth, she had worked for a large bank in the City for 10 years. She returned to her former job on a full-time basis with considerable difficulty following the births of both her children. On both occasions she gave financial pressure as a major reason for returning although she was also very committed to working. Her situation was made more difficult by a number of problems: an unhappy marriage, unsympathetic work colleagues (only her male colleagues had children), and only her childminder for support (she had no family or friends with whom she was in regular contact).

She suffered 'a mental breakdown' following a very difficult second birth and was admitted to hospital. She eventually returned to her job and requested a very significant downgrading, from a managerial job to a clerical grade, 'so I could drop my responsibility and work my lunch hours and clear off at 4 o'clock'. She was not at all happy with this solution but felt she had no alternative. That she is the only continuous returner to be occupationally downgraded is significant: in the face of so many problems most would have resigned. Although just over one half of returners experienced some kind of difficulty during the first 6 months or so when they were back at work – role overload, problems with the child or childcare – relatively few experienced such serious problems or more than one problem.

Within Occupations

Within-occupation downward mobility – where women moved to lower grades but remained in the same occupational group – was more evenly distributed across the work histories. There were seven cases among the continuously employed (Groups 1 and 2), four among returners who changed employers (Group 3) and five among non-returners who found new jobs (Group 4) (Table 5.2). Ten of the 16 cases of within-occupation downward mobility involved professional jobs, including five teachers, a radiographer, a publisher, and a midwife. Teachers, for example, found part-time school jobs or worked as supply teachers or took on private tuition working from home. In nearly all these cases of downgrading, teachers returned to work later on having given up their jobs at childbirth. By contrast, nearly all teachers who returned to their former jobs after maternity leave continued at work (many citing school holidays and the school working day as reasons) without downgrading, though many were unwilling to take on additional responsibility.

Only one teacher who resumed the same job after maternity leave experienced downgrading, and her case is indicative of the effects of the labour market upon women who have breaks in their professional (as opposed to employment) careers, however short. After the birth, this primary school teacher continued to travel to an inner London primary school from her home in a village some 30 miles from London. She took her child to a childminder near

Table 5.2 *Employment history groups by type of occupational mobility*

Employment history group		Downward mobility		Upward mobility		No change
		Between occupations	*Within occupations*	*Between occupations*	*Within occupations*	
Continuous returners (FT+PT) (Groups 1+2)	N	1	7	1	23	90
Returners who change employers (Group 3)	N	16	4	7	3	14
Non-returners who change employers (Group 4)	N	16	5	–	–	14
TOTAL	N	33	16	8	26	118

NB: Employment history groups 5 + 6 are excluded because women in these groups were not employed or only for a short.

the school; some nights they stayed near the school with a friend. However, it was only when her husband was made redundant that she resigned. She did so in order to help him run a pub but found that she was working even longer hours than before but without any help with childcare. She then sought a full-time teaching post nearer home but could only get supply teaching. The downgrading resulted from changes in her husband's employment situation and the lack of appropriate teaching opportunities locally. It is notable that, unlike many of the downwardly mobile who did not perceive their situations in terms of loss of status, this mother was unhappy with her new position.

Most cases of downgrading among the continuously employed occurred as a consequence of women *requesting* a reduction in hours. For example, a radiographer continued in her job after the birth of both her children but began to find the hours too demanding and requested a reduction. She was eventually offered the chance of working a 28 hour week on a basic grade, which she accepted without complaint because she was 'so grateful' for the concession. In a couple of instances women felt under pressure to apply for demotion. A senior scientific officer, for example, said she was unpopular at work because she refused to work overtime, and felt pressurized not to take time off when her child, who was at the workplace creche, was taken ill. Since there was no possibility of doing her current job on a part-time basis, she felt constrained to ask for a downgrading.

A second primary school teacher exemplifies within-occupation downward mobility among initial non-returners (Group 4). She had never been entirely certain about returning to her job – 'I think deep down I didn't want to go back at all. From the moment he was born I thought "How can I leave him?"' It also emerged, though not in response to a direct question, that a pressure to return to work was her husband's impending redundancy: 'If he'd been in a safe job I'd have made the decision (not to return) earlier'. In the end, she did not have to go back to her job because the woman who was going to look after her son became unavailable. At various points between the births of her two children she took on a few weeks' supply teaching on a very part-time basis. She also helped her husband with 'his books' when he started up his own company. She was not concerned about the lower status of her current job and did not allude to it; as with most non-returners and women who were not very committed to returning, the move to a lower status job did not lead to complaints or regrets (or rather, if they did so, they were not expressed).

Decisions to Move into Lower
Status Jobs

Women's decisions to move into lower status jobs after the birth involved a number of considerations among which the issue of downward mobility rarely figured. If it was referred to at all in the interviews, it was only mentioned in passing. The most common reason given for taking demotion or a lower level job concerned the child and the extra time the mother could spend with him or her, particularly if she reduced her hours at work and worked locally. Before the birth many women in the study had worked for large centralized organizations which involved long journeys to work in Central London. If they left these jobs and sought new work they confined themselves to local labour markets where they were likely to enter poorly paid jobs with much shorter hours and less travel time.

Financial cost was clearly an issue in many of these employment decisions. Where women changed to new part-time jobs they calculated that they would not have to pay out money in childcare. In some cases their children were looked after by fathers or by relatives while, in others, women took the children with them or they worked at home. Thus women calculated that a less well paid and less demanding job would be offset by lower financial costs (travel, childcare, etc.) and greater involvement with their children which, at the most, would give them satisfaction and, at the least, peace of mind.

The Labour Market Consequences of
Downward Mobility

Many of the women who were downwardly mobile, both within and between occupations, experienced a major change in their labour market situations as a consequence. Prior to the birth most women (whether or not they were intending to return) were clustered in relatively advantaged or primary sectors of the labour market (Doeringer and Piore, 1971; Barron and Norris, 1976; Althauser and Kalleberg, 1981). Forty per cent of returners and 19% of non-returners were in *professional* occupations before the birth, as teachers, nurses and paramedical workers. Fifty one per cent of returners and 68% of non-returners were in intermediate non-manual or clerical jobs located in *organizations*. On average, clerical workers had been in the labour market for 10 years prior to childbirth; many of the women in clerical jobs were at or near

63

Table 5.3 *Employment history groups by overall weekly pay and average hours at work at Contact 4*

	Monthly take-home pay	Hours at work per week
Continuous returners (FT) (Group 1) (N = 98)	£553	43
Continuous returners (PT) (Group 2) (N = 22)	£445	21
Returners who change employers (Group 3) (N = 44)	£239	21
Non-returners who change employers (Group 4) (N = 35)	£89	11

the top of their job hierarchies. Women in jobs in the intermediate non-manual category had been in the labour market, on average, even longer – 11.6 years – and again many had gained promotion during this time.

An examination of the jobs to which women were demoted suggests that leaving work and/or changing employers after childbirth entailed a number of 'risk factors'. The first was low pay which was also associated with particular types of work history and was not simply a function of downgrading (Table 5.3). Non-returners who took on new jobs after the birth (Group 4) brought home the lowest pay and worked the shortest hours of all the groups. Next came the returners who changed to new jobs (Group 3) and lastly, with the highest pay, were those who stayed with the same employer (Groups 1 and 2). When pay and hours are considered in relation to occupational mobility, the downwardly mobile group fall between the non-returners and the returners. By contrast the upwardly mobile have an average income and work an average number of hours which are identical to the averages for the continuously employed (Table 5.3).

A second risk factor was the gendered character of many of the jobs and, in particular, their association with mothering. For example, nine women took up childminding, a job which is seen to 'fit in' conveniently with caring for children at home. Indeed some women commented that it was the only job that they could do in the circumstances. As others have suggested, such jobs are accorded low status and value *because* they are done by women (Phillips and Taylor, 1980; Craig, Garnsey and Rubery, 1984). In practice childcare requires very considerable skill and yet it entails low remuneration (Moss, 1987). A further gendered feature of some of the jobs is their association with the servicing role of being a wife. Three women did typing or 'the books' for their self-employed husbands, who offset their wives' pay against tax.

Other risk factors included doing casual or temporary work and being home-based, conditions which are strongly, though not necessarily, associated with part-time work (Hurstfield, 1987). Twenty-two of the jobs were carried out from or within the home; most of the rest worked locally. Apart from the women who did childminding or worked for their husbands, several did home-based sales work – selling cosmetics and children's clothes, running a clothing catalogue and a book club. Some women made goods at home: one was self-employed making children's birthday cakes while another was paid piece rates for assembling paper goods.

Overall, nearly two thirds of the downwardly mobile worked on a temporary, casual or self-employed basis and three quarters were part-time, with one quarter doing less than 8 hours a week. Partly because of this, many did not qualify for any maternity leave, maternity pay, paid holidays, or sick pay.

UPWARD MOBILITY

Between Occupations

There was only one instance where between-occupation upward mobility occurred as a result of staying with an employer. A woman was promoted by her firm from sales assistant to training co-ordinator. In all other instances – 7 cases – women resumed their former jobs after maternity leave and then changed employers (Group 3). There were no cases of between-occupation upward mobility among non-returners (Table 5.2).

Only in two cases did women move to higher graded occupations for overtly 'careerist' motives. In both instances, women had completed occupational qualifications while on maternity leave. In one case, for example, the woman had previously been an environmental housing assistant and had passed her final surveyors' exams while on leave. After the birth she became a self-employed surveyor working with her husband two days a week. However, in practice her reasons were more to do with convenience than with status.

> I thought this is ridiculous working a seven day week. It was just basically getting too much. And also partly because neither of us do nine to five jobs [implying that she and her husband work long hours]. If I'd have carried on I would have looked for a local job. Also we had plenty of money coming in.

Clearly, in this instance the new job allowed the woman to work the hours she chose. In the short term at least the change was not defined primarily as career progression or financial betterment.

Other between-occupation upgradings were artefacts of the Registrar General's classification. For example, one woman resigned her job as a prison officer and helped her husband to run a fish and chip shop. A second woman gave up a caretaking job in the block of flats where she lived after returning from maternity leave. She wanted to look after her child full-time but soon found that the household could not manage on one income. So she took a job in a local betting shop. A third woman moved from being a sales assistant to a dental nurse. While all three examples involved an occupational upgrading on the Registrar General's classification, they are not convincing examples of upward mobility nor did the women appear to regard them as such.

Within Occupations

Within-occupation upward mobility was more common than within-occupation downward mobility (26/34 v. 16/49) (Table 5.2). Within-occupation upward mobility was confined to three groups: the continuously employed who were promoted by their pre-birth employers (Groups 1 and 2 – 23 cases) and those who changed employers in order to be upgraded and who remained in full-time work (Group 3 – 3 cases). Upward mobility within occupations was more common in higher status than lower status jobs (19/26 v. 7/26). Teaching apart, it was confined to those employed in bureaucratic structures – local government, the Civil Service, the NHS and large banks – since jobs with promotion structures are to be found in internal labour markets based on organizations. Promotion to higher grades within occupations normally occurred therefore among women who worked for large organizations with clear hierarchical structures; in some instances women applied for promotion within these organisations while, in others, they benefited from routine upgrading. Staying with the same employer therefore increased women's promotion chances substantially.

Women rarely considered promotion without a great deal of trepidation, sometimes legitimating their upward step in terms of their role as mothers rather than workers. The woman quoted below resigned her job as a theatre nurse in order to become a sister in a neighbouring hospital; yet the reasons for taking this step are not only to do with furthering her career.

> It was the first sister's post I could do with the hours that were set . . . You see I make myself responsible for my son. Because my husband is able to do overtime and do funny hours my hours have to fit in with the nursery . . . *Do you think in terms of having a career?* No, because I've reached where I want to be . . . *Would you ever consider taking a step down?* No I don't think so . . . Once you take a step down it's very hard to come back up if you find you need to.

It could be argued that this woman is merely tentative in *expressing* ambition but it is also notable that she does not allude to a significant pressure to work full-time, namely her husband's heavy financial commitment to the children of his first marriage. This factor was clearly influential in her original decision to return to work. Instead she focuses on the suitability of her working hours for the nursery: the child is her first priority rather than her own needs or those of the household.

In a second example, a woman legitimates her promotion to the headship of the school where she had been deputy in terms of her child.

> I didn't see the child as a constraint. In a sense I saw it as a reason for promotion. I put her name down for the nursery before she was born. It was something for us. I wanted to be responsible for the place, have her in my school, developing in a situation I was constructing . . . It's so convenient at the moment. I couldn't see it before she was at secondary school age me actually moving.

The Significance of Upward Mobility

Upward mobility is a less diverse phenomenon than downward mobility in that it occurs in three work history groups instead of four (Table 5.2). It also has a different significance in terms of the meanings women attribute to it. In the construction of their employment careers women did not set out to be demoted whereas a substantial number sought promotion. Others were promoted by their employers without having to seek it. Downward mobility was the unintended consequence of decisions to do with finding suitable work conditions to fit around childcare responsibilities. The loss of status was simply the price to be paid for these decisions, rather than the objective.

Despite relatively high promotion rates among those continuously employed with the same employers, Groups 1 and 2 were not unequivocally oriented towards promotion. At Contact 1 only 38% of intending returners and 17% of non-returners mentioned a goal related to employment prospects, with women in high status jobs twice as likely to do so. Even women who saw promotion as a goal saw themselves as 'treading water' for a time after the birth of children.

> I've got goals and ambitions. They are probably slightly tempered now having a son. But I'm certainly very ambitious workwise but I want to be able to balance two aspects of life now. I think it's going to be hard. My goals are still high but I've got to tread water for a little while . . . If a job came up next year it wouldn't stop me applying but it might be an idea for a while to do a job I know without having an extra. (Administrator; Contact 2)

At Contact 4, among those who had had continuous full-time work histories, just under half were categorized (in the qualitative analysis) as unwilling to be promoted, either as a matter of principle or practice. Just over half were classified as positively oriented towards promotion, though many also expressed reservations. A content analysis of these reservations suggests that in the construction of their employment careers many women themselves imposed limits upon their ambitions. They felt that they ought not to take more responsibility at work while having young children.

> When I was in [an interview for promotion] I thought 'What if I get this job and I'm having a second child?' This isn't going to go down very well . . . not going to help goodwill. I'll be sacrificing my short-term needs to my long-term desires – another child. So I thought – better to stay with (present employer) and have number two and sort out what I need now. (Administrator; Contact 4)

Women also showed themselves to be very aware of the finite

nature of their time and energy, in circumstances where they felt they could expect little support – from informal sources, employers or from the state.

> I fancied (moving to) college administration but I don't put in for it anymore because of the change in routine at home . . . It would mean a lot more work for my husband. As it is he has to see to him in the morning. (Typing pool superintendent; Contact 4)

Many, moreover, were unwilling to trade more of these personal resources if it meant reducing their involvement with their children.

> My aim in life really is to be able to work properly at a level where I'm competent and will be a good mother. (Nursing tutor; Contact 4)

The majority of women who remain in full-time employment with their pre-birth employers enjoy a relatively advantaged situation in the primary sectors of the labour market, the most significant benefit being an increased chance of upward mobility; they are also more likely to have access to occupational pension schemes, paid holidays and other benefits. In contrast women who find new part-time work after childbirth are vulnerable to downward mobility and movement into secondary sectors of the labour market; many make no further use of their former skills and experience. They also lose out on job security, pay and benefits. Deterioration in their employment situations is not only to do with part-time hours; it is also associated with self-employment, temporary/casual work status.

Competition for many of the new jobs mothers take on is based not on qualifications or experience but on gender and phase in the life course. Mothers compete with other mothers for local jobs with short, flexible hours because they can be fitted around the care of their children. In the great majority of these cases, women combine being workers with being the main carers of their children. Moreover, lack of childcare provision is rarely given as the sole reason for moving into these types of jobs; few women are prepared to take on 'the double burden' at this stage and most feel, at some level, that motherhood ought to be a full-time activity (Chapter 7).

In making changes in their employment careers women were clearly authors of their own actions. The downwardly mobile rarely sought downgrading but they were not necessarily unhappy when it occurred. Many of the upwardly mobile sought promotion but not wholeheartedly. The reasons in both cases were to be found in the overarching ideological and institutional contexts within which motherhood, childcare and mothers' employment were negotiated. We consider these issues in the following chapters.

6

Childbirth and the Meaning of Employment

In this chapter we shall consider the diversity of meanings which women attribute to their employment and earnings in the context of becoming a mother. The chapter is structured around two main themes concerning the meaning of employment: its importance in terms of individual attachment and its importance in terms of the household. The analysis will focus directly on those women who returned to full-time employment after maternity leave with some comparisons made with full-time housewives.

In the literature on 'working women' there is evidence which suggests that mothers' employment attachment is secondary rather than the breadwinning attachment that typifies the employment attachment of men with children (see Morris, 1989). This evidence includes findings which suggest that women regard themselves as earning 'pin money', as well as a growing body of data concerning women's discontinuous employment histories and the kinds of jobs many mothers do – part-time work which is fitted in around domestic responsibilities. A group of mothers who work full-time constitute a critical or extreme case according to the *a fortiori* principle (Platt, 1988). This group represents the most favourable set of conditions for the confirmation of the hypothesis – namely, that full-time employment leads to a breadwinning attachment to the labour market, rather than to the notion of a secondary wage.

INDIVIDUAL ATTACHMENT
TO EMPLOYMENT

In this first part of the chapter we examine the ways in which women describe employment as being important to them as individuals. As individuals, women develop particular employment orientations which in turn are reflected in their definitions of self identity. Two concepts are particularly important: occupational

71

identity and employment orientations. Occupational identity, it has been argued, is central to social identity – 'the activities [individuals] engage in during the course of their employment are socially recognised, valued, evaluated and rewarded, and those evaluations and rewards, in our sort of society, constitute an important, perhaps still the most important, element in overall social identity' (Brown, 1986, p. 2). If social identity is likely to be influenced by changes in occupational status, especially if they are forced rather than voluntary changes, loss of a job may provoke a change in women's identities when they withdraw from the labour market to have a child. However, since maternity leave constitutes only a temporary withdrawal, the conditions for confirming such changes are not critical ones. What is likely to be much more significant is the fact that women have become mothers during the period of withdrawal.

Like occupational identity, the notion of employment orientations has been developed by researchers in the study of male workers. It has been defined as 'the meaning men [sic] give to work and . . . the place and function they accord to work within their lives as a whole' (Goldthorpe *et al.*, 1968, p. 9). Central to the notion is the contention that different occupational groups hold different priorities and expectations in relation to employment. Following the fruitful work of Goldthorpe and his colleagues in this field there has been considerable debate within industrial sociology about the source of individuals' orientations and about whether orientations are stable or fluid, together with some criticism of the fact that most of the relevant research has been done on men. Where studies have been done separately on women different assumptions have been made, in particular that domestic responsibilities are the principal factor governing their attachment to work (Dex, 1984).

A central feature of the employment orientations approach is the distinction it draws between instrumental and expressive orientations and the links that are made between employment and other aspects of workers' lives. For the instrumental workers, the primary meaning of work is in terms of a means to an end, the end being external to the work situation (Dex, 1984). In so far as the instrumental worker seeks extrinsic rewards from employment, these are seen to be located outside the workplace, primarily in the privatized world of family life (Goldthorpe *et al.*, 1968). Expressive rewards, by contrast, are seen to be related to satisfaction with the job and/or aspects of the workplace environment. Contrary to expectations, the few studies which have compared men's and women's employment orientations have found that both types of orientations are equally present (for a review of these findings see Brown, Curran and Cousins, 1983). Moreover, the two orientations are not mutually exclusive (Dex, 1984).

This approach has several advantages. For example, it attempts to evaluate attachment to employment in qualitative rather than quantitative terms and thereby gets away from the debate as to whether women are more or less attached to the labour market than men. It also attempts to avoid the trap of locating the source of employment orientations in one particular sphere – the workplace as opposed to the domestic sphere – or in relation to one particular sector or point in the life course. While there is much criticism of the approach – in particular about the origins of orientations, their fluidity and how far they can be said to be mutually exclusive – nonetheless they provide a broad multi-faceted conceptual framework in which to explore the employment attachment of individuals (Dex, 1984).

Before the Birth

Before the birth of children women, judged in terms of their behaviour as continuous workers, were as committed to their jobs as most men; there was nothing to suggest that they had regarded their employment as anything other than a permanent and taken for granted feature of their lives (Chapter 4). On average women had worked without interruption for 9 to 10 years since leaving full-time education. Few had experienced any voluntary or involuntary unemployment. (The husbands' employment histories prior to becoming fathers were not investigated.)

At Contact 1 women were asked a number of questions about the importance of employment, including one about the pre-birth period. Those intending to return to work were rather more likely to say that work had been 'very important' or 'quite important', compared with those not intending to return; however, the difference was only statistically significant for the high status groups (73% v. 55%). A second pre-coded question asked the respondent to compare the significance of employment before the birth with other areas of their lives (marriage, home, social life, etc.). Those not intending to return again ranked employment less highly, but, as before, the differences were only statistically significant within the high status occupation group.

Such answers need to be interpreted cautiously. It seems possible that some women may have constructed their replies about the past in the light of the present, namely from the vantage point of

73

their new status as mothers and their decisions about returning to work. In the case of high status returners, the knowledge that they were returning to their former employment may have led them to over-emphasize its past importance in their lives; while in the case of high status non-returners, the opposite may have been true.

Women's employment orientations before childbirth were also explored, again using structured methods of questioning. Women were asked to rank the three features of a job they had considered most important to them before pregnancy. These responses yielded no differences between returners and non-returners: the main discriminating factor was occupational status (Table 6.1). Ninety per cent of those who, before maternity leave, had worked in low status occupations selected at least one instrumental feature (good pay, job security, good prospects), compared with only 48% of those women who had worked in high status jobs. Conversely, expressive or intrinsic features of jobs (varied and interesting work, having responsibility for one's own work, the opportunity to use one's abilities) were rather more frequently mentioned by women in high status jobs (93%), compared with women in low status jobs (70%). Since none of the women had childcare responsibilities at the time to which the question referred (before the birth), 'convenience factors' did not figure very highly although the 21 – 25% who did mention them may well have had in mind housework responsibilities; a study of newlyweds suggests that many women found more convenient jobs after marriage in order to 'fit in' the household chores (Mansfield and Collard, 1988).

On Maternity Leave

Focusing on the importance of employment in the immediate post-birth period, women were asked an open-ended question at Contact 1: 'If someone said to you what do you do, how would you answer?'. The question was intended to explore the salience of employment in women's identities on the eve of their return to work. Not surprisingly, those intending to return to work were more likely than those not intending to return to describe themselves as workers or by their occupational titles (68% v. 15%). On the other hand, those intending to remain at home were more likely to describe themselves as housewives and/or mothers (45% v. 15%). Occupational status affected employment identity, with high status returners significantly more likely to define themselves in terms of their employment roles than low status returners (76% v. 58%). Conversely, non-returners in high status jobs were less

Table 6.1 *Job features mentioned by women at Contact 1 as being three most important features of pre-birth employment*

Job features	Occupational status before birth	
	Low status (N = 114)	High status (N = 131)
	(%)	(%)
Instrumental (e.g. good pay, security, perks, good prospects)	90	48
Expressive (e.g. varied and interesting work, pleasant environment, responsibility for own work, opportunity to use abilities)	70	93
Social (e.g. friendly work colleagues)	48	48
Convenience (e.g. flexible and convenient hours, convenient workplace)	25	21

likely to emphasize housework and motherhood roles than non-returners in low status jobs (25% v. 62%).

Asked specifically about their identities as mothers, it is noteworthy that, at this stage, whatever their employment intentions women had not yet totally identified with the motherhood role. A substantial proportion still felt themselves to be in a process of transition (28% of non-returners and 42% of returners).

> I think of myself as a mother only that's not my idea of motherhood. In fact I kept saying [to the baby] 'I'm Lizzie!' I suppose I was wary first of all whether she would see me as a mother. *How do you feel about that now?* I still feel a bit strange. We say 'We're Mum and Dad'. You do that because you try and make them talk. But it's difficult, very difficult. (Local government administrator; Contact 1)

Since those not intending to return played down the importance of paid work during maternity leave, they might also be expected to emphasize the advantages of being at home. They were less negative than returners about the experience of being at home full-time on maternity leave (this rating of dissatisfaction with motherhood is discussed in more detail in the next chapter). Low status returners were the most negative of all about being at home full-time (though the difference with high status returners was not significant) and the difference between them and low status non-returners was greater than between high status returners and non-returners. As low status jobs provide lower rewards, both instrumental and expressive, than high status jobs it is to be expected that women are less attached to them. Yet many women in low status jobs in our sample were clearly attached to their work. It is possible that such commitment may exhibit itself in terms of complaints about being at home – boredom, isolation and lack of material resources – rather than in terms of satisfaction with the particular job.

Low status returners, therefore, might be expected to dwell on the domestic factors pushing them back to work rather than the pull of employment and job satisfaction. In effect this is what was found. Returners in low status jobs were more dissatisfied with being at home on maternity leave and gave finances as their main reason for returning to work. By contrast, those returners in high status jobs were more likely to emphasize the importance of the intrinsic rewards of work and gave these as the main reasons for returning.

After the Return

Women's responses about the importance of employment soon after the return to work (at Contact 2) were contrasted with their Contact 1 responses about the pre-birth importance of employment (Table 6.2). On this basis, employment remained as important after as before the birth for just over half the returners; among the remainder, employment was more likely to become less rather than more important. Women were also asked at Contact 2 to make their own assessment of whether the importance of employment had changed for them over time (Table 6.2). A comparison of the two sets of data reveal similar proportions for declining importance – 36% for the first data set compared with 40% for the second data set. There is much greater disagreement, however, over the increased importance of employment – 12% when comparing responses at Contacts 1 and 2, but 49% according to women's own assessments at Contact 2. It is hard to know what

Table 6.2 *Changes in importance of employment between periods before and after birth*

	Comparison of responses at Contacts 1 and 2 (N = 169) (%)	Respondents' own evaluations at Contact 2 (N = 174) (%)
Employment less important after birth	36	40
No change	52	11
Employment more important after birth	12	49

to make of such discrepancies. An analysis of respondents' accounts suggests assessments are indicators of different qualitative changes, concerning the way in which employment was now important in their lives.

A number of major themes emerged from women's accounts of the changed importance of employment after having a child. For some, motherhood brought the realization that there were more important priorities than employment; consequently, employment diminished in importance.

I think having a child has made me realize there is something else other than work. (Principal officer in local government; Contact 2)

Again associated with the diminution of employment, the ascendancy of maternal responsibility led some to re-evaluate the importance of their employment in purely instrumental terms; women now continued in their jobs for no other reason than the money, and given the opportunity would have resigned.

It's only important in so far as it provides the necessary money to pay the mortgage. In terms of companionship or change of scene it really doesn't offer that much. (Civil service executive officer; Contact 2)

While motherhood for some women overshadowed the previous importance of employment, for others it gave a new significance to employment. This could result from the experience of full-time motherhood while on maternity leave. In particular, the realization of the limitations to being at home all day with a young child alerted women, perhaps for the first time, to the sense of structure and perspective that employment gave their lives.

> If anything [my job] is more important now. It gives me perspective . . . makes your day seem more structured, perhaps because I'm the sort of person who has been working so long. (Careers Officer; Contact 2)

Being at home could also make women realize their need for a sense of fulfilment and challenge which might not be met by motherhood.

> If anything it [the importance of work] has gone up. I mean I was aware that my job was important to me. I think it was only when I was faced with a child and looking after a baby at home and thinking 'Well, it would be nice to stay at home' that I realized I needed something more. I mean the baby didn't fulfil everything. (Doctor; Contact 2)

Some women said that the experience of being a full-time mother made them want to take on more responsibility at work.

> More important than before. I don't know if it relates to the baby or not. I used to be happy to cruise along, being what I thought was a good classroom teacher. But since I've gone back I'm no longer happy to be just that. I actually want to be given more responsibilities. (Language school teacher; Contact 2)

A central theme was the enduring importance of employment for promoting psychological well-being, a role enhanced by the transition to motherhood. The mother quoted below thought employment was critical to her mental health, even before she had a child. Both during an earlier spell of unemployment and during her maternity leave she had undergone considerable psychological distress experienced as an acute obsession with thoughts of illness and death. Only after her return to work and her obsessive fears had diminished, was she able to reflect calmly on the benefits of working.

> In terms of mental health I think it's essential that I work . . . I have experienced being at home and I think I would have gone

completely off the rails if I'd stayed at home any longer . . . I need the stimulation of a job . . . It gives me a different sort of identity. (Librarian; Contact 2).

Other women alluded to the importance of employment in promoting psychological well-being less directly. There is now a fairly widespread recognition that being a full-time housewife frequently leads to isolation, boredom and loneliness and that being 'stuck at home' with small children and little money puts women at risk of depression. The work of Oakley (1974, 1980) on housework and motherhood and of Brown and Harris (1978) on working class mothers' high risk of depression may have permeated professional and public opinion. Apparently dismissive comments made by women about the importance of work in terms of 'getting out', 'not getting into a rut', 'having a break' and 'the contact with people' are essentially grounded in commonsense but are likely to have been influenced, albeit indirectly, by such research.

Identity Changes After
the Return to Work

As we have already described, before the return there were significant differences between returners and non-returners in the extent to which they defined themselves spontaneously in terms of their occupational or employment roles. After the return there were even greater differences: 95% of returners but only 13% of non-returners defined themselves by these roles. Nonetheless, many described themselves spontaneously in terms of multiple roles.

If someone asked what I did I'd say a housewife, a mother and a bank employee. I'd give all three. (Senior bank clerk; Contact 2)

An identity change may be experienced as a change in personal qualities, as well as the addition or loss of social role. Asked the extent to which they felt differently as persons, around one half of both returners and non-returners confessed to feeling no different at Contact 2. However, of those who felt different, returners were more likely than non-returners to feel entirely positive about their new selves (35% v. 14%). As employed mothers, some women described a feeling of enhanced self-esteem, brought on by the experience of motherhood, a state they described as transcending the whole of their lives. Others simply said they were more tolerant, responsible and mature.

79

I think I've become more responsible and mature than I was. Once you've got a child you've got to grow up. You can't be silly . . . I try to concentrate on my work. I don't have time to be childish. (Bank clerk; Contact 2)

The maturity that motherhood brought was typically associated with unselfishness; responsibility for children curtailed mothers' own wants and choices, both material and non-material.

I could be selfish before. We could go out and do what we wanted. I suppose again I've had to grow up . . . I've gained a bit more maturity because I've got more responsibility mainly because of him. (Clerical assistant; Contact 2)

Employment was also seen as salient to establishing a separate identity from that of domestic roles of mother, wife and house-wife, even though domestic childcare responsibilities might be valued more highly. This theme was particularly apparent at the last contact when children were three years old. Returners emphasized the importance of space in their lives to do something independently.

Sanity! Talking to other people. Doing something independently. (TV production assistant; Contact 4)

It's important . . . as it ever was that I have something important of my own to do. Getting out of the house and being in a different place and having contact with other adults. (Teacher; Contact 4)

The perceived advantages of employment in sustaining the individual's identity were constantly juxtaposed with the negative image of full-time housework and familial roles.

It is important to me personally because I tend to feel I need to have the sort of job where I've got to fulfil myself as opposed to just staying at home with the family. (Surveyor; Contact 4)

HOUSEHOLD MEANINGS OF EMPLOYMENT

Questions about the importance of work to women as individuals yielded one set of meanings, while questions about the importance of their earnings and, by implication, their importance to the household, yielded quite other dimensions of meaning. Much of the research reported in the literature concerning the importance of women's earnings focuses on two patterns. One is a marked desire on the part of women for financial independence (Rimmer, 1980; Cragg and Dawson, 1984; Martin and Roberts, 1984). The other is the tendency for women to use their wages to augment housekeeping (Morris, 1989). In the present study the importance of women's earnings is underlined by the fact that finances constituted the most frequent reason women gave for continuing in paid work after childbirth (Chapter 4).

Returners contributed very significantly to household finances; at Contact 2 their earnings constituted on average 44% of household income (see Chapter 9 for more details about earnings). What women spent their earnings on is also indicative of their importance. Most contributed to major items of household expenditure; at Contact 2 two thirds contributed to housing costs, including a fifth who said paying the mortgage was wholly their financial responsibility. Nearly two thirds contributed to such major bills as fuel and telephone bills and over three quarters to shopping and child costs, especially childcare fees. Men were more likely to contribute towards the costs of housing, fuel, phone and car, while women were more likely to contribute towards shopping and children (Table 6.3). Women also largely bore the brunt of the costs of the dual earner lifestyle – for example, second cars which some purchased in order to transport the children to and from the carers.

The Symbolic Importance of Women's Earnings

Questions about the ways in which women's earnings were spent were treated in the quantitative paradigm; the results have just been outlined. More subtle questions concerning what women *thought* their money went on were treated qualitatively on a subset of 70 Contact 2 interviews (see Chapter 2). In many cases these two sets of responses were contradictory. At Contact 2 roughly three quarters talked about their earnings being for 'basics' and 'essentials', with many women spelling out the household's primary needs: housing, food and the bills. The other quarter talked about their money going on 'additional expenditure', 'luxuries' and 'extras' or, as one woman put it, 'things we couldn't have had if I hadn't worked'. They also mentioned the costs of childcare and the dual earner lifestyle. In some instances, these labels conflict with women's reports of how they actually spent the bulk of their money

Table 6.3 *Contributions to household expenditure at Contact 2 by women and husbands where both in full-time employment (N = 184)*

Item of expenditure		Expenditure from		
		Woman's earnings	Husband's earnings	Both earnings
Childcare	(%)	49	17	34
Child's day to day needs	(%)	35	14	51
Daily household needs	(%)	31	23	46
Child's other needs (eg toys)	(%)	27	14	59
Housing	(%)	21	34	45
Telephone	(%)	21	25	54
Fuel	(%)	20	26	54
Car	(%)	12	27	61

(see Table 6.3) while, in others, they are at variance with the ways women organized it.

Where women put their earnings into joint bank accounts (at Contact 2, 32% organized their money in this way) some still continued to think of their own earnings as being earmarked to pay for particular items of expenditure. Even those who kept their money in separate bank accounts and covered the mortgage or regular household bills from their earnings, in some cases labelled their money in their heads as being for luxuries and extras (Contact 2). At the last contact some women who had worked continuously full-time through the three years of motherhood still regarded their earnings as being of secondary importance to the household.

> Well I had to [work] so we could have the things we wanted. It wasn't important for me myself. It was for getting things and going places. *For example?* We used to save a lot of it like to get carpets and do alterations. (Bank clerk earning £420 a month married to an electronics engineer earning £650 a month; Contact 4)

It is significant that this woman was planning not to return after her second maternity leave. Seeing her earnings in these terms helped her to justify her departure from the workforce despite the fact that, at an earlier interview, she had said that her earnings were 'essential' to the household. She further justifies her decision not to return – 'I'm at home at the moment so it wouldn't prove too much bother'.

The same process, of labelling earnings as used for 'non-essentials', can be seen in this second example.

If I wasn't working these would be just non-considerations. We say which shall I do this year and which next year? So I guess my money goes on non-essentials. We've had a new kitchen and I paid for the whole of that £3,000. If I hadn't been working we might have got a couple of new units. (Nursery nurse earning £508 per month married to a contract engineer earning £700 a month; Contact 4)

A third mother had been recently promoted at Contact 4 and her husband was about to be made redundant. Nonetheless she saw her earnings as providing not just the basics, but the things which the dual earner lifestyle make possible – holidays abroad, nice clothes and so forth.

As my husband said if I don't work we could afford it but I'd have to do without my car. My dad lives abroad – we won't be able to go and see him. My daughter has nice clothes. I have nice clothes sometimes. All the perks will have to go. (Secretary earning £640 per month married to a precision engineer with a similar basic rate but taking home substantial undisclosed overtime earnings; Contact 4)

The parents in this fourth account worked in similar occupations at similar grades, but with different local authorities. Their earnings were similar, though the wife was said to be more likely to be promoted.

[My earnings] are important. Yes, they're fifty per cent. We regard it as joint money . . . But I mean because of the earnings of one of us, it means that we can save and we can enjoy spending on things . . . *Last time you told me you were saving all your money?* Yes, that's still my – well I suppose it's my husband thinking 'I'm the one who tries to cover everything in case you give up.' But I mean it's really joint money . . . It's mine that's providing the savings and care for (our son). And for my clothes. [Laughs] I suppose sometimes if we have an extraordinary bill mine is the one that pays it. (Principal local government officer married to a principal local government officer, both earning £840 a month; Contact 4)

In this last instance, the father's earnings were treated as core income, covering routine expenditure. By contrast, the mother's money was treated as surplus or peripheral income, i.e. savings, in case she was forced or wished to give up work at some point in the future (although she had no intention of doing so at the time). This perception of her income constituted a coping strategy in the event of leaving work: as her money was earmarked for savings, she deemed that it would not be used on a day to day basis. It was also a way of anticipating withdrawal from employment: the treatment of earnings as marginal to household resources *before* a mother leaves work would make a decision to leave easier.

The way in which women took responsibility for childcare fees was a further mechanism by which women's earnings were marginalized and treated as peripheral income in the household. As already mentioned, in the great majority of cases childcare fees came out of women's earnings, the justification for this being that the decision to return to work was their individual 'choice'. They estimated the value of their financial contribution to the household on the basis of whether or not it was 'worth their while' continuing to work once they had paid for childcare and the other costs of the dual earning lifestyle. Husband's earnings were considered without such deductions.

We did work it out that after paying for these items how much I was going to earn. Say I am in a very low paid job and I ended up working for no money. I'm not sure I could really do that, i.e. pay somebody else to look after my children and end up working for no money. (TV production assistant; Contact 4)

The effects of defining childcare as a charge on the women's earnings were twofold. First, it marginalized women's earnings in both real and symbolic terms. Second, it provided a way of anticipating and hence of coping with withdrawal from the labour market if, for example, women had a second child. As we have already discussed in Chapter 4, when facing the possibility of two childcare arrangements to pay for, together with the complexities of the organization involved, women might decide it was no longer 'worth their while working'. Thus despite the fact that a majority of returners remained in full-time continuous employment for three years after the birth, there was a culture of impermanence surrounding the *symbolic significance* of women's earnings to the household, with women playing down the importance of its actual significance.

The Prioritizing of
Hubands' Jobs

Just as some women marginalized their own economic contribution to the household, so it was frequent for women to prioritize their husbands' employment and earnings. At Contact 2, over half the returners said that their husbands' jobs were 'more important' than their own, a quarter said they were equal and only one fifth that their own jobs were more important. The most common legitimation for prioritizing husbands' employment was that they earned more, which indeed the majority (75%) did. However, even when the reverse was true – that is, the wife earned more than her husband – this did not guarantee that the wife's job was given priority.

> His job is more important even though I earn more. He's the man of the house . . . *Is it difficult that you earn more?* Oh no! He doesn't care at all . . . It's not right a man being at home and woman out at work. It's the way I was brought up. (Bank clerk married to a bus driver; Contact 2)

Closely associated with men's greater earning power was the idea that men's investment in paid work was central to their ego, with the wives of manual workers more likely to make such comments. Since a man 'has to work', his job 'has to be' more important.

> Again, a typical thing because a man's job is more important. *Why?* Because it is a man's job. (Clerk married to a council worker; Contact 2)

Just as men were perceived as having a higher investment than women in their jobs so they were also seen as unlikely candidates for childcare. Typically they were not expected to adapt to being at home.

> I don't think he'd have the same time for the children . . . He'd become more home oriented than child oriented. (Teacher; Contact 4)

> I think I get more enjoyment out of my job than he does from his – certainly, yes . . . But it's ingrained in you. It's

85

what you expect . . . plus the fact that the society as a whole expects husbands to be out at work. Quite honestly if he were at home for any length of time he would hate it. (Telephonist; Contact 4)

The corollary was that, despite enjoying their own jobs a great deal, a number of women said they were more likely than their husbands to 'settle' at home and to be 'better' at looking after children.

I think a woman has more ability . . . There's no way I think he'd be able to take on the care of a two month old baby . . . I don't think he'd be able to cope . . . I think it's partly being a male . . . The baby used to terrify him, he didn't feel safe with her on his own. I don't know. I think it's a male thing as well. I'd have more ability. And I'd feel it was my duty to do it as a mother. (Programmer; Contact 4)

A further legitimation for the priority given to husbands' jobs concerned the husband's happiness and household harmony.

He sees his responsibilities as the man, the breadwinner – he's still got that . . . I think my husband's job is important to me because it's so important to him to do it effectively. I like him to be happy because if he wasn't happy in his job the whole house would be unhappy. (Senior accountancy assistant; Contact 4)

Although men and women had started off their marriages with a similar investment in employment, at least in behavioural terms, with the birth of children women had little choice but to curtail their time in employment to the standard working day or less; they took on or were left with the major responsibility for their children, including taking children to and from carers (Chapter 10). In the following example, the husband increased his involvement in work, a change which brought about major consequences for the wife. After the birth of the first child, he changed his job three times and by Contact 4 was a rising executive in a multi-national company, working late every evening and frequently abroad on business. His wife had returned full-time to her former job as a local government administrator after the first birth, taking the child with her to the workplace creche. On maternity leave for her second baby she grew increasingly uncertain about returning to work a second time. Undoubtedly her husband's heavy work commitments were an important factor, together with the fact that, at her husband's insistence, they had recently moved to a new house, making her journey to work even longer and more complicated. Before the first birth she said she had been the main breadwinner because she had earned more than her husband and also because she had been deeply committed to her job. After the second birth her story was very different.

> My husband's job is everything to him. I think it shouldn't be. But whereas I see getting out of the house and having a job that you don't put much into as important. I consider my job important to me but he thinks his job is far more important to him . . . Before we had kids we were both workaholics. I've just learned not to be . . . Yes, I do find it difficult that we went into having kids with a view that jobs would take their toll to the same extent. But it just didn't happen. (Local government administrator; Contact 4)

In cases where the husband was in the process of setting himself up in business on his own the wife's job was clearly the more important one, at least until the business started making a profit. The wife in this second example was a senior accountancy officer in the NHS, married to an ex-site-manager who was setting up his own company. At Contact 4 her job was more stable and hence more critical to the family finances. On the question as to whose job was the more important she was clearly ambivalent but anxious that her husband 'succeeds', not only for his own satisfaction, but also from the point of view of their marriage.

> [My job is] very important at the moment. I tend to think of it as a form of security probably . . . [Laughs] I do want him to succeed. That's very important really although I think my job is very important. A bit conflicting! Depends on which way you look at it. *From the point of view of your marriage?* His I suppose. *The household?* That's got to be as well . . . Again he's putting so much into it. For all sorts of things which, he believes, will hopefully make life a bit more comfortable for us later on. His is not a selfish – hopefully for what we'll all get out of it. I think mine is a little bit more selfish. (Senior accountancy assistant; Contact 4)

Thus in addition to her concern about her husband's happiness, this woman was looking forward (in both senses) to the time when he would be the higher earner. Notable is the way in which she describes her own employment as 'selfish', a definition connected with the notion of women's employment as optional. By contrast the husband's employment is presumed to be central and enduring even though his wife commands a breadwinner wage. She justified this definition in terms of wanting her husband to 'succeed' in his business but also, one suspects, as a breadwinner.

So far we have neglected those women who gave equal or greater priority to their own jobs. On balance these women were more likely to earn more or the same as their husbands – that is, compared with those who put their husbands' jobs first – but they did not always give this as the reason (see also Stamp, 1985). The following extract from a Contact 4 interview illustrates the awkwardness that confronting such issues may provoke in a marriage, and which therefore may have influenced women's interview responses. The woman, a local government administrator, earned £300 a month more than her husband, a lockkeeper in Central London. But she was reluctant to say her own job was more important financially as well as being higher status.

> That's a loaded question. From my point of view my job is more important because I'd be lost without it. But his job is more important because he couldn't do without his work.

She searches for justification for putting her husband's job first. Ultimately, it comes down to the fact that their flat is tied to his job. Moreover, it is clear that he was unhappy with the fact that his wife earned more (he was present during part of the interview).

> [Husband interjecting] I feel I'm not contributing as much as I should be able to. Perhaps it's chauvinistic but the man should be at least equal to the wife . . . But she's cool. She says it's our money. I don't want to feel at the end of the day that I'm poncing off her. Not a nice word but living off her like. [Later, when the husband is out of the room, the wife says] I wish he would get over the obvious difficulty he has. [Pause] I still have a slight hold on my money. I wish we could just pool it.

It is notable that rather than accept her own greater earning power, this mother resorts to the (equalitarian) ideology of 'pooling' and blames herself for being the possessive partner in relation to money.

In general, where women put their own job first their accounts were characterized by an absence of comment. Women were often 'hard put' to respond to these questions – that is, in contrast to their responses to questions concerning the superiority of husbands' jobs and earnings. In effect they appeared to lack a clearly and confidently articulated discourse with which to express their obviously vital contribution to household resources. The male breadwinner ideology thus remained powerful even for this group of full-time employed women, suppressing in great measure the emergence of counter-ideologies.

The absence of ideologies which run counter to the breadwinner ideology cannot be explained by women's fear of poverty in the event of the break-up of their marriages since they were in full-time employment. Rather this absence may be explained, at least in part, by a powerful ideology of marriage with its emphasis on marriage as a state of love, not conflict. A counter-ideology which emphasizes women's economic power inside and outside marriage would need to make material exchanges part of the 'affective bargain' of love. We return to this issue of the ideology of modern marriage when we consider why returners did not complain (much) about their husbands' failure to share the housework and childcare equally (Chapter 11).

After childbirth women's employment orientations were fraught with contradictions. As workers, women described their jobs as very important to them while, as mothers, they wanted to be 'proper' mothers to their children and to enjoy the rewards of motherhood (see Chapter 7). An attractive compromise was to consider working part-time even though in practice many did not relish the poor conditions of most part-time jobs. Moreover, most women agreed that if one partner had to give up their job (for example, if childcare arrangements failed) it would have to be the mother (63% at Contact 4), irrespective of whether or not the mother wanted to.

Despite the fact that women's earnings were very important, in both relative and absolute terms, to their households, they were not necessarily valued accordingly, with women themselves frequently playing down their significance and labelling them as dispensable and somewhat peripheral. The process of marginalization constituted one way of anticipating the possibility of giving up work or of going part-time. Conversely, women also prioritized their husbands' jobs on the grounds of men's greater earning power or the centrality of employment to male identity and to male happiness and hence to marital harmony. These ways of talking about the significance of their own and their husbands' employment contributed to the creation of a culture of impermanence in which women's full-time employment was treated 'as if' it was a temporary phenomenon. This culture was further sustained by an ideology of motherhood which was critical of full-time employment; we turn now to consider this issue in more detail.

7

Employed Mothers – Ideologies and Experiences

This chapter explores women's constructions of their careers as mothers in paid employment over the time span of the study: both before and after the return to work and, for those who have been continuously in full-time employment, from the vantage point of having a 3 year old. It relates these constructions to dominant ideologies concerning motherhood, especially when children are very young, the ways in which employed mothers' accounts of motherhood reflect and the ways in which they challenge dominant ideologies. While ideologies are powerful, we do not regard them as imposed upon and accepted by mothers as passive victims; women negotiate their own meanings of motherhood, both in their beliefs and practices. Prevailing ideologies are a resource to be drawn upon in the construction of meaning, as well as forming part of the social context in which mothers conduct their lives.

The chapter begins with a brief overview of the discourses surrounding motherhood in the twentieth century and some of the main themes that make up the ideology of modern motherhood. This sets the historical and ideological context in which mothers in the study returned to work.

DISCOURSES OF MOTHERHOOD IN THE TWENTIETH CENTURY

The main discourse around parenthood in this century has been a concern for mothering and the transformation of childhood into a motherland (Lilestrom, 1981). Despite their having fewer children, motherhood has expanded in most women's lives, attracting new duties and a new significance, and requiring new skills. No more are mothers seen simply as the main providers for their children's physical health and well-being; they have come to be regarded as crucial to children's emotional development and cognitive progress.

> Women's emotional role in the family and their psychological mothering role grew just as their economic and biological role decreased. We notice women's mothering role today because it has ceased to be embedded in a range of other activities and human relations. It stands out in its emotional intensity and meaning, and in its centrality for women's lives and social definition. (Chodorow, 1978, p. 6)

At the beginning of the twentieth century motherhood had already come under the influence of experts, principally the medical profession. Physicians required that mothers impose a regime of iron hard discipline upon themselves and their treatment of their children. The failure of working-class children to thrive was attributed to mothers' fecklessness rather than to the poor economic and social conditions of the time. Mothers were instructed in the art of managing their household resources to promote the health of their children (Oakley, 1986; Schutze, 1988).

By the Second World War, motherhood had been transformed from a medical to a psychological orientation. The strict disciplining of children became unfashionable, especially in Europe and North America (Hardyment, 1983). New experts, child psychologists, became influential. One psychologist in particular exerted great influence in the post-war years – John Bowlby (Tizard, 1986). On the basis of his work on orphanages, Bowlby argued that a child would suffer psychologically if a mother did not provide her child with 'constant attention, day and night, seven days a week, and 365 days a year' (Bowlby, 1965, p. 77). It was essential, Bowlby concluded, 'that the young child should have a warm, intimate, and continuous relationship with his [sic] mother' (Bowlby, 1951, p. 361). The detrimental effects of maternal separation became the single most important post-war theory of child development; the corollary of full-time motherhood was that mothers should not be employed, certainly while their children were young.

From the 1950s onward a new development in the motherhood discourse became discernible. No longer was it sufficient for the mother to be constantly available to the child in the satisfaction of its every need. The mother was also supposed to derive personal enrichment and joy from her devotion – 'the mother's pleasure has to be there or else the whole procedure is dead, useless and mechanical' (Winnicott, 1962, p. 27) . According to this model, successful mothering was no longer a matter of moderating and governing undesirable emotions. In contrast to the discourse at the turn of the century in which mothers had been urged to restrain their need to be tender towards their children, in this new discourse they were required to produce, consciously and calculatedly, desirable emotions (Schutze, 1988). The principal mechanism by which motherhood was decreed to be a pleasurable activity operated through the imposition of norms of child development – the process by which characteristics of positive value were fostered in the child (Urwin, 1985).

Whereas Bowlby had been largely concerned with the prevention of emotional disorders in children, the contemporary emphasis has increasingly been on optimal, as opposed to adequate, levels of achievement in children. Increasing emphasis has been placed on mothers as unfolders of their children's cognitive capacities, with maternal ambition goaded (by a variety of experts and, increasingly, a 'child development' industry of manufacturers, retailers and media) to have the best developed child (Schutze, 1988). However, elements of the preceding phase – namely the importance of mothers in their children's emotional development – have been carried over: mothers are supposed to be instrumental in fostering their child's cognitive and emotional development.

The allocation of responsibility to mothers for their child's development is sustained by a set of intrinsic rewards: the promise of seeing the child achieve each developmental milestone (Urwin, 1985). Thus enjoyment is to be derived from the means of achieving the goal as well as from achievement of the goal itself. A key aspect of this process is conducted through 'play', a phenomenon rediscovered by child development experts and transformed into an important constituent of the pedagogic repertoire. Thus a mother is positively rewarded if she spends every moment of the day with her child; if she fails to do this she is condemned to feeling guilty.

This discussion indicates one of the main themes that have constituted the dominant ideology of motherhood in the post-war years – that when children are small, 'normal' motherhood is a full-time activity precluding employment, and that the mother has the major responsibility for all aspects of the child's development. This theme has not remained entirely unchanged over the years. We have already noted an increased emphasis on the mother's role in fostering cognitive development. Ideas about mothers' employment have also evolved. For example, the proportion of women who agree with the statement that 'a married woman with children under school age ought to stay at home' has decreased in

92

recent years, from 78% in 1965 to 62% in 1980 and 45% in 1987 (Jowell, Witherspoon and Brook, 1988).

Closer examination shows that this represents an adaptation of existing ideologies, not a fundamental change. Even by the late 1980s, nearly half of all women still opposed maternal employment without reservation. Moreover, a majority of the remaining women (29% out of 55%) took the implicitly negative view that going out to work is only acceptable as the lesser of two evils, supporting the statement that a married woman with pre-school children 'should only work if she needs the money'. The remainder held that it was 'up to her whether to go out to work or not'. There continues to be no support for the proposition that women with young children 'ought to work', although it would be regarded as uncontroversial if applied to men with young children.

This evidence suggests a growing, if grudging, acceptance of maternal employment, but not positive approval. Moreover, the survey data quoted say nothing about the conditions attached to this acceptance. It may well be, for example, that there is much less acceptance of women working full-time or working when they have very young children (under 2) – in other words to the course of action taken by most women in our study. Moreover, it seems probable that the growing acceptance of maternal employment assumes that the major responsibility for children and their development remains with mothers; maternal employment, therefore, is only acceptable if women continue to discharge this responsibility.

Some support for this interpretation comes from the 1986 British Social Attitudes Survey where respondents were asked to choose which of six work arrangements they thought was best for a family with a child under 5. The great majority (76%) selected an arrangement where the mother was at home; virtually all the rest preferred the mother in part-time, as opposed to full-time, employment. Moreover, the overwhelming proportion of respondents (93%) chose an arrangement where men with children under 5 worked full-time; only 3% opted for an arrangement where both parents worked similar hours. In other words, the preferred arrangement involved fathers in full-time jobs, together with full-time motherhood or, failing that, employment clearly subsidiary to the motherhood role.

The ideology of motherhood in the 1980s emphasized women's continuing major responsibility for children and their development – and, as a corollary, the male breadwinning role and the unacceptability of full-time maternal employment. Closely related

93

to this was the belief that the care of young children was a private responsibility to be managed within the household, without external social support. As discussed in Chapter 3, this view of childcare as a private issue was given increasing prominence by the Government in the 1980s as a justification for not intervening to support employed parents. It is expressed clearly below by two women – one from our sample, the other a politician and former Minister.

> I feel really we had him, he's really up to us or one of us . . . I suppose it's just an old fashioned view really. They are your responsibility and I feel it should be me, not somebody else. (Health service technician; Contact 1)

> I start off by believing that people should provide for their own children and provide their own childcare – it's not that difficult. (Edwina Currie, former Department of Health Minister with responsibility for childcare)

The significance of this belief that childcare is a totally private responsibility is brought into relief by the situation in some other societies, for example France or the countries of Scandinavia, where it is accepted that there is some degree of social responsibility for the care of children. In Denmark, for example, 'the social structure (of childcare services for employed parents) which has developed during the last 20 years is based on the concept that the responsibility for children's upbringing rests jointly with parents and society . . . basically the attitude on the left wing as well as the right wing is that the society has extensive obligations to ensure children fair and good conditions during the years of growth' (Schmidt, 1987, p. 11). Similarly, in Sweden, there is 'agreement that society must ensure that all children . . . who need care outside the home can obtain care of good quality' (Broberg and Hwang, 1990, p. 98).

ATTITUDES TO MATERNITY LEAVE

At Contact 1 women were asked whether or not they thought mothers of young children ought to resume employment after childbirth. Not surprisingly, those intending to return to work were much less hostile to the idea than those not intending to do so. Eighteen per cent of intending returners were opposed compared with 59% of those not intending to return. It is important to

94

note that mothers were asked specifically about mothers' working full-time and from choice rather than necessity, a question which might be expected to have led to more negative attitudes rather than the broader question asked in national surveys.

Although women were coded as being more or less in favour of mothers of young children's being employed they were also in many cases equivocal. A qualitative analysis shows that their responses were marked in many instances by nuance and reservation. Some felt it was only admissible to be employed in certain circumstances – if the mother needed the money or had a career. Other women were reluctant to be judgemental or dogmatic – 'It's up to them', 'It's a matter for the individual'. But a substantial number then went on to spell out the considerations to be borne in mind in cases where mothers did return to work – 'It's O.K. but . . .' 'It's O.K. unless . . .' . The principal reservation concerned the child – ensuring that he or she didn't 'suffer'.

In general, women ignored the contradiction between being unbiased and the setting of conditions under which mothers' employment was admissible. What interpretation should be put upon this apparent contradiction and women's failure to confront it? It might be seen as an indication of 'anomalous consciousness'. Alternatively, it might be seen as a 'way of talking' which is highly contextual (Frazer, 1988). According to this second view, women exhibit 'communicative competence' (Hymes, 1971), switching positions according to the context – in this case between their own individual situations (which for those intending to return to work involved contravening the dominant ideology), and their stance as to what is acceptable within the general dominant ideology. The 'truth' is probably somewhere between the two.

THE EXPERIENCE OF
MATERNITY LEAVE

As maternity leave drew to an end, the majority (67%) admitted to anxiety or doubts about their decision to return. This finding emerges from responses to a direct question, though women also frequently confessed to anxiety once the interview had ended. Not surprisingly, some seized upon the interview as an opportunity to express their concerns since, as we will describe elsewhere (Chapter 13), sources of advice and support – both formal and informal – frequently proved inadequate or inappropriate on these issues. Many of women's doubts and anxieties hinged upon the

95

ideologically salient question of the harm and disruption which might be caused to the mother–child relationship by the separation. The conflict was typically experienced and expressed as a feeling.

> I don't know if I'd say it was right. I don't think it's wrong. Difficult to be objective. I suppose inside myself I don't feel it's right. I feel I ought to be at home. But I've rationalized it to myself so much it's difficult to step back from that . . . I've always known I was going back to work . . . Originally I was going back in July. But as the time approached I put it off and then I thought 'I've got to go back'. I've tried to make the best arrangements for the baby that I can . . . I suppose it's because he's so little and you're so attached to him. It's very very hard and the break is very very hard. I feel that attached to him and he must feel that attached to me. It *feels* like you're abandoning him at a time when they need you [our emphasis]. (Librarian; Contact 1)

These anxieties also had a material basis in women's individual situations. Since the birth, women had been responsible for the child day and night (though returners were likely to anticipate the return to work by leaving the child in others' care for short periods). Some women had not yet found a childcare arrangement by the time of the first interview (Moss, 1986), while a few women did not yet know what job they would be doing or where they would be working once they had returned to work. Furthermore, mothers on maternity leave had yet to accomplish the organizational feat of getting the child to the carer and themselves to work. These material circumstances were themselves likely to provoke considerable anxiety about the return.

Women employed a number of strategies in order to deal with their doubts and anxieties; they were not victims of these material constraints. They anticipated their return to work with, for example, 'dummy runs' – practising for the day when they had to get the children ready and take them to the carers' before getting themselves to work. Some returned before the end of statutory maternity leave, specifically so that their children would not become 'too attached' to them (others, of course, returned early for other reasons). Various mental coping strategies or 'cognitive manoeuvres' (Pearlin and Schooler, 1978) were adopted – for example, taking the view that 'I can always give up my job if it doesn't work out' or waiting 'to see how it goes', a strategy which parcelled up time and reduced it to small manageable portions. Another way was to take a realistic stance – expecting it to be difficult at the beginning (Brannen and Moss, 1988).

The ideology of the inseparability of the mother–child bond was brought to the fore when women contemplated the return to work. There is a level at which the ideology of mother love parallels the ideology of monogamous love between adults. Both types of love emphasize the desired and desirable situation of one person forming a close, unique relationship with only one other person at a time. Mothers talk about their love for their babies as 'special' and exclusive – as the 'be all and end all' (Oakley, 1980, 1986). In describing their search for childcare mothers referred to finding substitutes for, rather than additions to, themselves, as if the child could only be 'properly' attached to one person. Notably, women never alluded to the impact of fathers' separation from the child. Such 'monogamous' notions of the mother–child relationship are likely to induce feelings of conflict as women think about resuming their jobs and putting the child in someone else's care. The language which they drew upon in describing the anticipated separation is highly suggestive – 'breaking the bond', 'abandoning' or 'leaving' the child.

The conflict that women experienced in contemplating the separation did not appear to affect their accounts of .the pleasurable aspects of full-time motherhood. Indeed, they largely constructed the rewards of motherhood according to features of 'normal' (i.e. full-time) motherhood, though in response to direct questions returners were more likely than non-returners to complain about the conditions of full-time motherhood. Despite their employment intentions and their reservations about being at home, returners' accounts of motherhood as a positive experience focused on the centrality of the mother–child relationship – namely, the child's responsiveness to the mother and the pleasures of witnessing and enabling the child to develop. It was notable that in response to these questions intending returners did not articulate anxieties about the effects of their employment.

As well as coded answers to single questions and qualitative analysis of responses to open-ended questions and probes, at Contacts 1 and 2 separate ratings were made of women's satisfaction and dissatisfaction with motherhood. These four-point ratings (none, minimal, moderate, high) were made on the basis of responses to questions about the pleasures and pains of motherhood, as well as respondents' non-verbal communication. These

Table 7.1 *Motherhood dissatisfaction ratings while on maternity leave by employment intentions*

Employment intentions at Contact 1	Last occupation before birth		Dissatisfaction ratings		
			None/low	*Moderate*	*High*
To resume employment after maternity leave	HS (N = 100)	(%)	47	38	15
	LS (N = 77)	(%)	43	35	22
	Total (N = 177)	(%)	45	37	18
Not to resume employment after maternity leave	HS (N = 27)	(%)	67	26	7
	LS (N = 39)	(%)	77	18	5
	Total (N = 66)	(%)	73	21	6

Key:
HS = High status occupations (professional and managerial)
LS = Low status occupations (clerical, sales, manual)

ratings showed that returners were more likely to describe the experience of being a mother on maternity leave in negative as well as positive terms: 55% of returners compared with 27% of non-returners were rated as moderately or severely dissatisfied (Table 7.1). Complaints focused mainly upon the social conditions of being at home on leave – in particular the isolation and loneliness of being at home all day – rather than on the totality of maternal responsibility. Many returners claimed that they had been able to put up with being at home only because they knew it was a temporary phase. Boulton (1983) also found that mothers' assessments of the context of motherhood are largely independent of the way they described their feelings for their children.

Returners were perhaps more ready than non-returners to confront the negative aspects of being a full-time mother while on maternity leave because they had already made up their minds to return to work. The process of articulating their reasons for returning may have helped to open up the issue. Since the researchers tried hard not to associate themselves with a particular value position respondents were not required to give 'public accounts' of their individual experiences which were consistent with dominant ideological definitions of motherhood as a full-time career. (For a discussion of public and private accounts see Cornwell, 1984.) On the other hand, asked about the rewards of motherhood, returners' and non-returners' accounts were similar.

THE TRANSITION BACK TO
WORK

Analysis of changes between Contacts 1 and 2 in individual women's satisfaction with motherhood shows that twice as many returners as non-returners had increased their satisfaction ratings (32% v. 16%); conversely, non-returners were more likely to have increased dissatisfaction ratings (75% v. 56%). In response to specific questions at Contact 2, nearly half the non-returners (48%) claimed to have felt bored at home, rather more than when they were interviewed on maternity leave (38%). Forty-six per cent said the social side of their lives could be better, compared with 37% at Contact 1 (these questions were not asked of returners at Contact 2). Overall therefore, returners were likely to become more satisfied and less dissatisfied with motherhood over the return to work period compared with non-returners, and after nearly a year at home, non-returners were more dissatisfied with motherhood, a reverse of the situation at Contact 1.

Although by Contact 2 the returners' and non-returners' experiences of motherhood were not directly comparable, their accounts, especially concerning the positive aspects of motherhood, do not appear to differ significantly in substance. This is important in terms of an earlier argument concerning women's experiences of maternity leave. It reinforces the conclusion that feelings are not necessarily synonymous with the conditions that give rise to them.

On the rewards of motherhood, both returners and non-returners said that they enjoyed their children more at 10–11 months than at 4–5 months because they were older. The rewards of motherhood were couched in the ideology of child development. In a qualitative analysis of responses at Contact 2 about the positive aspects of motherhood, 70% mentioned the rewards of observing their children's development – their greater co-ordination, competence and 'responsiveness' (N=47); (the other 30% were split between those who did not find any aspect enjoyable, those who mentioned other features and those who did not venture any particular features).

Few returners drew any connection with their employment when discussing either the positive or negative features of motherhood. On the negative side, for example, they dwelt on characteristically restrictive features of motherhood – sleepless nights, not being able to have a lie-in, times when their children were irritable, ill or over-demanding. Non-returners, by contrast, emphasized different features, many of which were connected with the condition of full-time motherhood – the 'need to have a break' from their child and the social and physical isolation of being at home all day.

Women's accounts therefore reflect the divisions in our questions. Feelings of guilt and loss at separation from their children, discussed below, did not intrude upon their responses to motherhood questions. Similarly, mothers did not link the difficulties which they experienced on their return to work – overload, problems with the child and childcare and which were reported by 59% of returners in response to direct questioning – to their answers to questions about motherhood.

This evidence suggests two conclusions: dominant ideologies do not totally determine how people feel about an experience; but they do affect how people 'package' their responses. This may be understood as a strategy, albeit an unconscious one, by which women avoided confronting the conflict between the normative model of the 'good mother' and their practices as mothers in full-time employment. Non-employed mothers who had been at home for some considerable time expressed their dissatisfactions even when their actions concurred with dominant ideologies. Similarly, employed mothers, whose actions conflicted with dominant ideologies, expressed greater dissatisfaction with maternity leave and greater satisfaction with their experiences of being a mother than women at home. Such findings indicate the varied and contradictory nature of human experience and, in particular, the lack of fit between ideologies and lived experience: the ways in which actors draw upon the language of dominant ideologies in their accounts of their experiences and the way in which these accounts are at times in conflict with their feelings. A measure of the power of the ideology of full-time motherhood is the extent to which it precludes the development of new discourses and ideologies which legitimate new models of motherhood.

Leaving the Child

The separation of a mother from her child if she returns to work, especially from a very young child and to a full-time job, calls into question the very essence of what it is to be a 'proper' mother in Britain. As we have suggested, it is significant that returners' considerable distress about 'leaving' their children was not referred to by the women in their replies to questions about the pleasurable and painful aspects of motherhood. Yet women talked very readily about the matter when asked about it.

Asked specifically at Contact 2 how they had felt about the separation in the first week or so of the return to work, 74% described themselves as considerably distressed. This finding is not surprising in one sense since, in the great majority of cases, it was the mothers who took and left the children at the carers (see Chapter 10).

> It seemed very odd walking around without the baby . . . I used to carry her in a sling and all of a sudden I was standing there on the pavement without anything. It feels as if you are missing something. I felt apprehensive, worried. (Secretary; Contact 2)

Women described a variety of other feelings over the first weeks away from their children, particularly feelings of anxiety, loss and guilt. These feelings were fuelled both by ideologies of motherhood and by their material circumstances. Anxiety manifested itself in a variety of ways. Some women said they had to restrain themselves from continually ringing up the carer in order to check on their children. At the end of the working day many could scarcely contain themselves, rushing off to be reunited with their child. Undoubtedly their anxiety was increased by ideological prescriptions that only mothers' care is 'good enough'. However, in addition, women were made anxious by situational factors. For example, nearly two thirds (65%) had had no opportunity to settle their children at the carers before their first day back at work.

The second predominant feeling described was an acute sense of loss or impending loss at the separation from the child. In accordance with the primordial significance which is accorded to the emotional tie between mother and child, women feared that they might be giving up their child to someone else and that that person might supplant the mother in the child's affections. For some, this fear was an influential factor in their choice of childcare. In particular, those who found nurseries for their

101

children frequently justified this choice of care in terms of the child 'not growing too attached' to any one person. Similarly, some of the mothers who used their relatives for childcare said they would be unhappy with a childminder because the child might become over-attached to a 'stranger', the implication being that attachment via a blood tie was acceptable, desirable and (in any case) natural. Women were also undergoing a real loss since they had spent most of the past months in intimate contact with their child.

The third feeling was guilt – guilt that the child might suffer or not progress because the mother was not with them all the time. 'Proper' mothers are supposed to devote all their time to their children. Such feelings were anticipatory since, as yet, they had no evidence that their actions would damage their children.

Coming to Terms

After a few months back at work most mothers said they felt differently and had come to terms with their sadness and worry. Moreover, they came to see it as their own loss rather than the child's.

> I really felt in that first week as if my heart was breaking – leaving her. I thought 'I'm never going to get over this'. But it's got much easier now. It's a bit like a broken love affair, I suppose. It mends. (Teacher; Contact 2)

Coming to terms with the separation from the child was typically described in similar terms to the process of grief following the death of a loved one. Women said they felt initially overcome with the trauma of separation and anguish at the physical absence of the child. With time and the realization that the child was happy and settled at the carer's and showing no signs of missing them, they accepted the separation.

> Leaving him was a wrench. I'm not sure if it was depression or what. Or whether it was a sort of selfish feeling. I just missed him. It was worst at the time I had to drop him off. I was running to the tube crying my eyes out. It was a difficult time those first two weeks. I had been very obsessed with the baby. Obviously, he is the main thing in my life. But he's not the only thing I think about now. I'm forced to think of other things. *Do you feel O.K. about that?* I think so. He still has all my love and loads of attention. Now I don't worry at all about him at work. At first it was difficult because I

had to come to terms with my relationship to the baby. *Do you feel guilty?* Yes I think you do. I think most of us would. (Solicitor; Contact 2)

Another mother said she eventually overcame the common fear that a baby will forget who its mother is.

It was a lot easier than I thought it would be. I had fantasies in my head that nobody could look after the baby. Nobody will do it the same way, which is a load of nonsense. The baby survives willy nilly. (Doctor; Contact 2)

Although the great majority of returners came to terms with the separation, at Contact 2 nearly a third (31%) said they continued to feel guilty from time to time. Feelings of conflict and guilt were described as occurring in particular kinds of situations. Typically, women said they were brought on when children were ill or 'off colour'. Here was the ultimate situation in which only mothers' care was considered 'good enough'; children were said to 'need' their mothers when they were ill. Practical constraints also came into the matter since it was the mother who was usually faced with the responsibility and the dilemma as to whether to keep the child at home and take time off work (Chapter 10). If the mother considered the child's illness to be only slight, she frequently felt torn about taking time off work. Where the mother decided that the child was fit enough to go to the carer's she often felt bad about it.

Guilt was sometimes said to be experienced fleetingly, provoked by reminders of how 'proper mothers' ought to behave.

On sunny days when I see lots of mothers and their babies – there's a playschool nearby – I think 'I really should be with him'. I feel guilty. (Local government administrator; Contact 2)

Women said they started to think about their children when they were under-occupied at work. They felt unable to enjoy this leisure because of the more important priority – namely, their sense of duty to their child. They felt both that they ought to be with them and wanted to be with them.

When I'm busy I'm happy and when I'm not I sit there thinking 'I could be downstairs with the baby'. (Local government administrator whose child was in the workplace creche; Contact 2)

Because 'proper' mothers are expected to assume primary responsibility, returners wanted to compensate their children for

103

their absence when they were not at work. They felt guilty if, because of tiredness or having household chores to do, they were unable to devote all their time and attention to their children. Some also felt guilty if they suspected that the carers were not investing as much effort in their children as they considered, perhaps somewhat unrealistically, that they themselves would have done if they had been at home.

Although most mothers came to terms with separation, a few did not and experienced acute and persistent guilt feelings. Most resigned soon after their return to work, although a small number 'soldiered on' mainly because of financial pressure.

> I still have my cultural guilt about the fact that I'm not looking after him and maybe people are right when they think I should be. I enjoy my work. *Do you think people think that?* Good question! An element of me thinks that and then I feel angry with myself for being so stupid as to think that. But I know that when I first went back to work I felt certain people might think I was a bad mother. And the reason I thought that as well was this voice inside me – and the guilt is still there. (Language teacher; Contact 2)

Other Negative Feelings

We probed for other negative feelings – jealousy and feelings of rejection – which might arise in the context of placing children in others' care. These feelings were less common than guilt. Thirty-two per cent said they had felt jealous at some time, mainly of the child's carer, though by Contact 2 only 4% of mothers still often felt jealous. Eighteen per cent described feeling 'a bit left out' at some time, typically when they came to collect their children from the carers. Though most women claimed never to have felt jealous or rejected, they did not appear surprised by or defensive about the questions, and some women indicated they had expected to experience these feelings. Women who admitted to such feelings frequently said that they were balanced out by the realization and relief that the child had formed a good relationship with the carer.

Feeling Positive

Despite the initial trauma at leaving their children and the recurrence of guilt, by Contact 2 the great majority of returners said they were happy with their decision to continue working. Asked a specific question which required them to make an overall judgement, four fifths were on balance positive, while the rest were wholly or mainly negative. Women felt positive from several vantage points – their children's and their own, both as mothers and individuals – and described a number of benefits; (similar benefits were described at Contact 4, and they will be presented in detail in the next section). It is likely that one of the principal benchmarks for evaluating their decisions concerned their experiences at home on maternity leave which, as we noted earlier, were not very positive. Returners' emphasis upon the benefits of working was therefore one of the ways in which ideologies of conventional motherhood were challenged, though these assertions did not emerge in their responses to questions about motherhood.

WORKING MOTHERS AND
3 YEAR OLDS

In this last section we consider data from Contact 4, when the first born children were 3 years old, and specifically from the qualitative analysis of the sub-set of women who were still working full-time at Contact 4. We consider in detail the three main themes which emerged from women's responses: the pleasures of motherhood, the losses incurred in being a working mother and the benefits.

The Pleasures

As outlined earlier, current ideologies of motherhood emphasize mothers' contribution to cognitive and emotional development. They construct mothers as the principal figures in bringing about 'normal' developmental progress. At each contact mothers talked a great deal about 'development', were highly conversant with behaviour appropriate to each developmental stage, and saw this as one of the most rewarding aspects of having young children.

> I enjoy just sort of seeing her different behaviour patterns that she has and the way she is changing. (Secretary; Contact 4)

> I enjoy his development. Each day is a new day. I still think it's fun to see all the new things he can do. I think that's what I really enjoy – his development. (Hospital cook; Contact 4)

Asked specifically about losses entailed in being employed, mothers feared that this was the reward they would most likely be denied. Yet at the same time they were at pains to demonstrate that they had not missed out by drawing attention to the occasions when

105

they had witnessed their children's first steps and first words. By implying that they were exceptional in this respect, working mothers constructed their experiences according to the dominant paradigm.

> I've been very lucky. I've seen firsts with both of them. And I gather that's quite unique not being there all day. The chances of them doing something . . . I sometimes wonder if [nanny] isn't telling a fib so I'll get the pleasure out of saying it. (Surveyor; Contact 4)

The ideology of mothers as developers of their children emphasizes not simply the benefits for the child but also the rewards for the mother – namely, the fun element of it all (Urwin, 1985). Mothers were very largely in tune with this element and talked about the delights gained from teaching their children and 'bringing them on'.

> You put a lot of love and work into them and now it's being rewarded. She'll come and cuddle you spontaneously and tell you she loves you. And the way she's developing (is a pleasure) because a lot is down to yourselves. I do enjoy trying to teach her. (Bank clerk; Contact 4)

It was not universally regarded as fun, however, as the comments below suggest. Significantly, this mother associated 'bringing on' children with full-time motherhood.

> I try to bring her on but I'm not sure I'm active enough . . . like getting her to drink from a cup. That's because she blows bubbles and I can't stand the mess. So I only do it every now and again. But I keep on telling myself that I'll do everything like that when I've given up work . . . I'm putting off being a super mother. (Administrator; Contact 2)

In talking about the pleasures of 'seeing children develop' mothers also suggested that each stage has its own specific rewards. When their children were babies and toddlers, mothers dwelt on their physical development – 'watching him grow' – and on their responsiveness. When children reached 3, mothers' accounts highlighted new aspects of their development: they were valued for being 'older', for their ability to do things for themselves, for the companionship they provided.

> It's very nice when they become less physically dependent on you. It's very nice when they can talk and can communicate

properly with you. I think they go through a very frustrating period when they want to communicate but can't do it properly. (Solicitor; Contact 4)

Just the fact that she's my daughter and she gives me pleasure and she's fun to be with. You can take a pride in her . . . She's done something. It's as if you've achieved something as well. (Computer programmer; Contact 4)

The significance women attached to witnessing their children's development emerged in a second context. At the end of the last interview, women in the study were asked about their experiences as respondents. One quarter were interviewed on the subject while the whole sample was invited to write about their experience and to return their comments by post to the researchers; approximately 60% did so. Among the most frequently mentioned aspects of the research considered to be rewarding was the developmental assessment carried out at three of the four contacts. Mothers enjoyed seeing what their children were capable of, but there was also a concern as to whether their children were doing as well as other children of the same age. Since women had been told that the study was about the progress of children in different types of caregiving environment they were, not surprisingly, anxious to know which groups were doing 'better' and which 'worse'. Their comments also suggest that they saw the findings on the children's progress as the most important outcome of the study. In response to a direct question most wanted to be told the results, especially about the progress of children in different types of daycare. These findings underline women's concern about any negative repercussions of their employment upon their children's development.

Regrets and Losses

One of the main preoccupations of working mothers is time and the concern that they may not be giving sufficient time to their children. It has been noted that there are two ways in which mothers conceptualize the giving of time to children.

The conception of 'the child as being' means that both parents and children . . . are subject to certain limitations and rules to which they must be resigned . . . Development is not something that can be achieved as a goal set by parents. Rather there is a 'natural order' of things to which one must submit. Similarly, the concept of 'child as project' can be linked to the idea of planning. Individuality is seen as a goal . . . A child

107

is not born possessing certain traits . . . but rather develops
these traits through interaction . . . This notion is linked to
a psychological perspective whereby the role of the parent is
productive rather than reproductive. (Hallden, 1988, p. 5)

Mothers in the study viewed their children from both perspectives and worried about the lack of time for both. As children got
older the notion of 'the child as project' assumed more significance.
When their children were younger the notion of 'the child as being'
was more salient; the giving of time was more important as an end
in itself rather than a means to an end. In general, mothers in the
study suggested that giving their children time was less likely to
have tangible results at a younger than an older age. In the first
year of life mothers' concern with development was defined more
as a reward than as a goal of motherhood. At this time, they
appeared to feel less obviously influential in terms of producing
particular outcomes, subscribing to the notion that children grow
willy nilly.

Yet at the same time they may have also felt that, as new mothers,
they could not be certain of this. A parallel can be drawn with the
Protestant Ethic, according to which the individual urges herself
to work hard to ensure salvation since there is no certain way
of knowing during life on earth that a place in heaven has been
secured. So it is with first time mothers; they feel they must continually stimulate their children in order that, in later life, the child
fulfils its promise. At the time they have no way of forecasting the
results of their efforts but dare not risk not making the effort. With
greater experience such anxieties may wane. A mother in another
study summed up the matter succinctly.

> You know all these 'stages' of development that children are
> supposed to go through? Well, I've been thinking. If children
> everywhere are supposed to do the same things at round about
> the same ages, what difference does it make anyway what I
> do? (Urwin, 1985, p. 200)

But at all ages, a superabundance of mothers' time, both directed
and undirected, was seen as desirable – yet difficult to provide
since time was a resource in short supply for working mothers.
Two women convey this idea succinctly.

> The woman who works hasn't got time for her family . . . I
> wonder if I'll regret it in years to come. I may not be giving
> her what I should be giving. (Deputy head of a residential
> hostel; Contact 4)

I don't feel I am a full-time mother. When you say about being a mother, to me it's somebody who is there quite a lot of the time. In a sense, the childminder must be the mother because she is fulfilling a lot of physical and emotional functions as well. So, in a sense if she's any good, which I think she is, then she's kind of got two mums . . . Do they know I wonder who their real mum is? (Careers officer; Contact 2)

The Child as Being

Mothers compensated their children for not being there all the time by spending as much time as possible with them when not at work. It was also a way of expiating guilt for not being a 'proper' mother. Setting aside 'special times' for their children was a common strategy (the literature talks about the notion of 'quality time' (Hoffman, 1980)). Typically, these 'special times' included the period following the mothers' return from work, while some mothers also set aside time at weekends.

Sundays are our day. I try to get everything done so I can have Sunday free with her. We go out together and play a lot. (Librarian; Contact 4)

Most mothers said that at weekends they normally went out as 'a family' rather than as a couple. This was a way of devoting time to children but also a way of giving children greater significance in the life of the household – a corporate identity as opposed to the separate identities of couple versus the child.

In their great anxiety to compensate their children for the time they were not with them some women worried that they might be overindulgent. But on balance many felt that this was a risk they had to take, especially as they also harboured the fear that the child might, at some later point, interpret lack of time as lack of care.

The Child as Project

When children reached 3 years of age, mothers' concerns about giving time were focused more on the results of their efforts, principally with the child's cognitive development, though they were also concerned with social development – learning how to mix with adults and other children. This was a major concern of all mothers at this stage, whatever their employment status. Middle-class mothers, in particular, were concerned about their children's intellectual progress, especially the possible limitations of their children's current daycare environments as they approached

109

3 years of age. This concern about a lack of 'stimulation' (the operative language) in the daycare environment was reinforced by anxiety about a lack of maternal care.

> I'm a bit more worried now that opportunities may be passing. *How do you mean?* I think he's getting to an age when he needs more input. He's growing so fast. I think he needs more input before he starts school. I feel we don't have enough time for him. I'd like to take him to a lot more things as well, more stimulation perhaps . . . Before, it didn't really matter. I feel he's coming to an age where we must concentrate on him. (Executive officer in the Civil Service; Contact 4)

> I was wanting to change his childminder anyway [They now had a second child and the childminder was unable to have both children] . . . For various reasons actually . . . Basically [the childminder's family] are a completely different social class from us. It began to be important to me, just that he was in a more similar kind of house . . . He was beginning to watch TV an awful lot . . . Things were cropping up like racist comments . . . and the husband thought school was a total waste of time . . . And the language he was beginning to pick up! (Teacher; Contact 4)

As children got older, women's concern and guilt about time was aggravated by additional demands. Those with two children felt they had insufficient time for both children. Others regretted not being able to participate with their children in important new experiences, in particular starting playgroup or nursery school. Some felt that their children would miss out on the 'social round' because they had insufficient time to organize activities with other children.

Some women worried that they might jeopardize future relations with their children by being 'only' part-time mothers. They feared their children might turn against them when they were older.

> That's my greatest fear, her turning on me when she's 14 and saying 'You didn't love me because you shoved me into a nursery'. (College administrator; Contact 4)

Another mother expresses a similar fear, alluding directly to full-time motherhood as the norm and stressing the importance of playing with her child as a means of developing her.

> I sometimes think I don't play enough with her . . . because of

110

my work. In the morning she might get up and want to play. I dare say for a lot of people at home they can do that. It doesn't matter when they have breakfast. But because we're always working to a timetable and a very strict timetable, I feel we're always trying to push it into her head 'Oh, Mummy's got to catch the train', that Mummy's more important in a way. I sometimes wonder when she goes to school, I daresay there will be loads of mothers who don't go to work – whether she feels then 'Why should Mummy go to work?' (Secretary; Contact 4)

By the age of 3, some children were already wise to the dominant construction of full-time motherhood. Mothers regarded their children's disapproval as the ultimate sanction: it was one thing to have to leave a child at the carer's when he or she was 'under the weather' but quite another when the child said she didn't want her mother to go to work.

Those sort of piercing questions: 'Why do you have to go to work, Mummy? I don't want to be here. I want to be with you'. They are quite traumatic. (Physiotherapist; Contact 4)

She screams blue murder in the morning when I go to work. She knows when it gets to about 8.45 – 'Mummy, don't go to work'. Before I used to hide from her but now I thought 'No, this has got to stop'. (Bank clerk; Contact 4)

The Gains of Being
a Working Mother

In response to direct questions at both Contacts 2 and 4, the great majority (80%) felt that, on balance, there had been more gains than losses from combining motherhood with full-time employment. The gains were justified on three grounds: the effects on the mother–child relationship, the child and the mother.

Despite the ideological salience of giving time to children, women asserted that working motherhood resulted in a heightened quality of the mother–child relationship because they were not with their children all the time. In some instances women gave the normative notion of 'giving time' a new twist in talking about 'quality time' (Hoffman, 1980).

I really believe it's not the quantity so much as the quality of mothering. And certainly I rarely get fed up with her. Never to the point where I would smack her. Whereas if

111

I was at home with her all the time I think I would do.
(Nurse; Contact 4)

Em, I wouldn't say all the time he has with me is quality
time because a lot of the time I'm actually tired. But I think
I'm certainly a lot more patient with him on a daily basis
than I would be if I was with him all the time. (Doctor;
Contact 4)

Mothers readily gave instances in support of their assertions that
they were better mothers for working. Some commented that they
felt able to devote themselves exclusively to the task when they
were not at work. Others mentioned looking forward to seeing
their children at the end of the working day, coming home to them
refreshed, with feelings of renewed vigour, energy and patience to
care for them. Many had clearly reflected a good deal on these
matters, concluding that they would have been less involved and
less patient with their children had they been at home with them
all day every day.

I think we may have a better relationship. I think I might
have been quite short with her, if I'd been at home. I feel
that my patience [now] is just right for her. (Administrative
assistant; Contact 4)

Children were also seen as gaining in other ways from their mothers
being employed. In some cases, children were thought to be more
outgoing, independent and sociable as a consequence.

I think he's benefited. He's more outward. He's more happy
and he's very approachable – never sort of wary. He goes
straight in there. If he was stuck at home with me I think
I wouldn't have been able to give him as much . . . He gets
on with other children as well. (Clerical officer; Contact 4)

Others said their children benefited from the broadening experience of being in more than one environment. In some cases
nurseries and childminders were felt to provide what the women
felt they, as relatively inexperienced mothers, could not. Other
mothers said that only by virtue of their own employment had
they been able to afford material goods and beneficial experiences
for their children.

Finally, women emphasized the overall benefits of combining
motherhood and employment by invoking personal gains. As
discussed in Chapter 6, a strong personal commitment to work
constituted an important factor, both in women's original decisions

to return to work and in the ongoing significance they attributed to employment. In talking about the gains of being a working mother they said they benefited from having 'another topic of conversation', from 'being interested and informed' people, from 'being able to communicate with other adults' and so on. Again, allied to their identities as workers, women mentioned personal changes, describing themselves as happier and more self-confident people.

> I think I'm probably the sort of person who needs something to motivate me. I'm not very good at motivating myself. (Librarian; Contact 4)

WORKING MOTHERHOOD AND THE DOMINANT IDEOLOGY

Motherhood continued to be mainly constructed according to the dominant ideology. The mother was regarded as the person responsible for the child's development and for giving the child time and attention. Moreover, in order to be a good mother, it was also necessary to enjoy it.

The continuing power of the ideology of the 'all responsible mother' among full-time working women is not surprising given the political and institutional context concerning childcare and parental employment in Britain. Women's images of motherhood were also influenced by their own mothers' attitudes and experiences. The mother quoted below concluded that having a working mother was better for a child than having a bored mother at home, a view reinforced by knowing that her own mother felt and did the same.

> Perhaps at the beginning I thought I'd like to stay at home. But basically I take after my mother. She went back to work when I was two for the simple fact that she was bored. She did five hours a day and a friend looked after me. And she said 'Sometimes I felt a bit guilty about it'. She said 'But I needed it. I think I was a better mother for having gone out and had a break'. I think I take after my Mum. I'm not really child-oriented. I think I'm more tolerant than perhaps I would have been if I was at home full-time. (Secretary; Contact 4)

But the mothers of the great majority of women (74%) had not

113

been employed when their own children were under school age; of the 26% who were said to have been employed at this stage, just over half (only 14% of the whole sample) had worked full-time at any time during this period of early parenthood (returners were no more likely than non-returners to have had mothers who had been employed when their children were of pre-school age). In so far as women had identified with their non-employed mothers, they were presented with a problem when they themselves returned to work. Women were also subject to images in the workplace of what it means to be and not to be a mother. In this respect, the following constitutes a critical case – a woman who consciously distances herself from her own mother and the stereotype.

> My mother never had anything within her own life. It was totally child oriented. She always had her apron on. There was always at the back of my mind that my mother enjoyed what she did. If only she'd had the opportunity to do something else. I get up, do my hair, put my make-up on. And the reason I do is that it's almost like saying 'Look it's all right, I still have time. It's OK. Women can do it. You can still be yourself. You don't have to look bedraggled. You can have a happy home life'. (Worker in a residential home; Contact 4)

In emphasizing the gains for the mother–child relationship, especially the notion of 'quality time', and the reflected benefits for the child of having a happy and fulfilled mother, women began to contribute towards the creation of a new discourse around working motherhood – namely, that if a woman cannot be happy as a full-time mother then it might be better to work, both for herself and her child. These developments, however, should not be exaggerated. The new themes may best be described as emergent, and in many respects modest, not questioning for instance women's primary responsibility for children; notably absent was any developing notion of 'shared parenthood' with fathers, involving an expectation of shared responsibility for children's development and time with children. Similarly, while the possibility of compensating for the absence of full-time motherhood to some extent is recognized, the status of full-time motherhood, as the standard against which other 'deviant' types of motherhood should be judged, is not questioned.

These new themes – in which women negotiated their own meanings of motherhood – represent one way in which women attempted to reconcile the dominant ideology about motherhood with their actions as full-time employed mothers, which contra-vened this ideology. A degree of integration was also achieved through a process of compartmentalization and through applying various coping strategies – for example, using limited time as effectively as possible. For some women, reconciliation proved so problematic that they were forced out of full-time employment; but most were able to come to some resolution, even though this usually meant settling for a tolerable level of guilt.

8

The Well-being of Mothers

In this chapter we consider the relationship between employment and various indicators of well-being among the women in our study. Two broad models have been proposed about the relationship between employment and well-being among women (Arber, Gilbert and Dale, 1985). In the first, paid employment has a protective and beneficial mediating effect. Employment protects women against certain negative aspects of being full-time housewives and mothers – for instance, isolation and the monotonous nature and low social status of housework; it may also increase self-esteem and lessen dependence on male partners for financial and emotional support. A more specific protective role for employment has also been suggested. Brown and Harris (1978) concluded that employment might protect women from the consequences of severe life events, but only in the presence of an intimate, confiding relationship. A more recent study similarly found evidence of employment effects 'for mothers at higher risk of psychiatric symptomatology because of life event stress' and suggested that employment outside the home may 'increase the threshold of the level of life event stress that can be tolerated before psychiatric symptomatology results' (Parry, 1986, p. 204).

In the second model, employment has a harmful effect through making additional demands. The several roles required of women – housewife, mother and paid employee – may lead to role strain because of fatigue and role overload. Their competing demands may also lead to role conflict and psychological stress. (For an overview of the extensive research on role strain and conflict in dual earner households, see Lewis and Cooper (1988).)

These two models are not mutually exclusive. It is possible to conceptualize employment creating strain in some cases and being protective in others, or even having these effects for the same person, perhaps creating role overload on the one hand yet at the same time reducing isolation and feelings of frustration.

Developing both models further, the impact of employment may depend on interaction with other factors. One of these may be the ages and number of children; employment for a mother with two or three very young children might be expected to create more overload and stress than for a mother with one older child.

A second factor concerns the demands of employment itself. One type of demand is the hours of employment. Looking at physical health using data from the 1975 and 1976 General Household Survey, Arber and her colleagues (1985) conclude that part-time employment may have beneficial effects for women with children, but that full-time employment appears to be detrimental. She argues that this is caused by the strain of occupying multiple roles – as a full-time employee, mother and housewife – and that such effects are likely to continue until there is 'a substantial change in the sexual division of labour, so that women who work full-time are no longer expected to have the primary responsibility for childcare and housework'.

Arber, however, qualifies her conclusions and in so doing introduces a third factor – occupational status. While the GHS data

> consistently confirm the benefits of part-time work for women in all occupational classes . . . those (women under 40 with children) who work full-time in professional and managerial jobs report only marginally higher levels of illness than full-time housewives, whereas in the other two occupational groups (intermediate and junior non-manual + skilled manual and semi- and unskilled manual) women working full-time report over 50% more illness than housewives. (Arber *et al*, 1985, p. 393)

Arber suggests these occupational differences may arise from the nature of the work itself and the material rewards of different jobs. Women in higher status jobs have greater financial resources, and are likely to have more flexible hours and more control over their work, both of which are likely to ease some of the role strain.

Occupational status may affect material constraints: but it may also be important for other reasons. Parry concludes that the 'findings of most studies of married women do not establish any statistically significant differences between homemakers and employed women' (Parry, 1986, p. 94), and finds no employment effect on mental health in her study. Her sample however is confined to working-class mothers in part-time jobs, and in discussing the possible impact of full-time employment, Parry also suggests

117

that it may depend on the nature of the job. Full-time employment for mothers might, following the role strain hypothesis, be expected to increase some aspects of psychological distress: but for mothers with high employment commitment it might be expected to reduce distress. For this reason Parry explicitly cautions against generalizing the results from her study to mothers employed full-time, particularly in 'high-commitment career occupations'.

This reference to 'high-commitment career occupations' suggests that the meaning and salience of employment may be significant factors in determining the relationship between employment and well-being. Women in 'high-commitment career occupations' may be more likely to feel satisfied with their employment situation and find employment an enhancing experience; such role satisfaction or congruence may also mediate, it has been suggested, between women's employment status and aspects of child development (Gottfried and Gottfried, 1988). Other women may be less likely to feel satisfied, and more likely therefore to feel conflict between their roles as employee, mother and wife.

In this chapter we consider how the relationship between employment and well-being is affected by occupational status and whether employment is full-time or part-time. The impact of numbers and ages of children cannot be taken into account, since the design of the study limited the sample to women having a first child. Nor have we assessed the incidence of severe life events or major difficulties; we are not therefore in a position to replicate the work of Brown and Harris or of Parry on the potential for employment to protect women from the consequences of these events and difficulties. We have however considered the impact on well-being of one severe life event – becoming a lone mother – though we are unable to relate this to employment status because of the small numbers involved. Finally, we have examined the relationship between employment status, congruence and one aspect of maternal well-being, psychological distress.

WELL-BEING AND
EMPLOYMENT STATUS

Measures

In examining the impact of employment on well-being, women in the sample were divided into three employment status groups: employed full-time; employed part-time for 8 hours or more a

118

week; and not employed or employed less than 8 hours. Four aspects of well-being were considered: psychological distress, self-esteem, physical ill health and tiredness – each one of which was covered at each Contact. For psychological distress and self-esteem we used well-established measures based on self-completion inventories: a shortened scaled version of the General Health Questionnaire (GHQ) and Rosenberg's Self-esteem Scale. Assessments of physical ill health and tiredness were based on questioning. In the former case, a Score of Physical Ill Health (SPIH) was produced, using a method developed for a previous project at Thomas Coram Research Unit concerned with the transition to parenthood. Tiredness was rated on a four-point scale developed for the current study. (For full details of the measures used, see Appendix A at the end of this chapter.)

For each Contact and for each mother there are four measures of well-being, or lack of it. How far, though, do these measures overlap? There was a moderately strong relationship between GHQ on the one hand and self-esteem and tiredness on the other ($r=0.3$ – 0.49 except for tiredness at Contact 4), while the relationship between GHQ and SPIH was the most marked of the other relationships ($r=0.17 - 0.3$). The relationships between self-esteem, tiredness and physical ill-health were weaker but statistically significant at the 5% level, except for self-esteem and physical ill-health where the correlations were very weak and not significant at the 5% level. Overall, then, the degree of overlap was greatest between the psychological distress measure (GHQ) and the other three measures, which reflects the inclusion of some items in the GHQ which are symptoms of physical ill health, tiredness and low self-esteem.

Comparisons between Contacts
1 and 2

Did resuming employment in the early months of parenthood have any impact on well-being? Comparing the results from Contacts 1 and 2 provides some answers. Several qualifications, however, need to be made at the beginning. First, a number of women were already back in employment at Contact 1; two separate sets of analyses have been done, one including them and one excluding them. Second, many women reported acute feelings of conflict and guilt in the early weeks back in employment, which in most cases abated over time (Chapter 7). Our measures of psychological distress and self-esteem however only covered feelings at the time of each Contact; they would not reflect any temporary periods of heightened distress during, for example, these early weeks back in employment. Finally, Contact 1 was just one point during a period of transition, and not a static baseline when women were unaffected by employment and other considerations. Contact 1 was just before most women resumed employment and the prospect of resumption, as well as the work involved in making childcare and other arrangements, might be expected to have an effect on the well-being of at least some women. Similarly, for some women an expectation of not resuming employment could have an adverse effect; thus, women expecting to resume employment felt better able to put up with the negative experiences of being at home full-time (Chapter 7).

What we can assess is whether there was any relationship between employment status at Contact 2 and (i) measures of well-being at Contact 2; and (ii) changes in these measures between Contacts 1 and 2. For example, did women employed full-time at Contact 2 show higher levels of psychological distress than women who were not employed? Had their psychological distress score changed more or less compared with what it was at Contact 1?

On both types of assessment, there was no apparent effect of resuming employment for three of the four well-being measures. The exception was tiredness. Women in full-time employment had significantly higher tiredness ratings at Contact 2 than women who were not employed, while at Contact 1, before they resumed employment, there was no difference. Women in part-time employment at Contact 2 were much nearer the non-employed group, but the difference between them and women in full-time employment was not statistically significant (the numbers in part-time employment at Contact 2 were, however, very small).

The impact of employment on tiredness can also be seen by comparing tiredness ratings at Contacts 1 and 2 for individual women not employed at Contact 1. The group in full-time employment at Contact 2 was twice as likely to show an increased rating for tiredness between Contacts 1 and 2 (38% v. 19%) and were less likely to show a decreased rating (16% v. 31%); the difference was statistically significant. An even more marked trend is apparent if women's own perceptions of change between these two Contacts are considered. Women who were not employed at Contact 2 mostly said they felt less tired than at Contact 1 (63%); only 16% reported feeling more tired. Among those employed full-time, the most common response was to report feeling more tired at Contact 2 than at Contact 1 – 33% compared with only 27% who felt less tired. The remainder were divided between those who said they felt the same (27%) and some who described their tiredness as similar in level but different in type (12%). For example, several women referred to feeling less mentally tired or lethargic but more physically worn.

Comparisons between
Contacts 2, 3 and 4

For these three contacts, covering the period after most women had resumed full-time employment, we applied four types of analysis. There is a 'cross sectional analysis', of the relationship between each well-being measure and employment status at Contacts 2, 3 and 4. This type of analysis, however, has major limitations; it takes no account of change over time and how this may relate to employment status. Two women may, for example, have the same score on a measure at Contact 3, but have had very different scores at Contact 2 or Contact 1.

We have examined the issue of change and employment status in three ways. First we have compared scores at Contacts 2, 3 and 4 with scores at Contact 1. To take an example, women in full-time employment at Contact 4 had a mean GHQ score of 17.3, slightly higher than the 16.8 for non–employed women; however, the Contact 1 scores for the respective groups were 15.1 and 13.5, so that an analysis of change over time shows a slightly higher increase in GHQ for women in the non-employed group. Second, we have compared changes in well-being measures over time for women who remained in the same employment status. To do this, we have organized women into three 'long-term' employment status groups: those employed full-time between the end of their first maternity leave and their child's third birthday (and including those taking a second maternity leave who had resumed full-time employment again); those never employed for more than 8 hours a week over this period; and the rest, a 'mixed' group consisting of some women who had had a spell of full-time or part-time employment. These two measures involve some comparison with Contact 1, and the reservation made earlier about viewing Contact 1 as a baseline should be re-emphasized.

Finally, we have looked at change in well-being measures between Contacts 2 and 3, 3 and 4, and 2 and 4 in relation to changes in employment status in these periods, using a regression model described by Plewis (1985). If there is a relationship between, for example, GHQ and employment status, then women changing employment status between Contacts should also show a change

121

in GHQ score between Contacts. This analysis is designed to test for such relationships.

There was no relationship between psychological distress or self-esteem and employment using any of these analyses. There was a continuing relationship between employment status and tiredness, on both the cross-sectional analysis and comparing long-term employment status groups, but it got weaker after Contact 2; the regression analysis however shows no relationship in this period between changes in employment status and changes in tiredness. Non-employed women got more tired over the period, while women in full-time employment showed some improvement between Contacts 2 and 3, followed by increased tiredness between the next two Contacts. For both groups, therefore, there was a marked increase in tiredness between Contacts 3 and 4. Part of the reason for this upturn was that women were more likely to have a second child or to be pregnant at Contact 4, and this group had higher tiredness ratings which applied to both non-employed and full-time employed mothers – though in neither case was the difference statistically significant. The impact of further pregnancies or births does not though fully explain the increase in tiredness ratings between Contacts 3 and 4. Another possible factor is that as children got older they were more active and mothers tried to do more for them. There may also have been a cumulative process at work, with women feeling steadily tireder the further they proceeded into motherhood.

Our analyses showed two relationships between the physical ill health measure (SPIH) and employment status. Among women who retained the same employment status throughout, there was little difference between the 'non-employed' and 'full-time employed' groups at Contacts 1, 2 and 4 – but at Contact 3, the 'full-time employed' group had a higher score, suggesting more ill health, the difference being statistically significant. Mothers in the 'full-time employed' group increased their scores more than the 'non-employed' group between both Contacts 1 and 2 and Contacts 2 and 3, and the change between Contacts 1 and 3 reached statistical significance (2.8 v. 0.6). The situation then reversed between Contacts 3 and 4; the score for the 'full-time employed' group dropped, while the score for the 'non-employed' group rose, the difference again being statistically significant (-0.5 v. 2.0). This brought them back to a similar relationship to that at Contact 1, when the 'non-employed' group had a slightly higher score.

The reason for these divergent changes between Contacts is not clear. It might however be a reflection of the demands made on mothers in the early months back at employment, when their children still required a lot of physical care. This would not however account for the increased score for 'non-employed' mothers after Contact 3.

A second feature concerns part-time employment. Cross-sectional analysis shows that the SPIH for women in part-time employment increased over time, relative to women in the other two employment groups. At Contact 2 they had the lowest score, but by Contact 4 they had the highest, the difference between this group and the other two being around the 5% significance level. Similarly, women who were employed part-time at Contact 4 showed a significantly increased SPIH between Contacts 3 and 4. The meaning of this is difficult to interpret; there were three women not employed at Contact 3 but who had part-time jobs at Contact 4 and whose scores increased substantially between these two Contacts – from 1 to 19, 4 to 17, and 8 to 20. It is possible that these were unusual cases giving a result which is significant by chance. Overall, then, there is no strong evidence that women in part-time employment had either more or less ill health, though women in full-time employment appeared to have worse health for a period of time after resuming employment.

WELL-BEING AND
OCCUPATIONAL STATUS

The relationship between employment status and well-being was limited. Women who resumed full-time employment experienced more tiredness, especially in the early months back at work, while their physical health worsened temporarily in the middle of the study. Otherwise, there was no apparent employment effect. Was this, however, true for women in different types of employment?

Occupational status was classified in two ways: 'higher status' (professional and managerial jobs) and 'lower status' (other jobs); and according to the WES classification of employment (see Chapter 4). For non-employed women, occupational status was based on their last job before childbirth; for employed women, this was supplemented by a second classification based on the job they were doing at the time of interview.

Analyses, using these two classifications, were conducted for all mothers and, at Contacts 2 to 4, separately for mothers in full-time employment and for mothers who were not employed. The only statistically significant relationships with well-being measures were with psychological distress (using the GHQ measure) at Contacts 1 and 2. At both Contacts there was a relationship for all mothers between GHQ and mother's occupation (grouped into high and low status); at Contact 2 there was a relationship between GHQ and both occupational classifications for mothers in full-time employment, but not for non-employed mothers. In all cases, the relationship was for GHQ score to be positively related to occupation. Women in higher status jobs, therefore, began with rather higher GHQ scores (implying rather poorer well-being on this measure), but this difference had disappeared by Contacts 3 and 4.

In considering the paucity of significant or consistent relationships between occupation, employment and well-being, the socio-demographic characteristics of our sample should be remembered. In particular, the sample had low representation from groups likely to have fewest material resources and highest levels of ill health and psychological distress – for example, women in semi-skilled and unskilled manual jobs, women born outside the British Isles, lone mothers and women with 3 or more children.

WELL-BEING AND LONE PARENTHOOD

Psychological Distress

Some studies have found an association between lone parenthood and psychological distress (Pearlin and Johnson, 1977; Colletta, 1983; McGee *et al.*, 1983). In her sample of mothers, which excluded women in full-time jobs, Parry did not find much evidence of such a relationship. In our study, the GHQ score for women who were lone parents at some stage up to Contact 4 was lower than for other mothers at Contact 1 (13.5 v. 14.6), though not statistically significant, and even lower at Contact 2 (13.1 v. 16.2), by which stage the difference was significant; in other words, women who became lone mothers showed less signs of psychological distress at these first two Contacts.

Most mothers (15/18) however did not become lone parents until after their child was 18 months. The events leading up to separation and the early months of separation largely occurred therefore after Contact 2; and it was between Contacts 2 and 3 that the major changes in GHQ occurred. At Contacts 3 and 4, the situation on GHQ scores reversed; women who experienced a period of lone parenthood had higher scores (implying they were more distressed) and the differences were statistically significant (Contact 3 – 19.5 v. 15.5; Contact 4 – 22.1 v. 16.8).

The large difference at Contact 4 was accounted for almost entirely by the two non-employed mothers who had become lone parents, and the one lone mother employed part-time; they had GHQ scores, respectively, of 38, 45 and 36. Excluding them, and comparing only mothers in full-time employment at Contact 4, the GHQ score for lone mothers was only slightly higher and the difference not significant (18.4 v. 17.2). The score for the lone mothers in this group had however increased by 6.6 between Contacts 1 and 3 and by 5.4 between Contacts 1 and 4, compared with 0.4 and 2.6, respectively, for mothers in full-time employment at Contact 4 and who still lived with their child's father.

Nearly all the women who experienced a period of lone parenthood were employed full-time throughout once they had resumed work after maternity leave (13 out of 18). If we compare this group with the mothers employed full-time throughout who did not experience lone parenthood, the same trend emerges – the lone parent GHQ scores started lower, at Contacts 1 and 2, then increased rapidly to move ahead. Limiting the comparison even further, to those women not employed at Contact 1, both groups (lone parents and others) showed a slight average increase in GHQ to Contact 2. The lone mothers' scores then rose between Contacts 2 and 3 by 5.7, while the others fell by 1.0. Change between Contacts 3 and 4 was less marked, with lone mothers up by 0.5 and other mothers by 2.1. As a result of these changes, the lone mothers went from having a score 3 points lower at Contact 1 (12.18 v. 15.8) to a score 2.5 points higher at Contact 4 (19.5 v. 17.1).

None of the differences for this analysis reaches statistical significance, partly because the number of lone mothers involved was small. Taken overall, however, the evidence does suggest that the experience of becoming a lone parent was associated with an adverse impact on psychological state, at least for some time. If this was so, it still leaves unclear how far this was a result of the process leading up to becoming a lone parent, as opposed to the additional demands of lone parenthood itself. Moreover, because we had so few non-employed lone parents, we cannot assess whether and how employment status interacts with lone parenthood to affect psychological distress.

Self-esteem, Physical Ill Health and Tiredness

Trends on self-esteem for women who experienced lone parenthood between Contacts 1 and 4 were similar to psychological distress – though the three women who had experienced lone parenthood and were not employed full-time at Contact 4 did not have very high scores on the self-esteem inventory as they did for the GHQ. At Contacts 1 and 2, the lone parent group had lower scores (Contact 1 – 6.9 v. 8.2; Contact 2 – 5.6 v. 7.1), implying rather better self-esteem; they then climbed to overtake the other mothers at Contact 3 (8.1 v. 6.9), but fell back at Contact 4, though they still ended the study ahead (7.2 v. 6.7). None of these differences was statistically significant. Between Contacts 1 and 3, lone mothers' scores increased while other mothers' decreased, and the difference was statistically significant (1.2 v. −1.4); the trend is the same between Contacts 1 and 4, although less marked and indeed no longer significant (0.2 v. −1.4).

The same pattern is apparent if the lone mother group who were employed throughout are compared with other mothers in continuous full-time employment (and in both cases excluding mothers already employed at Contact 1). Between Contacts 1 and 3, the lone mothers' score increased, while for other mothers it dropped; the difference was again statistically significant (0.3 v. −2.4). As with GHQ, therefore, there is evidence to suggest that becoming a lone parent was associated with adverse effects on well-being, and that this was most apparent between Contacts 2 and 3.

The analysis by Arber and her colleagues shows that lone mothers reported higher levels of illness. There was also an adverse employment effect even among lone mothers with part-time jobs. They conclude that this is a consequence of the considerable role strain that arises from coping with children, housework and paid employment without a partner.

As for other measures of well-being, the numbers of women who experienced lone motherhood in our sample were too small to assess whether there was an employment effect within this group. Up to and including Contact 3, the pattern for physical ill health among this group, employed or not, was similar to that already described for GHQ and self-esteem, and supports Arber's conclusion of a relationship between illness and lone parenthood. Mothers who experienced lone parenthood at some point during the study had lower or similar SPIHs (implying less ill health or similar levels) at Contacts 1 and 2 compared with other mothers.

However, at Contact 3 lone mothers had a higher score (7.1 v. 5.3), which reflects a more rapid increase in SPIH between Contacts 2 and 3 (3.3 v. 1.9). Unlike GHQ and self-esteem, however, this was followed at Contact 4 by a return to the preceding pattern; lone mothers ended the study with a lower score (4.6 v. 5.7). None of the differences was however statistically significant.

The same pattern is apparent if the analysis is confined to women employed full-time throughout, excluding those already back at work at Contact 1. The lone mothers had a much higher, and statistically significant, increase in SPIH between Contacts 1 and 3 (5.1 v. 2.4), and a higher Contact 3 score (7.5 v. 5.2) suggesting they were experiencing more ill health at this point. They then showed a more rapid, and again statistically significant, fall between Contacts 3 and 4 (-2.6 v. -0.2), ending the study with a rather lower score.

Unlike the other three well-being measures, there was no relationship at any stage between lone parenthood and tiredness.

CONGRUENCE

Assessment of Congruence

At each Contact mothers were asked what employment status they would like 'if they had the choice' – to be non-employed or employed. At Contacts 2 and 3, women were offered the choice of 'part-time' or 'full-time' employment, while at Contact 4 those who said they would prefer paid work were asked what hours they would choose to work; those who chose 30 hours a week or more were classified as preferring full-time employment. Answers on preferred employment status were compared with actual employment status to produce a three-point rating:

1. 'Congruent', where actual and preferred employment status coincided.

2. 'Partly congruent' where mothers either were not employed but wanted to be employed part-time; *or* where mothers were employed part-time but wanted to be employed full-time or to stop employment altogether; *or* where mothers were employed full-time but preferred part-time employment.

3. 'Not congruent' where mothers were not employed but wanted to be employed full-time; *or* vice versa.

Addressing issues of preference in this area is inherently problematic. Given the strong ideological opposition to women with

127

young children's working full-time, expressing a preference for part-time work may have appeared a more socially acceptable answer. Our questioning was also limited in certain important respects. It confined itself to just one paramenter of choice – being employed or not, and being employed part-time or full-time. A comprehensive approach would need to take account of preferences about other employment conditions – for example, place and type of work, when hours were worked, flexibility of working hours and so on.

It is likely that the preference questions were interpreted differently by different women. Some might have assumed that all or many conditions (for example, childcare provision or the journey to work) remained constant; while others assumed that all or most other relevant conditions were also ideal. Related to this, we did not ask women to consider their preferences in the context of what they would choose for themselves *and* for their partner and child. Women's personal preferences may differ depending on whether or not they assume that full-time employment for their partner is a given condition.

The example of Denmark may help to illuminate this last point. The employment rate among mothers has increased rapidly over the last 20 years, to the point where 90% are now either employed or seeking paid work. There has also been a large increase in publicly funded childcare provision; Denmark now has more provision of this kind than any other Western developed country and indeed is the only country where a majority of children with employed parents are cared for in publicly funded childcare services. At the same time, changes have also occurred in what mothers say they would prefer. The proportion stating a preference for employment has increased from 47% in 1970 to 83% in 1985, though nearly all preferred part-time employment. These personal preferences, however, were given in the context of questioning about preferences for all household members (including care arrangements for children). While more mothers have, over the years, expressed a preference to be employed, there has also been a marked growth – from 15% to 46% – in the proportion who would prefer their partners to be employed part-time. In 1970, the two main preferred choices, cited by equal numbers of women, were for the father to be in full-time employment and the mother to be at home, and for the father to be in full-time employment and the mother to have a part-time job. By 1985, however, the most popular preference was for both parents to have a part-time job (Vedel-Petersen, 1988).

In Denmark, it is apparent that mothers' preferences have

changed over time, in the context of changed views about their partners' employment as well as a large actual increase both in employment among mothers and in publicly funded childcare services. The Danish experience illustrates the significance not only of the form and scope of questioning used in seeking preferences, but the impact on preferences of changes in the wider society which affect both expectations and support.

Congruence at Each Contact

At Contacts 2, 3 and 4, only a small proportion of women in full-time employment (14–15%) were 'not congruent'. The great majority expressed a preference to be employed. However at Contacts 2 and 3, women were twice as likely to prefer part-time to full-time employment, while at Contact 4 the two groups were equally sized suggesting some movement from partial congruence to congruence between Contacts 3 and 4. The difference in the distributions of congruence ratings between Contacts 3 and 4 reached statistical significance.

This increase in congruence might have arisen, in part, from selective losses from the full-time employment group, with women who were not congruent being more likely to give up full-time employment. In practice, the congruence rating at one Contact did not predict employment status at the next; women who were employed full-time at Contacts 2 and 3 but preferred to be not employed were just as likely to be employed full-time at Contacts 3 and 4 as women who preferred full-time jobs. Further support for this conclusion – that the increase in congruence between Contacts 3 and 4 was not caused by selective drop-out from full-time employment – comes from an analysis of congruence at different Contacts among women who remained in the same employment group throughout. This shows the same movement: among the group who remained in full-time employment throughout, more women were congruent at Contact 4 than at Contact 3. The most likely explanation of the trend towards increased congruence is that employment preferences among women in full-time jobs changed somewhat as children got older.

Non-employed women were more likely than women in full-time employment to be congruent. At each Contact, between 56% and 63% fell into this category, and the difference in the overall distribution of congruence ratings between the two groups was significant. A substantial proportion of non-employed women, however, did prefer employment, though few opted for full-time work. Between 36% and 41% at each Contact chose part-time employment as their preference, illustrating the strong 'pull' of this type of employment both for women who were not employed and for those with full-time jobs. Indeed, at Contacts 2, 3 and 4 women in part-time employment were most likely to be congruent; the difference for congruence ratings between part-time and full-time was highly significant at all three Contacts, and was significant between women in part-time employment and non-employed women at Contact 4.

A preference for part-time employment covered a wide variety of hours. Of the 116 women who expressed a preference to work less than 30 hours a week at Contact 4, 25% chose less than 15 hours a week (though only 3% less than 8 hours), 23% between 15 and 19 hours, 30% between 20 and 24 hours and 12% between 25 and 29 hours. Women currently employed full-time were more likely to opt for longer part-time hours than women currently employed part-time or not employed at all.

Factors Related to Congruence

Congruence might be influenced either by job-related or household-related factors, including the nature of the job done, the salience of employment, feelings about full-time motherhood, domestic workload and perceived support from a partner. We explored these possible factors by looking at the relationship between the congruence rating at Contact 2 for mothers in full-time employment, and a number of variables from Contacts 1 and 2:

(a)   Occupational status, classifying jobs held before childbirth into higher and lower status as described above.

(b)   Pre-birth commitment to employment. This was assessed on the basis of women's responses to a Contact 1 question 'How important is work to you?', which was coded as 'very', 'quite' or 'not very' (Chapter 6).

(c)   Dissatisfaction with motherhood at Contact 1. Women were rated for negative feelings about motherhood, using a four-point scale (Chapter 7).

(d)   Proportion of housework and childcare done by the mother at Contact 2 (see Chapter 10 for a description of method used).

(e)   Perceived supportiveness of partner. Three measures were used: satisfaction expressed with the partner's contribution to housework and childcare at Contact 2 (Chapter 11); the mother's perception of how understanding her partner was about her experience as a working mother at Contact 2 (Chapter 11); and the mother's perception of her partner's preference about her employment at Contact 1, which was coded into prefers or accepts full-time employment, prefers employment but with qualification and prefers non-employment.

The initial analyses showed that there was a statistically significant relationship between congruence, and occupational status, commitment to work, proportion of housework done and the three supportiveness variables. Commitment to work, proportion of housework and childcare done and partner's perceived preference on employment were, however, related to mother's occupational status, at a statistically significant level. Since congruence was also related to occupational status – women in high status jobs being more likely to be congruent – a further analysis was carried out to control for this variable (using a proportional odds model, with the explanatory variables treated both as unordered and as linear scales). This further analysis showed that, once occupational status was controlled for, proportion of housework done was no longer significantly related with congruence, and the mother's perception of her partner's degree of understanding showed a weaker relationship that fell just outside the 5% level of statistical significance. The other three variables – satisfaction with partner's contribution, partner's preference on mother's employment, and commitment to work – remained statistically significant, with the last two variables having the strongest relationship.

This analysis suggests that women in full-time employment were more congruent the higher their commitment to work and the more supportive their partner was perceived to be, supportiveness covering attitudes to mother's employment, the perceived adequacy of the partner's contribution to domestic work and his level of understanding about being an employed mother and what it involves.

Congruence and Psychological Distress

Psychological distress (as measured by GHQ score) increased as congruence decreased. Women whose preferred employment status coincided with their actual employment status had, on average, the lowest GHQ scores (that is, the lowest levels of psychological distress). This relationship held both for women in full-time employment and for women who were not employed, and was statistically significant for both groups of women at each Contact.

As well as these cross-sectional analyses, we examined the relationship longitudinally. We looked at change in congruence between Contacts 2 and 3, Contacts 3 and 4, and Contacts 2 and 4, to see whether this resulted in a change in GHQ score (again using a multiple regression model as described by Plewis (1985)). For each of the three periods, there was a relationship between change in congruence and change in GHQ, though the relationship was not statistically significant between Contacts 3 and 4: in each case, increased congruence was related to reduced GHQ scores, implying reduced distress, and vice versa.

While there may be a statistical relationship between congruence and GHQ for the sample as a whole, this disguises considerable individual differences. For example, women in full-time employment at Contact 4 who were rated as non-congruent had an average GHQ score of 22.6. This was above the threshold point of 19/20 for the measure which has been found most discriminating in distinguishing between 'cases' and 'non cases' (see Appendix A). Within the group, however, there was a wide spread of scores, with a standard deviation of 18.5. Altogether there were six women in full-time employment at Contact 4 who were rated non-congruent and also had a GHQ score of 20 or over. Closer examination of these women provides some insight into the relationship between lack of congruence and psychological distress.

Two had had recent specific problems – one with childcare arrangements, the other linked to moving house and job. In the latter case, the mother had moved to a new job in Lancashire 9 months prior to the interview. Moving house from London was described as difficult and traumatic, and the father had still not found a job in Lancashire; he continued to work in London, and went home only at weekends. In both cases, at the previous Contact the mothers had been 'not congruent' – but had had much lower GHQ scores (7 and 12 compared with 23 in both cases at Contact 4).

A third woman, a teacher aged 39, was rated 'non-congruent' at Contacts 2, 3 and 4, and at the last Contact described herself as 'totally lacking in motivation and thoroughly jaundiced with the education system'. Her situation and feelings about it had changed little since resuming employment: 'I feel the same as I did when you first asked me [at Contact 2] – the answer is I'd rather not work . . . it's financially vital, that's the only reason I'm working'.

She felt 'permanently worn out and [had] done since [her child] was born', ascribing this to 'overwork and probably over-age'. Her partner was described as very unsupportive: 'I gather from other friends that their husbands do quite a bit in terms of the child [but] mine doesn't, so strictly speaking a more supportive husband would have been very helpful to me'. Her GHQ at Contact 4 was similar to the previous two mothers (26); unlike them, however, her GHQ at Contact 4 showed little change from Contacts 2 and 3 (25 and 22).

Another teacher, aged 35, had always felt ambivalent about being at work, and was rated 'non-congruent' at Contacts 2, 3 and 4. She had a senior post which, though demanding, was also a source of some satisfaction. Since returning to work, her child had woken at least once a night, with the mother always getting up. At Contact 4, the child still often woke more than once a night, before waking for the day by 6 a.m. when 'I have to keep her company'. Not surprisingly, the mother had slept badly since the child was born and was constantly tired. At Contact 4, she reported anxiety and stress symptoms put down to general overload, and had been on sick leave for the previous two months. Her GHQ score was high at each Contact, but increased between Contacts 3 and 4, reflecting her recent stressed condition (35, 28 and 59).

Tiredness was again a theme for the fifth mother, a 26 year old clerical worker in the civil service. Like the previous mother this was linked to a child with difficult sleep patterns. Up to Contact 3, the child woke at least once a night and was always difficult to put to bed. At Contact 4, the child slept through the night, but only after she had settled to sleep at around 10 p.m. The mother always saw to the child at night and put her to bed. She described herself as getting headaches several times a week and feeling tired 'most of the time . . . I wake tired, I wouldn't ever say I'm full of energy'. She put this down, however, to another factor – her deep-seated and continuous feelings of guilt at working, a dominant theme at all Contacts. Her partner provided little support. He did little childcare or housework, but also applied pressure on the mother to stay at work, despite saying he would 'ideally' prefer her to stay at home.

> [The tiredness] is just an overall weariness . . . it's more mental than anything . . . I suppose it's mental exhaustion. If you're consciously worrying, feeling guilty, it does have an effect on you mentally . . . I don't want to continue at work. I'm very, very bitter at the moment. The past 6 months have

been really bad, I'm finding it really difficult workwise. *Why?* I don't know whether it's perhaps come to a head. Perhaps because I've been considering starting with another child and I've started to think now, 'Well, what when two come along'. Quite honestly I don't think I could cope mentally as well as physically . . .

. . . I feel I should be at home. I don't feel we spend enough time together. I feel I should be at home bringing her up myself . . . I've got this idea in my head a mother should be at home, and because of that concept that I have, that's my feeling of guilt, because I feel I'm letting her down . . . I feel I'm not being a good mother and that because I had her I should have stayed at home. *You feel guilty?* Yes. A hell of a lot . . . I don't think I've benefited – it's made me a nervous wreck . . .

. . . [My husband] would love me to stop and stay at home, but obviously he's a bit more practical than I am. Money is the main objective [for him]. He's a little bit materialistic, more so than I am. He likes to have money to buy things if he wants to.

Although her GHQ scores were high at each Contact, they rose significantly between Contacts 3 and 4 (29, 27, 35), again reflecting increased stress reported by the mother in recent months.

The final mother was a 35 year old bank worker, and at Contact 4 had returned to work after a second child and taken a demotion at her own request, trading a lower grade job for working fewer hours with less pressure – 'I'm doing a lesser job and I'm more and more bored and fed up with the whole thing'. Like the previous mother, she had a strong preference to be at home, but was under pressure to remain at work – in this case because of the large maintenance payments that her partner made to his first wife. Her partner was also extremely unsupportive in all ways, and there were many stresses connected with the marriage.

Again, like the previous mother, she reported frequent headaches – 'I've had dreadful migraines since the second child'. She had had a miscarriage in the preceding year, followed soon after by a breakdown involving in-patient psychiatric treatment.

Deep down I felt resentful for being at work with a child and I wanted to be home. So I thought if I had another pregnancy, that would give me time to be at home – although in the cold light of day I knew it was too soon for me to have another baby and I didn't feel I could cope physically or mentally

134

with it. But right at the back of my mind somewhere I kept thinking I could have time at home . . .

. . .I think it's dreadful to try and combine full-time work with two young children. One child's not too bad but with two it's a hell of a time . . . the thing that got me to the point of breakdown was the guilt. I'd got myself so hyped up and so tired and when I couldn't cope with them I shouted at them. And I saw my little boy go from a happy-go-lucky little boy to one who permanently had his fingers in his mouth, looking at me. I wanted to cuddle him and love him and say 'I'm sorry' but I hadn't got the time. And I had this terrible guilt inside me . . .

. . .*What would have helped?* A more understanding husband that was more helpful . . . He was totally unsympathetic [about the miscarriage] . . . He isn't happy about my working. He wishes that financially it wasn't possible. All his friends I've met have been to public school, they're all the same, they can't do anything. They expect their wives to be there and be supportive and to run all sorts of little charity works – but not to have a full-time job . . .

. . .I always wanted [my family to be] two lovely children and happy parents that had time for each other . . . It hasn't worked out like that. The first child has had ear infections and a snotty nose, the baby has been crying. I've lost complete interest in what my husband does and his work and I seem to have lost a lot of my interests as well. We have more arguments. I haven't got the time . . . I would like some time with him, but I would feel too guilty since I've been at work all week to leave [the children] at weekends as well . . . If the children were 15 or 16 and we went through the period we went through last year, I think one of us would have moved out.

Employment, Psychological Distress and Congruence

What do these cases, considered together with the statistical analysis, suggest about the relationship between psychological distress and the degree of congruence between employment preferences and actual employment status? One interpretation is that congruence mediates the relationship between employment status and psychological distress, and is itself the product of various factors such as low commitment to employment or perceived lack of support from a partner.

An alternative interpretation starts from the premise that in the circumstances current during the study – for example, a generally unsupportive social and ideological context and women carrying a disproportionate share of childcare and domestic work and responsibility (Chapters 3, 7 and 10) – employed mothers were at considerable risk of experiencing role overload and conflict. The presence, extent and nature of role overload and conflict varied between women and over time, depending on various factors, some of which have been identified above, including the type of job done, commitment to employment, the perceived supportiveness of a partner and, as illustrated in two of the cases, child-related factors, such as night waking or other particularly demanding behaviour or illness.

Role overload and conflict affect congruence, and may also contribute towards psychological distress. Lack of congruence and poor psychological state are, in this interpretation, both expressions, the one cognitive and the other affective, of the same role strain. There is not however a simple relationship; lack of congruence does not automatically mean high psychological distress. Some women may cope better with role overload and conflict, using coping strategies which reduce feelings of psychological distress. In some cases, these coping methods may be temporarily less effective when faced by some additional difficulty or stress. This may have been the case with the first two women described above, who were not congruent at each Contact, but whose GHQ score only rose substantially after problems respectively with childcare and moving house; these problems may have temporarily increased the level of role overload to the point where it affected psychological stress as well as congruence.

A rather different example is provided by the clerical worker who expressed continuous feelings of guilt. She is in marked contrast to most mothers whose feelings of guilt, as we described in the previous chapter, became less over time and troubled them only occasionally. She also had a husband who was unsupportive both in terms of what he did in the home and his contradictory attitude to his wife working. She was not congruent throughout, and had a high GHQ at Contacts 2 and 3 – but it was the prospect of having a second child which made her feel even worse at Contact 4 and made it harder for her to cope with her feelings of conflict and overload.

Psychological distress was not however only dependent on role conflict and overload. Other factors, not directly related to employment status, could have an impact. In the last case described above, there was a major marital problem. A stressful marriage such as this can create its own tensions, directly increasing distress, though it may also work indirectly via increasing the wife's overload if the husband's lack of support is part of the wider problem.

A similar model can be applied to non-employed women. The extent to which full-time motherhood was experienced negatively depended on a variety of contextual factors. The more negative the experience, the lower the level of congruence and the greater the level of psychological stress.

Overall, there were no consistent and marked relationships between employment and well-being. The mothers in our study in full-time employment were neither markedly better nor worse off than other mothers during the course of the study on the indicators applied, although they were significantly more tired and had worse physical health at Contacts 2 and 3 respectively. Neither did occupational status have a major impact, although this may be because our sample was insufficiently representative to allow the relationship between occupation and well-being to be adequately tested.

Most significant in affecting well-being – or at least psychological distress – was becoming a lone mother and lack of congruence. The meaning of these relationships, however, needs to be carefully considered. It is not clear from our data whether the relationship between lone parenthood and lack of well-being is most acute before or after separation. Moreover, separation was most common among employed women, and it is possible that the fact of employment, and financial independence, made this course easier for women to follow. It may be that women in unhappy marriages, but unable to separate because of material or other constraints, would have shown similar signs of diminished well-being; unfortunately, we had no adequate measures of the state of marital relationships. Similarly, the relationship between congruence and psychological distress is not necessarily causal. Indeed, both may be viewed as consequences of the same stressors, which may in turn both be varied and fluctuate over time.

Appendix A
Measures of Mothers' Well-being

For *psychological distress*, mothers were asked to complete a shortened scaled version of the General Health Questionnaire (GHQ). The version used has 28 items and respondents can select one of four points on each item. Each item can be scored in one of two ways, the first involving a 1-2-3-4 system, the other a 0-0-1-1 system. In validating the measure, the authors of the GHQ found a threshold score of 4/5 using the 0-0-1-1 scoring system most discriminating in distinguishing 'cases' from 'non-cases' (Goldberg and Hillier, 1979). Using the 1-2-3-4 method, as we have done, a threshold score of 19/20 was found to correspond closely to a cut-off point of 4/5 using the other method.

For *self-esteem*, Rosenberg's (1965) measure was used. This is another self-completion inventory, with 10 items, each scored 0-1-2-3. The higher the score for each item, or for all 10 items summed, the lower the level of positive self-esteem or the higher the level of self-depreciation.

For *physical ill health*, we asked mothers at the First Contact whether they had any longstanding or recurring conditions that affected their health or what they could do, and at subsequent Contacts enquired about these conditions. We also asked at each Contact if mothers had had any periods of illness or any conditions that had caused pain or discomfort, and prompted for certain specific conditions such as colds, infections, stomach or bowel upsets, backaches or headaches. At the First Contact, mothers were asked about the month preceding interview, but at subsequent interviews they were asked about longer periods – since Contact 1 at Contact 2 (between 5–6 months on average), since Contact 2 at Contact 3 (between 7–8 months on average) and in the 6 months preceding interview at Contact 4. The periods covered therefore varied, especially between the first and subsequent Contacts. For each condition mentioned, mothers were asked for a description of the condition, how long it lasted and any treatment received.

To convert these descriptions of conditions into a Score of Physical Ill Health (SPIH), we used a method developed for a previous project at the Thomas Coram Research Unit which had been concerned with the transition to parenthood (Moss, Bolland and Foxman, 1980). The approach adopted owes much to the concept of the significance of illness used by Wyler and his colleagues (1968) in developing a 'seriousness of illness rating scale'. Each condition reported is assigned to one of four categories according to an assessment of its 'significance' or threat to health, which is assessed on the basis of the potential consequences for health posed by a condition, rather than its immediate adverse effects. The four 'significance' categories used in rating each condition were:

Category A (score 1) – mostly conditions and symptoms in which, although a loss of well-being occurs, the prognosis is good and the condition is usually short term and not very incapacitating, e.g. colds, sprains, headaches, indigestion.

Category B (score 3) – conditions with a good prognosis, but more intense and persistent in character, e.g. 'flu', hayfever, eczema, small bone fractures, piles, bronchitis.

Category C (score 5) – potentially more serious, often definitely incapacitating, posing a mild to moderate threat to general health, e.g. colitis, arthritis, asthma, fibroids, toxaemia.

Category D (score 7) – serious conditions implying a definite threat to general health, e.g. eclampsia, diabetes, polio, skull fractures.

For classifying most reported conditions, use was made of the seriousness of illness rating scale drawn up by Wyler and his colleagues, while other conditions were classified for the previous 'Transition to Parenthood' study by four doctors: two consultants and two GPs. The basic score for each condition was augmented – if other factors were present which seemed to increase the significance – by 1 if the condition recurred once in the period covered by the interview, by 2 if it recurred more often or if the condition involved in-patient hospital care, and by 3 if it required an operation. The scores for each condition were then summed to give a total score for each mother. Reliability of the method was tested in the earlier 'Transition to Parenthood' study, when two independent raters scored all conditions reported at over 400 interviews; this produced a high level of inter-rater agreement (kappa=0.9). For the current study, all scoring was done by one researcher, who had been responsible for developing the approach in the previous study.

The great majority of conditions reported on each occasion were in Categories A or B – colds, backaches, headaches, migraines, 'flu', hay fever, stomach upsets and so on. In-patient hospital stays and operations were rare. A few examples taken from Contact 1 illustrate how the SPIH worked:

Teacher, aged 28. Recurrent migraines – score 3 for condition + 2 for recurrence; recurrent backache – score 1 for condition + 2 for recurrence. Total SPIH = 8

Clerical worker, aged 29. Cold for few days and sore throat for few days – score 1 for each condition. SPIH=2.

139

Physiotherapist, aged 34. Continuous hypothyroid condition – score 5 for condition + 2 for being continuous; several colds – score 1 for condition + 2 for recurrence; gastroenteritis – score 3 for condition. SPIH=13.

Tiredness was the most difficult area to assess. At each contact, mothers were asked whether they got tired. If they did, as the great majority did, aspects of their tiredness were covered – for example, how often they felt tired, when they felt tired, how their tiredness felt, if it interfered with doing things, what they put it down to and what they tried to do about it. On the basis of the replies, tiredness was rated using a four-point scale:

No tiredness reported (Score=0).

Mild tiredness (Score=1). Occasional tiredness reported or regular but mild and short patches of tiredness, with little associated stress; tiredness easily shaken off by brief rest or other break in routine. For example – 'I get tired some days . . . sort of late afternoon, and then after tea I sort of wake up again'.

Moderate tiredness (Score=2). Tiredness reported most days, or bouts when feels very tired; not easily shaken off. For example – 'I get tired some days. The mornings are my worst times. I feel I have just no energy'.

Severe tiredness (Score 3). Tiredness felt most or all of the time, with only occasional relief; physical exhaustion of an extreme kind, with terms used such as 'shattered', 'exhausted', 'drained'. For example – 'I do get tired, every day . . . I feel mentally and physically drained, lethargic. I just want to, not necessarily sleep, but sit down and read a book'.

9

Fathers' Employment

The preceding chapters have concentrated on employment, especially full-time, of women with young children. A small proportion of women in this position are lone parents; the great majority, around 90% with a child under 5 (OPCS, 1987; Table 6.6), are in two-parent households. Moreover, in two-parent households, mothers are more likely to be employed if their partners also are employed. Consequently, most mothers with young children who are in full-time employment are in a dual earner household.

In general, far less attention has been paid to paternal employment than to maternal employment. The dominant ideology of parenthood views paternal employment as unproblematic, a given feature of family life. Within this discourse, the main problem with respect to fathers and employment concerns men who are unable to earn a breadwinning wage, either because of unemployment or low pay.

This is reflected in research, which 'focuses on the influence on children of working mothers' (Hochschild, 1989, p. 236). Earlier work on men's work and family roles was mainly concerned with extreme examples – for instance, where occupations involved long periods away from home. More recently, there has been some increase in interest in men's 'family–work' management and conflicts in more common circumstances. However, there are still relatively few studies of paternal employment, and how it relates to maternal employment at the household level, and there is little information on actual patterns of employment, beyond average times spent in paid work per day (Moss and Brannen, 1987).

In this chapter, we examine some features of paternal employment in our sample – in particular, type of occupation, earnings and hours of employment – and how these compare and relate to maternal employment. We also look at an issue already discussed for mothers – occupational mobility and its relationship to continuity of employment – and consider it in relation to fathers and their employment. As already explained (Chapter 2) the original emphasis of the research, on mothers' employment rather than dual earner households, meant that fathers were not interviewed. This chapter therefore has to depend very largely on quantitative data, taken from interviews with mothers.

EMPLOYMENT HISTORIES
DURING EARLY
PARENTHOOD

Parenthood leads to most women entering a prolonged phase of unemployment and part-time employment, reflecting the pre-vailing ideology about how mothers should behave. The same ideology emphasizes the role of father as breadwinners at this stage and the importance for them of remaining in full-time employment. In terms of affecting continuity of employment, therefore, parenthood has little impact on men, apart from the short break – between 1 and 2 weeks on average – that most men now take at or soon after the birth, to provide some support to their partners (Moss and Brannen, 1987).

Although parenthood does not lead directly to unemployment among men with children, as it does for most women, in the years leading up to the study there had been an increase nationally in unemployment rates for men with dependent children. Between 1973 and 1985, unemployment among this group grew from 3% to 10% (OPCS, 1987, Table 6.7). During the same period unem-ployment among men without dependent children grew from 3% to 7% in 1983, then fell back to 5%. Having started from the same point, therefore, by the mid-1980s unemployment among fathers had grown to double the level among men without children. Moreover, unemployment among fathers was highest among men with children under 5, at 12%, then reduced for men with older children – to 9% where the youngest child was aged 5–9 and 6% where the youngest child was 10 or over. In addition, a very small number of men with children under 5 – 1% according to the 1985 Labour Force Survey – are employed part-time (Moss, 1988).

In our study, 12% of men were unemployed at some stage during the 3 years after the birth of their first child, and 2% had a period of part-time employment. Most, 7%, were unem-ployed for 6 months or less, and only 2% for more than 12 months. Unemployment at particular points of time – at each of the four Contacts – was much lower, between 1%

and 3%, well below the national rate for men with children under 5.

Why was unemployment so much lower among the men in our sample compared with fathers with young children in general? There are probably three main reasons. First, unemployment rates vary between areas. Our study was based in the south-east of England, an area of lower unemployment; and few of our sample lived or worked in those parts of the region – for example, certain areas of London – where unemployment was highest at the time of the study. Second, unemployment rates are highest for men with 3 or more children: in 1985, 9% and 7% of men with 1 or 2 children were out of work, compared with 14% with 3 and 31% with 4 or more (OPCS, 1987, Table 6.7). By the end of our study, no household in our sample had more than 2 children. Finally, unemployment rates are closely related to occupation. In 1981/2, unemployment among men with children under 5 was 2% among men who normally worked in professional or managerial jobs and 4% among men in 'intermediate and junior non-manual' jobs; it then rose to 14% for 'skilled manual and own account non-professionals' jobs and to 27% for 'semi-skilled and unskilled manual' jobs (OPCS, 1985, Table 6.24). As we shall show below, the majority of men in our sample had jobs in the first two 'low unemployment' groups, and very few had jobs in the very high risk fourth group.

Nearly all the mothers in our sample who were not in employment were either on maternity leave or else were not seeking work, and had given up paid work to care for their children. The situation among the relatively few non-employed fathers was very different. Only two fathers gave up their jobs voluntarily, specifically to care for their children. The first, a 36 year old civil engineer, looked after his son between the ages of 7 to 17 months, then resumed employment and passed over childcare to a nanny. The second, a 39 year old self-employed carpenter, took a similar period away from work, combining attendance on one day a week at a college course with caring for his son on the other 4 weekdays.

Otherwise, men became involuntarily unemployed as a result of losing their jobs. Sometimes, they then took over most or all of the care of their children while their partners were out at work – but stopped as soon as they found a new job. They cared for their children because they were not employed, and did so as a stopgap measure, with no intention of entering into a long-term commitment as a carer. One father, for instance, was a sales representative for medical supplies and lost his job when his son was 2 months old. His wife resumed employment 4 months later and arranged care with a friend; the father, however, looked after the baby for most of the time for the next 5 months, until he got a new job. In a second example, the father was a driver. He was also out of work when his wife resumed employment, and looked after his daughter. This arrangement, however, lasted for only 2 weeks, when the father got a new job; the child was then temporarily cared for by a relative while the mother found a childminder. This case also provides an unusual example of how childcare in general, and in particular making childcare arrangements while parents were at work, was regarded as primarily the mother's responsibility (this is discussed further in Chapter 10).

OCCUPATIONAL STATUS

Comparing Fathers and Mothers in the Sample

We have already described how the women in the sample included few manual workers, and that the women who resumed full-time employment were less likely to have clerical, secretarial and sales jobs and were more likely to have professional or managerial jobs than women who did not. The difference on professional and managerial jobs was due to the 'returners' including more teachers, nurses and other health and welfare professionals.

Table 9.1 shows the occupations of fathers at Contact 1 using the WES classification of occupations (see Chapter 4); the table also shows the occupational distribution for all men in full-time employment nationally, taken from the 1981 Labour Force Survey (LFS). There was little change in the occupational distribution of the fathers in our sample between Contacts 1 and 4. Half the fathers were in professional and managerial jobs, 10% in clerical or sales jobs and 40% in manual work; more than three quarters of the manual workers were in skilled jobs. Direct comparison with the 1981 LFS figures must be qualified because these national figures are for men of all ages, and occupational distribution is likely to differ somewhat between men of different ages. It seems probable, however, that our sample under-represented men in semi-skilled and unskilled manual jobs and over-represented those in professional and managerial work – similar differences to those already noted when comparing women in our sample with national samples of women having children.

144

Table 9.1 *Occupational distribution of fathers at Contact 1 by employment intentions of partners (mothers); and of all full-time male workers in UK*

	Occupational group								
	Professional/Managerial				Clerical/Secretarial/Sales		Manual		
	1	2	3	4	5	6	7	8/9	10/11
Contact 1									
Group A (N = 185) (%)	12	11	4	24	7	3	31	8	1
Group B (N = 70) (%)	19	1	1	21	10	–	36	12	–
A + B (N = 255) (%)	16	8	3	23	7	2	33	9	1
1981 Labour Force Survey: all men in full-time jobs in UK (%)	6	3	1	19	7	4	39	10	11

Key:
Group A = Fathers with partners who intended to resume full-time employment after birth.
Group B = Fathers with partners who did *not* intend to resume full-time employment after birth.
For definition of occupational groups, see Table 4.1.

Comparing men whose partners intended to resume employment after maternity leave with those whose partners did not, there is little difference in distribution between the three main categories of jobs – professional or managerial, clerical or sales, and manual. Men with employed partners were more likely to be teachers and less likely to be in higher professional occupations; the numbers involved, however, are small and the differences suggestive rather than conclusive.

The differences between the occupational distributions for fathers (Table 9.1) and mothers in our sample (Table 4.1) are pronounced, reflecting more general differences between female and male workers shown in the LFS figures. Mothers were concentrated in clerical, teaching and professional health and welfare jobs, fathers in skilled manual, higher professional and intermediate non-manual jobs.

Occupational differences were matched by differences in the types of industry in which men and women worked. Over 80% of full-time employed mothers in our sample worked in two industrial groups: 'professional and scientific services', which includes schools, hospitals and Social Services; and 'insurance, public and local government administration', which includes the full range of financial services as well as large parts of government. Men's jobs were rather less concentrated, although three quarters worked in just three industrial groups. The largest number, just under half (43% compared with 9% of women), were in 'other services', which includes post and telecommunications, transport, hotels and catering, engineering and public utilities. The two other main industrial groups were 'professional and scientific services' and 'insurance, public and local government administration', though each accounted for less than 20%. Men with wives in full-time employment were, however, more likely to be in 'professional and scientific services' (27% v. 6% at Contact 2) and less likely to be in 'other services' (37% v. 55%).

Fathers were more often self-employed than mothers who had full-time jobs (15% v. 5% at Contact 4); but the highest rate of self-employment – 20% – was among women in part-time employment at Contact 4. Self-employment had, in most cases, a very different meaning for fathers and mothers. Most self-employed fathers were self-employed before their child was born. Those who had changed since had done so either after being made redundant or because they had chosen to set up their own company or work on their own account. Nearly all had skilled occupations, most in manual work (for example, as bricklayers, plasterers, mechanics or decorators), and most worked by themselves on their own account, although a

146

few did have businesses employing others; nearly all worked most of the time outside their homes. Earnings were comparable to those of men who were not self-employed.

One father, for example, had been a contracts manager with a company that went bankrupt while his wife was pregnant. He set up his own company, doing shopfitting and renovation work, and also did some freelance design work. At Contact 4, he worked at home on Saturdays and most evenings, but spent the rest of his time at jobs; he worked over 70 hours a week and had net earnings of over £200 a week (end of 1985). A second father was a mechanic, and had had his own garage for some time before the birth of his daughter. He did no work from home, and put in over 55 hours a week at his job; his wife did not know what his earnings were.

Mothers, by contrast, had all become self-employed after the birth of their child, and the move to self-employment was usually associated with parenthood; it was a way of coping with childcare and employment, through working shorter hours, having some control over hours worked and often being able to keep their child with them while they worked or else working at a time when their partner could care for the child. The work itself was usually part-time, badly paid, and of lower status than work done before the birth. Mostly the work was done wholly or partly at home.

A typical example was a mother who had been head of a reference library before she had her son, but did not resume her employment after maternity leave. She remained unemployed until her son was 28 months old, when she became a childminder. At Contact 4, she minded for 28 hours a week, for which she received £25. Childminding was the most common self-employed occupation for women; other self-employed mothers made jewellery or assembled paper goods at home, sold clothes, organized sales parties and parties for children, ran a 'nappy service' and owned a fast-food cafe. The highest status work was done by a surveyor and a physiotherapist, both of whom worked full-time. Self-employment, therefore, was linked with discontinuity of employment and downward occupational mobility for most women (Chapter 5) – but not for men.

Comparing Fathers and Mothers in the Same Households

So far, we have concentrated on comparing occupational differences among all the men and all the women in our sample. We now consider occupational differences within households, where

147

both parents were in full-time jobs. Using the WES classification of occupations, fathers were in higher occupational groups than mothers in under a fifth of cases at Contacts 2, 3 and 4 (between 15% and 18%), and both parents were in the same occupational group in just over a quarter of households (between 27% and 30%). This leaves just over half the women in full-time employment at Contacts 2, 3 and 4 (between 51% and 55%) who were in a higher occupational group than their partners. In over 90% of cases this involved a difference of 2 or more groups; the most common difference, accounting for around a fifth of all households where both parents were in full-time jobs, involved a mother in secretarial or clerical work (group 5 in the WES classification) and a father in skilled manual work (group 7).

Grouping jobs into three broad classifications – professional and managerial (WES groups 1–4), clerical, sales and skilled manual (groups 5–7) and semi-skilled and unskilled manual (groups 8–11) – not surprisingly increases the proportion of households where both parents were in the same grouping to just over two thirds at Contacts 2, 3 and 4 (between 67% and 71%); households where the woman has a clerical job and her partner is a skilled manual worker now fall into this equal status category. In the remaining households, however, as with the other classification system, women were two to three times more likely to be in a higher group than their partners (between 21% and 22% at each Contact) than vice versa (between 7% and 10%).

Most mothers in full-time work therefore either had the same or a higher occupational status compared with their partners. This was not however reflected in pay. At Contacts 2, 3 and 4 we asked mothers about the 'take-home' pay of themselves and their partners. There are a number of problems about this approach. A proportion of mothers did not know what their partner's 'take home' pay was. Many employees also had their regular earnings supplemented from various 'perks', either in cash (for instance, bonuses) or in kind (for instance, a company car). A particularly valuable benefit for some parents who worked in financial services, such as banks or building societies, was a low interest rate mortgage. This type of preferential mortgage, or low interest rate loans for other purposes, was received by 11% of mothers in full-time employment, but by only 2% of fathers, reflecting the higher proportion of women working in financial services; by contrast, fathers were more likely to benefit from company cars. While we asked about such perks, we were unable to convert them to a cash equivalent and include them in our assessment of earnings.

Finally, differences in parents' 'take home' or net pay are not
accurate reflections of differences in gross pay. In a few cases,
where children were cared for in workplace nurseries, the cost
was stopped out of the earnings of the parent whose employer
provided the childcare. More generally, the married man's tax
allowance affected take-home pay. In nearly all cases, these factors
benefited men, increasing the proportion of gross earnings that
they retained compared with women. Unfair or inaccurate as it
may be in theory, it is probably the case that in practice most
parents view their own, and their partner's earnings, not in terms
of gross pay but in terms of what they actually get, in the hand
or in the bank, at the end of the month.

In comparing mothers' and fathers' earnings we have concentrated on the Second Contact, because we had the lowest
proportion of 'don't knows' for fathers' earnings. Altogether we
got 'take home' pay data for both parents in 77% of households
where both mother and father were in full-time employment. For
this group of households, average monthly 'take-home' pay was
£574 for fathers and £469 for mothers. In 19% of the households,
mothers and fathers had the same monthly take-home pay or a
difference of less than £30, while in 15% the mother earned at
least £30 a month more than the father. In the remaining 67% of
households, the father's monthly take-home pay was higher than
the mother's by £30 or more a month.

OCCUPATIONAL MOBILITY

In Chapter 5 we considered occupational mobility for women
in the sample, and related this to their employment histories
after birth. Occupational mobility included not only movement
between different types of occupation, but also movement within
occupation, for example a teacher moving up to a higher scale or
down to a lower one. Unlike the women, nearly all the men were in
continuous, or near continuous, full-time employment during the
early years of parenthood. Consequently, the relationship between
occupational mobility and employment history cannot be explored
as it was for women.

What we have focused on instead is a comparison of occupational
mobility between men and women. We have divided the women in
the study into three groups, similar though not identical to those
used in Chapters 4 and 5: women employed full-time throughout;
women not employed throughout or only employed for less than 8

149

hours a week; and other women, which includes those who worked full-time for part of the study period or had a part-time job of more than 8 hours a week. For each group, we have compared the women's mobility with that of their partners.

Occupational mobility mainly occurs when people change jobs. The employment histories show that women who were continuously employed changed jobs at a similar rate to men. Around half had only one job for the whole 3 year period, and just under a fifth (18% for men, 14% for women) had 3 or more jobs. Occupational mobility was also very similar for these women and their partners. A small number (5%) experienced downward mobility, most were unchanged and a quarter went up; slightly more men than women moved up (29%, 24%), but the difference is small and not statistically significant.

This initial analysis, however, needs qualification. Opportunities for upward mobility are likely to be lowest in manual jobs, and greatest in managerial and professional jobs, with clerical and sales jobs coming somewhere in between. As already described, mothers and fathers had different occupational profiles; more fathers than mothers were in manual jobs, while more mothers than fathers were in clerical and sales jobs. In comparing mothers' and fathers' occupational mobility, therefore, these differences in occupational profile need to be taken into account.

Men in professional and managerial jobs at Contact 1 were more than twice as likely as men in manual jobs to have been upwardly mobile during the study (38% v. 16%); the difference between men in sales and clerical jobs and men in manual jobs was less, but also statistically significant. The number of women in manual jobs was too small to make comparison with men; but in the two non-manual occupational groups men were more likely than women to move upwards, the difference in each case being greater than between all mothers and all fathers in continuous full-time employment. In neither case, though, does the difference reach statistical significance; if, however, the two non-manual groups are combined, then the difference just reaches a significant level. In other words, among non-manual workers in full-time continuous employment, men with young children were more likely to be upwardly mobile than women.

We cannot be certain how far these differences in occupational mobility for mothers and fathers in non-manual jobs were due to the differential impact of parenthood on men's and women's employment. Given the attitudes of mothers to promotion at this stage in their lives and the way in which many played down the importance of their work in contrast to their husbands' (Chapter 6), it seems probable that this was an important factor and that as parenthood progresses, it would lead to increasing differentials in occupational mobility for mothers and fathers in full-time employment.

The men whose partners were not in continuous full-time employment over the course of the study had a similar pattern of mobility to men whose partners were in continuous full-time employment. But the women's patterns were quite different. In the group with a record of broken full-time work or of part-time work with longer hours, two out of five women were downwardly mobile and only a few moved up. While in the third group, three quarters of the women who worked at some point after childbirth, but only for less than 8 hours a week, had moved down.

HOURS OF EMPLOYMENT

Given the high level of part-time employment among women with children, comparison of the work hours of employed fathers and mothers is not very revealing unless this factor is controlled for. Where this has been done and a comparison is made only between men and women with children under 5 in full-time jobs, fathers' work hours are still longer on average. The 1985 LFS, for example, shows that two thirds of mothers in full-time jobs normally worked 30 to 39 hours a week, just over a quarter (28%) 40 to 49 hours and only 8% over 50 hours; for fathers, the proportions were 21%, 49% and 30%, respectively. In other words, most mothers in full-time jobs were working under 40 hours a week in 1985, most fathers worked over, and fathers were nearly four times as likely to work over 50 hours a week (data come from a re-analysis of the 1985 LFS by the Statistical Office of the European Communities).

At the Second Contact for mothers and at Contacts 3 and 4 for both parents we collected information on 'hours at work' for the week preceding the interview; 'hours at work' included travel time, overtime in the main job and any time spent on a second job or studying. We also asked whether the preceding week had been typical or not; it was described as 'typical' in over 80% of the cases, except for fathers at Contact 3, when only 75% were 'typical' and 13% were described as 'usually working longer' compared with 6% who 'usually worked less'. Otherwise the 'usually works longer' and 'usually works less' groups were between 2% and 6%. In

Table 9.2 *Hours at work for fathers and mothers at Contacts 3 and 4*

	Hours at work in week before interview									
	30–39		*40–49*		*50–59*		*60+*		*Average (mean)*	
Contact	3	4	3	4	3	4	3	4	3	4
Fathers										
– partner in full-time employment (%)	4	4	22	29	42	42	32	25	55.6	53.5
– partner not employed (%)	5	4	29	17	41	41	25	37	53.7	58.1
– all fathers (%)	4	4	25	21	42	42	28	32	54.8	55.8
Mothers										
– in full-time employment (%)	12	10	53	54	33	34	2	1	47	47

addition 7% of fathers' hours at Contacts 3 and 4 were described as 'not typical' because their hours varied so much from week to week, while for women the proportion was 1–3% at different contacts.

At both Contacts 3 and 4, fathers' 'hours at work' averaged 55–56 a week, 8–9 hours longer than for mothers in full-time employment. Over a quarter of fathers were at work for 60 hours or more in the week, compared with 1–2% of mothers. At the other end of the range, fewer than 30% of fathers had 'hours at work' of less than 50 a week, compared with just over 60% of mothers (Table 9.2).

Among fathers, there was some difference between those with a partner in full-time employment and those whose partner was not employed. At Contact 3, men whose partners were not employed had rather shorter 'hours at work', though the difference was not statistically significant; but at Contact 4 they worked over 4 hours more a week, a statistically significant difference. This change in average hours between the two contacts was mainly due to actual changes in 'hours at work' for some fathers, and not to changes in employment status between contacts by women with partners working particularly long or short hours. Men with partners employed full-time at Contact 4 showed a decrease in 'hours at work' between Contacts 3 and 4 (55.6 to 53.5), compared to increased 'hours at work' (53.7 to 58.1) for men with partners not employed at Contact 4.

Other evidence also suggests a steady upward drift in average working hours among fathers whose partners were not employed or left full-time employment. Our ability to look at change over time for mothers and fathers is limited because we have no 'hours at work' data for both parents either at Contact 2 or for the period before the birth; we cannot say how 'hours at work' changed for fathers, or mothers, after the birth or between Contacts 2 and 3. However, at Contacts 2, 3 and 4, we did ask mothers if their partner's working hours (or their own) had changed since the preceding interview (or, for mothers at Contact 2, since before the birth) and, if so, in what way – longer or shorter hours or a different pattern of hours.

Some indication of the validity of these reports can be gained by comparing mothers' reports at Contact 4, about changes since Contact 3, with the actual 'hours at work' information collected at both contacts. This shows a clear correspondence between reported change and changes as measured by comparing the 'hours at work' data from the two contacts. Mothers who said at Contact 4 that their partners worked less hours compared with Contact 3 had partners whose 'hours at work' were, on average, 6 hours a week less at Contact 4 than at Contact 3; and those who said their partners were working more hours, had partners whose 'hours at work' were up 12 hours on average.

Mothers' reports of change in partners' working hours between Contacts show some consistent trends over time (Table 9.3). Where mothers were not employed at either the current or previous contacts, fathers were more likely to be reported as increasing their hours than reducing them; this was also the case for mothers who left full-time employment between Contacts 2 and 3 but not between Contacts 3 and 4. Where mothers were in full-time employment at both the current and previous contact, reported changes were more evenly balanced between fathers whose working hours were said to have increased and those said to have decreased.

Table 9.4 shows changes in mothers' working hours as reported

153

Table 9.3 *Mothers' reports of changes in partners' hours at work between contacts, by mothers' employment status*

| | | Reported change in fathers' hours at work | | | |
		No change	Hours increased	Hours decreased	Other change
Change between Contacts 1 & 2					
Mother NE at C2 (N = 67)	(%)	54	28	8	8
Mother FTE at C2 (N = 155)	(%)	45	21	23	1
Change between Contacts 2 & 3					
Mother NE at both contacts (N = 58)	(%)	62	22	9	10
Mother FTE at C2, NE at C3 (N = 28)	(%)	64	36	–	11
Mother FTE at both contacts (N = 124)	(%)	64	19	6	14
Change between Contacts 3 & 4					
Mother NE at both contacts (N = 51)	(%)	31	43	16	24
Mother FTE at C3, NE at C4 (N = 35)	(%)	37	26	10	27
Mother FTE at both contacts (N = 85)	(%)	40	26	21	22

Key: FTE = full-time employed; NE = not employed; C = Contact.
Rows add to more than 100% because 'other changes' (e.g. working a different shift) might also involve increased or decreased hours.

by mothers in full-time employment. At Contact 2, mothers were asked how their hours compared with those worked before birth. Just over half reported they had reduced their hours or changed when they worked their hours, or both, suggesting a substantial amount of adjustment on resuming employment. Very few reported their hours increased – 5% compared with 21% who said their partner's working hours had increased since they had resumed employment. At Contact 3, most women in full-time employment then and at Contact 2 reported no change in their

154

Table 9.4 *Mothers' reports of changes in own hours at work between contacts*

| | | Reported changes in own hours at work | | | |
		No change	Hours increased	Hours decreased	Other change
Change between before birth and Contact 2 Mother FTE at C2 (N = 155)	(%)	42	5	34	29
Change between Contacts 2 and 3 Mother FTE at C2 and C3 (N = 124)	(%)	87	4	4	8
Change between Contacts 3 and 4 Mother FTE at C3 and C4 (N = 85)	(%)	57	20	16	18

Key: FTE = full-time employed
Rows add to more than 100% because 'other changes' (e.g. working a different shift) might also involve increased or decreased hours.

work hours over this period. Fewer reported no change between Contacts 3 and 4, as might be expected given the longer period of time involved. But at both Contacts 3 and 4, those who reported a change since the previous contact were evenly divided between increased and decreased hours and other changes in hours.

Comparing within households where both parents had full-time jobs at Contact 3, 14% had parents who had similar 'hours at work' – that is, within 1 or 2 hours per week of each other – and in 13% of households the mother had longer 'hours at work' than the father. In most cases, 73%, the father had longer hours. Between Contact 3 and 4, as already noted, the 'hours at work' of fathers with partners in full-time employment decreased on average; this is reflected in more households at Contact 4 where parents' 'hours at work' were roughly similar (23%) and fewer where the father's hours were longer (60%). At both Contacts 3 and 4, mothers who worked longer hours also tended to have partners who worked longer hours, though this relationship between parents' 'hours at work' was only statistically significant at Contact 3. At that Contact, women whose 'hours at work' were less than 40 had partners who, on average, worked 50 hours a week. For women

155

who worked 45 – 49 hours a week, their partners' average was 56 and for women who worked 55 – 59 hours, the average was 62.

Finally, there was no consistent or statistically significant relationship at either Contact 3 or 4 between 'hours at work' and occupational status for either men or women in full-time jobs.

In dual earner households with young children, women's employment was often treated as secondary and temporary (Chapter 6), while men continued to be main and permanent breadwinners; ideologies about motherhood and fatherhood sustain these differences. There were also differences in actual employment circumstances between mothers and fathers. In general, fathers were more likely to be self-employed and work in the private sector; they earned more and worked longer hours; they remained in continuous full-time employment; and were more likely to be occupationally upwardly mobile, at least within non-manual jobs.

There appeared to be a trend during the early years of parenthood of increasing hours at work among fathers whose partners were not employed. This would be consistent with data from the 1975 Family Expenditure Survey which showed fathers' working their longest hours in employment when they had a youngest child aged 2–4 (Moss and Brannen, 1987). This may reflect career-building behaviour but also increasing financial pressures in households with only one earner, as children get older and more expensive, as second and third children are born and as financial reserves, built-up during the dual earner period before having children, are depleted.

Finally, there was no evidence of parents in dual earner households' adopting strategies to adapt their hours of work to each other. Instead men who worked longer hours were more likely to have partners who worked longer hours. This may reflect the growing phenomenon of 'workaholic couples', putting in long hours for high pay and depending heavily on paid domestic help. We return to this variant of the dual earner household in the concluding chapter.

10

Managing the
Dual Earner Lifestyle

Managing the dual earner lifestyle may involve a wide range of activities and commitments, ranging from necessities of existence to optional leisure and social activities. We have focused on three areas of activity at the 'necessity' end of the spectrum: paid work, childcare and certain types of domestic work. Paid work has been discussed in previous chapters. Here we consider the management of childcare and domestic work. This involves how these activities were divided within the household in the sample, between parents, but also the use of resources to reduce the amount of childcare and domestic work parents had to do and methods adopted by individual parents, and particularly mothers, to manage the demands of paid and unpaid work. While the focus is on dual earner households, we have also considered how far the role of fathers in childcare and domestic work differed between dual and single earner households.

Nearly all the households in our study were dual earner before having a child. The main new issue for them was accommodating the additional demands made by having a child. We conclude by considering the process involved in making this accommodation, and how the management of the dual earner lifestyle after parenthood compared with that beforehand.

THE WORKING DAY

At Contact 2, we asked mothers to describe the family timetable on a 'typical working day', starting with the time members of the family woke, and running through the day up to the time children and parents went to bed. Most mothers in full-time jobs (71%) reported that their 'typical working day' began before 7 a.m. – earlier than non-employed mothers, only a quarter of whom were awake by this time. Children with both parents employed full-time woke earlier than other children – 54% before 7 compared with 27% of those with mothers not employed. The difference in waking hours between employed and non-employed mothers, and between their children was, in both cases, statistically significant. Fathers however began their day at much the same time whether or not their partners were employed full-time – around half woke before 7 – and on average woke rather later than mothers with full-time jobs.

Employed mothers got up earlier not because they left for work earlier. In fact mothers and fathers (and children) left home at very similar times; over 75% left after 7.30, with the median time for departure being between 8 and 8.30. Mothers, however, as we shall discuss later, did most of the childcare and domestic work; getting up early was one way to cope, making time to catch up on housework, prepare meals for later and get their child up and ready. In some cases, the early morning provided women with the one period in the day when they had some peace and time to themselves.

Mothers and children got home at similar times, largely because mothers were mainly responsible for collecting children from caregivers, an issue discussed later. A third, many of them teachers, were home by 5, the remainder between 5 and 7; the median time for return was between 5 and 6. Fathers got home later; their median return time was between 6 and 7, and a quarter were not in until after 7.

The median bedtime for children where both parents worked was between 8 and 9, compared with between 7 and 8 for children whose mothers were not employed; despite this, the difference in the distribution of bed times between the two groups was small and not statistically significant. During the course of a day and night, there was also no difference in the amount both groups of children were said to sleep. Since children with employed parents woke earlier and went to bed no sooner than other children, this implies they spent more time asleep in the day at their carers'. Employed mothers were the first adults to bed, starting and finishing their day, on average, earlier: just over half (54%) retired by 11 p.m. compared with 34% of their partners. Non-employed mothers and their partners had similar bedtimes; most – 58% and 63%, respectively – retired after 11 p.m.

CHILDCARE WORK

The Division of Time

Mothers' accounts of the 'typical working day' at Contact 2 con-firmed that fathers spent, on average, longer at work (Chapter 9). The obverse of this was that fathers spent less time with their children while the children were awake – between 3 and 4 hours a day compared with 4 to 5 for mothers. Children on average were cared for 8 hours a day by someone other than their parents.

A more comprehensive and accurate view of how childcare time was organized comes from the diaries which mothers completed at Contacts 3 and 4 over a 7 day period (these asked for information about the child's day, and were left at the end of each contact for mothers to complete over the following week and return by post). The results for both contacts are summarized in Table 10.1. Excluding for the moment children with lone mothers, children were in the *sole charge* of their mothers for over 50 hours a week where the mother was not employed, roughly twice as long as for children whose mothers had full-time jobs. Fathers with partners in full-time, or indeed part-time, jobs were more likely to have sole charge of their children than were fathers with non-employed partners; the difference was statistically significant.

The main reason for this difference is that fathers with employed partners quite often cared for their children for part of the time their partners were at work; for instance, at both Contacts 3 and 4, about a fifth of children with both parents employed full-time were looked after by their fathers in this way. The amount of time for which fathers had sole care of their children in these arrangements, which involved 50 children at some point in the study, varied considerably. Seven of the 50 fathers shared the care of their child equally with a non-parental carer. An example was a father who worked a double-day shift as a fitter in a factory. When on 'early' shift, from 6 a.m. to 1.30 p.m., he collected his son from the childminder at 1.50 p.m., then had sole charge of him until his wife returned at 4.45; when on 'late' shift, the father looked after his son from 7.30 a.m., when his wife left home, until the time he left for work at 1 p.m., when he took the child to the childminder. Most of the remaining 43 fathers had sole charge of their child, while their partner was at work, for shorter periods but every week – 10 for between 10 and 19 hours a week, 21 for less than 10 hours a week. The remaining 8 fathers had sole charge less regularly, for example during school holidays in the

159

Table 10.1 *Distribution of child's week between caregivers at Contacts 3 and 4*

Person caring for child	Type of family	Contact 3		Contact 4	
		Hours in week	*% of total hours*	*Hours in week*	*% of total hours*
Mother only	MNE	53	31	57	33
	MPT	49	29	45	27
	MFT	28	17	33 $\begin{array}{l}(a = 25)\\(b = 100)\end{array}$	20 $\begin{array}{l}(a = 15)\\(b = 59)\end{array}$
Father only	MNE	3	2	3	2
	MPT	7	4	6	4
	MFT	6	4	7 $\begin{array}{l}(a = 6)\\(b = 12)\end{array}$	4 $\begin{array}{l}(a = 4)\\(b = 7)\end{array}$
Both parents	MNE	107	64	98	56
	MPT	95	57	97	58
	MFT	95	57	91 $\begin{array}{l}(a = 100)\\(b = 11)\end{array}$	54 $\begin{array}{l}(a = 60)\\(b = 6)\end{array}$
Non parent	MNE	5	3	17	10
	MPT	17	10	20	12
	MFT	37	22	37 $\begin{array}{l}(a = 36)\\(b = 45)\end{array}$	22 $\begin{array}{l}(a = 22)\\(b = 27)\end{array}$
Child asleep	MNE	88	52	83	47
	MPT	89	53	82	49
	MFT	86	52	80	48

Key
MNE = Mother not employed; MPT = Mother employed part-time; MFT = Mother employed full-time.
a = Hours in week for mother in two-parent family employed full-time
b = Hours in week for lone mother employed full-time

case of some teachers or on certain Saturdays or evenings where their partners had to go into work occasionally at these times.

Because fathers generally had longer 'hours at work' than mothers, it was more common for mothers to have sole charge of children for part of the time their partners were at work. Mothers in full-time jobs, though, spent longer in sole charge than can be explained simply in terms of these differences in 'hours at work' – on average, over 20 hours a week more than fathers at Contacts 3 and 4. This suggests either that fathers' 'hours at work' were under-reported by mothers, or that fathers were apart from their children for substantial periods for non-work reasons.

Unfortunately we have no way of knowing how much time fathers, or mothers, spent away from their children for non-work reasons. At Contact 2, we asked mothers to go through a checklist of 'things that working mothers sometimes do to cope'. This included cutting down on social life and on hobbies and activities: for both items, a third of mothers in full-time jobs said they had cut down 'to a great extent', while half said they had cut down 'to some extent'. The greater time mothers spent in sole charge may therefore result from fathers' greater involvement both in employment and leisure and social activities, and fathers being less willing or able to reduce the time they devoted to these activities. This interpretation receives some support from the findings of an Australian study:

> Employed mothers were significantly less likely to spend time on personal leisure than non-employed mothers (1.3 v. 2.8 hours a week), whereas the difference between fathers in these two types of family was relatively minor (4.2 v. 4.7 hours a week). Thus it seems that mothers adjusted their lifestyles to accommodate the extra pressure and demands of having both parents employed. (Russell, 1983, p. 60)

The main bloc of time in the child's week, around 100 hours altogether, was when he or she was in the charge of *both* parents. At Contact 3, 'joint' care was higher for children with non-employed mothers, the difference being statistically significant, but there was no difference at Contact 4. Indeed, between Contact 3 and Contact 4, the period in 'joint' care fell for children with non-employed mothers, while the period in 'sole' care with the mother increased; in other words, fathers in these single earner households spent less time with their children. This change is consistent with the increase that occurred between these two Contacts in 'hours at work' for fathers with non-employed partners (Chapter 9).

161

The term 'joint' care needs to be qualified. 'Joint' simply meant that the child was at home, or in some other place, at the same time as both parents. Since our diary method did not give more precise information about this period of time, we have no means of knowing how the demands of care were actually divided between parents during this period. 'Joint' care could mean anything from both parents actively playing with their child or taking equal turns to do so, to one parent being in the house but closeted away with no actual child contact.

Many mothers in our sample felt the need to give their child considerable, even exclusive, attention after work (Chapter 7), and some felt that they gave more attention during this period than their partner.

> *Do you have enough time with [your child]?* I think I do because I do spend my time with her when I get home . . . [But my husband] is always doing something, and I won't do that because my time is with Jane, whereas he's quite happy to do [decorating] . . . [men] don't see it's important. I wouldn't go out in the evenings straight from work unless I took time off in the day, whereas for my husband, it really wouldn't matter. (Senior clerical worker; Contact 4)

A second woman provides a particularly clear example of how a mother could spend more time in 'sole' charge because her 'hours at work' were shorter than her partner's; and also how 'joint' care could mean in practice 'mother' care because of the mother's feelings about the need to have and give 'special time' with her child – in this case at night.

> [After work] I tend to do very little apart from be with her and do what she wants to do. I let her direct it fairly much. By the time I collect her [at 4.30], then it's her world until she's tired out and wants to go to bed. That's how I want it to be. *Does your husband have a special time with her?* It's difficult with his work hours. No. He sees her in the morning, usually plays with her for a while, and when he gets in. But there's no specific time . . . Obviously [because of breastfeeding] I was the one who got up every night to see to her, and once established for 8 months, that's hard to break [the child had only just begun to sleep through the night at Contact 4]. And I think that's where the guilt thing comes in. If you're at work all day, you want every minute you can spare. So if she woke 6 times in the night, that was great, fine, that was my time,

that's what I owed her. (Headteacher married to self-employed computer consultant; Contact 4)

In other families, however, mothers saw the times after work and weekends as 'special times' for children which were *shared equally* by both parents, rather than being, by necessity or preference, primarily the mother's domain.

I try to [make special time to be with child] in the week when she's home. We try to get her to bed by 8, 8.30 – invariably 9. Until she goes to bed the time is hers, I'd say from 6 to 9 on average. It has to be hers, because I'm not with her all day, so she's got to have that time. *Does your husband have a special time with her?*. No, no more than just in the week we both are really with her. I think he knows he has to make the effort to give her his attention. (Secretary; Contact 4)

Children from dual earner households spent around 130 hours in a 168 hour week – or about three quarters of their time – in the care of their parents. For part of this time they would have been asleep. At Contact 3, when they were 18 months, children slept on average for 86 hours a week, and for 80 hours at Contact 4 when they were 36 months; some of this time would have been during the day, when they were not being cared for by their parents; but most would have been during the evening and night at home, largely during the 'joint' care period. Even so, it seems likely that children with both parents in full-time employment spent, on average, around 50 hours a week of waking time in parental care, mostly at the weekend and in the late afternoon and evening after work. Taken over the year, the average would have been higher, because parents usually looked after their children during public holidays and when on leave. Most of this time would have been either spent with both parents or with the mother alone. By contrast, children spent on average 37 hours a week in non-parental care – just under a quarter of their total week or, making allowance for sleep periods at non-parental caregivers, around 40% of their waking hours (though less taken over a full year, because of holidays).

Children whose mothers were not employed spent a small period of time in non-parental care at 18 months, $5^1/2$ hours a week on average. By 36 months this figure had increased substantially, to $16^1/2$ hours, reflecting the high proportion (53%) who were going to playgroups or other forms of part-time group care by that age. In addition, children probably spent more time with other adults as they got older – for instance, playing at friends' homes.

163

The pattern of care for children in lone parent families, with a mother in full-time work, was considerably different. Not surprisingly, these children spent very little time in the 'joint' care of both parents. Instead they spent much more time in the mother's 'sole' charge, nearly 100 hours a week, and 10 hours a week more in non-parental care – presumably, because fathers were not available to provide care for part of the time while mothers were at work. At the same time they spent twice as long in their father's 'sole' care, possibly during weekend or overnight visits.

Organizing Non-parental Childcare
Initially

Some period of non-parental childcare has to be organized in almost all dual earner households. In our families, the average period was just over 35 hours a week, though the length varied depending on when and for how long mothers and fathers worked, while for lone parents, as already noted, the period was longer. The type of care and how it is organized will depend on a number of factors – in particular, on public policy on the provision of childcare for employed parents. In the UK, publicly funded childcare is not available for dual earner families, nor in practice for most lone employed parents. Only two children in our sample received care in publicly funded services during the whole course of the study, and in both cases this was because their mothers were employed in the day nurseries concerned. A number of mothers, unaware of the situation, looked into the possibility of using local authority day nurseries, but quickly found that these were not on offer.

> I did phone the Council about nurseries, but they said you can only have a place if you're a single parent. I said, I'm not. If you are married you can have one if you are in danger of battering your child – I'm not. (Teacher; Contact 1)

In the absence of publicly funded services, parents had to rely on informal social networks (relatives, friends and workplace contacts), the private market (largely childminders, but also the few private nurseries then available) or employer provision (in nurseries). The actual work involved in making initial arrangements fell very largely to mothers. Excluding initial placements that resulted from unsolicited offers from relatives and friends, 81% were described by mothers as being made by themselves, compared with 4% by fathers and 14% where both parents were said to have shared the work. Fathers made some contribution, except for a

164

few cases (12%) where women said their partners had played no part at all; this contribution mainly involved rubber-stamping the mother's decision or visiting proposed placements, often the one that the mother had chosen. Only a third of women said the final decision was joint. Most (57%) said they had made the decision, after discussion with the child's father; in the remaining 10% the decision was reportedly made without discussion.

Just under half the mothers felt that making childcare arrangements should be the mother's job. They regarded mothers as primarily responsible for childcare; some also considered mothers to be more competent to judge what was on offer – 'It should be down to the mother, because it's her choice she's going back to work'; 'Mothers usually [should make arrangements] because you're the one who has to feel happy about leaving the baby'; 'the mother because [she] knows the child more than the father would do . . . she would know instinctively if it was alright for her child to go to that person.'

The remainder (57%) felt that making childcare arrangements should be shared by both parents or might be done by either parent depending on who had most time or opportunity. Those mothers who took the latter view regarded – implicitly or explicitly – themselves as having more time and opportunity. There seemed, though, to be no practical reason why fathers could not have been more involved. In only a few cases (19%) was more than one placement visited in the course of making arrangements; even where several visits were involved, fathers could have made ample time to be actively involved by using evenings and weekends or even taking a day's leave.

Later Changes in
Non-parental Childcare

In many cases further childcare arrangements had to be made subsequently. Nearly half (45%) of children had at least one change in childcare arrangements while their mothers were in full-time employment. Put another way, of 331 placements made for children in the sample while their mothers were in full-time employment, 132 ended with the child being moved elsewhere. Placements in nurseries were least likely to end in changes – 23%, compared with 42–43% for placements with childminders or relatives or other carers such as nannies. Over half the childminder placements (58%) ended because parents were unhappy, the child did not settle or because the childminder was unable to cope or stopped childminding. These reasons accounted for 47% of changes from relatives, but most of the remainder were due to relatives being used to provide temporary care between or before permanent placements.

Each change involved a new arrangement to be made. On some occasions, the new placement might be suggested or even arranged by the previous carer. Mostly, however, the new placement had to be arranged from scratch, again mostly by mothers. The work and stress involved varied according to the notice given, the circumstances surrounding the change, the availability of alternative carers and the frequency with which changes occurred. In all cases, some work was involved but this could be part of a relatively orderly and unpressured process. Alternatively, the whole episode could create major problems and pressures, bringing the mother close to breaking point.

> On the Tuesday evening, [the nanny] said she was a little bit lonely and I said I'd speak to the health visitor to see if there was any local group she could join or other nannies in the area . . . [then] I got a phone call on Wednesday when I was at a meeting – 'Nanny has taken James to your mother's'. It was a *fait accompli*, and when I phoned my mother in the afternoon, she had had to come home from work because the nanny was overwrought. When I got home, my mother and the nanny were there and the nanny couldn't cope and was leaving and that was it . . . it was a disaster, it was my most miserable time. It was so catastrophic. (Surveyor; Contact 4)

Maintaining Non-parental Childcare Arrangements

The organization of non-parental childcare does not end once an arrangement is made. In a minority of cases – 7% at Contact 3, rising to 16% at Contact 4 – the carer came into the child's home. Mostly, though, children had to be got ready and taken to the carer's, then be collected at the end of the day. At Contacts 2, 3 and 4, just over 70% of children were taken always or mostly by their mothers; for the rest, the task was either shared by the parents (who either took turns or travelled together) or done mostly or always by the father. Collecting children and bringing them home showed a similar pattern, with the mother slightly less likely to be responsible. At Contact 4, for instance, 73% of children were always or mostly taken by their mothers, compared with 64%

always or mostly collected by their mothers; of the remainder, the collection of 17% was shared and 19% were usually brought home by their fathers.

Taking a child to and from a carer's makes several demands on the person involved. There is the travel which takes time and effort. Both can be reduced by access to private transport; most, though not all, mothers (64%) in full-time jobs had the use of a car for half or more of the time. Before being taken, children need to be got ready, and to a fairly tight schedule if they are to be out on time; everything they are likely to need for their day must be prepared and assembled. In most cases, this preparatory task fell mainly or wholly to the mother as the person taking the child, and was one reason why many mothers got up early. Finally, taking and collecting a child usually also entailed maintaining the arrangement, a task requiring the investment of some time and effort to establish and sustain a good, or at least tolerable, relationship; to discuss any problems that might arise on either side; and to ensure that, where due, payment was made.

Routine Childcare Tasks
in the Home

As well as the time that mothers and fathers spent with their children, we also looked at how some of the actual tasks involved in childcare were divided. At Contacts 2, 3 and 4 mothers were asked to indicate, on a checklist of childcare tasks, what proportion of each task they had done in the last week – all the task (scored 4), most of it (3), half (2), some (1) or none (0). There were five childcare tasks at Contact 2 (bathing and washing, dressing and changing clothes, feeding, changing nappies and seeing to the child after he or she had been put down for the night) and at Contact 3 (seeing to the child on a potty being substituted for feeding). At Contact 4 there were seven items, supervising meals and getting child ready for bed being added.

The scores for each item were summed to give, for each mother, a 'total childcare score', with a range of 0 (if the mother had done none of the items in the last week) to 20 or 28 (if she had done all of each item). The difference between the mother's total score and the maximum possible score was accounted for by two factors. A small proportion would be due to the task not arising at all in the week, in particular because the child had not needed attention after being put down for the night or, at 18 months, because the child was not yet using the potty. The greater part was accounted for

167

by others doing the task, which was nearly always the father. In broad terms, therefore, the higher the mother's score, the less the father did, and vice versa.

We were interested in comparing the division of childcare tasks between households where the mother was employed full-time and households where the mother was not employed. A straight-forward comparison would not however be very interesting; employed mothers were bound to do a lesser proportion of childcare tasks because they spent less time with their children, and a substantial proportion was done by non-parental carers. We therefore asked all mothers to assess what proportion of each childcare task they did *for the period when their partner was not at work*, to give a rough basis for comparability. Finally, we also asked mothers to indicate how often their partners did each childcare task, offering five options: every day, most days, weekly but not most days, less than weekly, and never or only in emergencies.

Table 10.2 summarizes the situation at Contact 2, both for the total childcare score and the frequency with which fathers performed individual tasks; it also shows the actual division of seeing to children at night in those families where the child had woken at least once in the week preceding the interview. On total childcare, mothers scored well over half the maximum possible score; and only a minority of fathers were reported to perform individual tasks every day or most days (or in the case of seeing to children at night, on half or more occasions). Fathers' performance on childcare tasks contrasts strongly with their participation in play: over 90% were said to play with their child every day or most days, and 80% of mothers rated their own contribution to this activity at half or less. In other words, while most fathers were involved in play on a regular and equal basis, this was true of only a small minority when it came to the day-to-day work involved in caring for a very young child.

The table makes comparison between mothers who were in full-time jobs and those who were not employed. Non-employed mothers had higher total scores, but the difference is small and not statistically significant. However, on all five tasks, fathers with employed partners were reported to do these tasks more often than fathers whose partners were not employed; the difference was statistically significant for four of the tasks. This apparent inconsistency may arise from the rather imprecise nature of the method used to calculate the total childcare score. The categories 'does some' and 'does most' of a task are very broad; a mother who chose 'does most' to describe how much of the nappy changing she

Table 10.2 *Division of childcare work in household at Contact 2*

			Mother's employment status	
			Not employed	*Employed FT*
Average total childcare score			14.3	13.5
Frequency father				
Changes nappies	A	(%)	28	14
	B	(%)	28	46
Feeds child	A	(%)	13	8
	B	(%)	27	43
Bathes/washes child	A	(%)	22	17
	B	(%)	22	31
Dresses child	A	(%)	18	8
	B	(%)	14	33
Sees to child at night	A	(%)	82	62
	B	(%)	18	39
Plays with child	A	(%)	2	1
	B	(%)	90	94

Key
A = % of fathers do task 'never' or 'in emergencies only' or for 'sees to child at night' less than half.
B = % of fathers do task most or every day, or for 'sees to child at night' on half or more occasions.

did might mean she did just over half or that she did nearly all of it. It would therefore be possible for an employed mother to be doing a lesser proportion of childcare tasks than a non-employed mother (say an average of 60% for each task, compared with 80%), yet still have the same overall score; the difference would show up in the frequency with which fathers did each task, the partner of an employed mother scoring higher than the partner of a non-employed mother.

A further item of data supports the conclusion that fathers with partners in full-time employment did more childcare tasks. At Contact 2, mothers were asked if 'the help your partner gives with the child had changed' since Contact 1, during which time most women had resumed employment. Mothers working full-time were more than twice as likely as non-employed mothers to say their partner's help had increased over this period (57% compared with 24%). Indeed, decreased help was nearly as often reported as increased help by non-employed mothers (16% compared with 5% for mothers in full-time work).

Total childcare scores for Contact 3 still show mothers were doing over half the work involved in the tasks; but the average (12 both for mothers in full-time jobs and non-employed mothers) was lower than at Contact 2. This might mean that fathers were doing more as children get older. However, as there was little change between the two Contacts in the frequency with which fathers were reported to do individual tasks, a more likely explanation is that there was an increase in tasks that neither parent performed – especially, fewer children requiring attention after being put down to sleep and a number of children not yet being potty trained.

Managing Unpredictable Childcare Demands

As well as routine childcare, working parents have to manage unpredictable events that require a parent's attendance or making a special arrangement for childcare. The major causes of such events arise from the child's health – some illness or the need to go to a medical appointment – or some problem with the carer, which means she is unable to have the child. We considered these events at each contact, but concentrate here on the data from Contact 4, because it is the most detailed; the overall patterns, in particular how parents divided the work, were similar at Contacts 2 and 3.

In the long interviews at Contact 4 we asked mothers to tell us who made the decision that the child should go to the doctor, who took the child, who took time off work if the child was ill and whom the carer would contact if something was wrong with the child. Most commonly, these events were dealt with mainly or wholly by the mother, followed some way behind by both parents sharing; it was rare for the father to deal with them by himself. Two thirds of the mothers (67%) said they decided when their child should see the doctor and a quarter described it as a joint decision; only 6% of mothers said the father decided. Once decided, it was usually the mother who took the child (74%).

The need for parents to take time off work for a sick child depends to some extent on the attitude and circumstances of the non-parental carer – whether she is, for example, ready to take a child with a minor ailment or whether, as in the case of some relatives, she is prepared to come to the child's home; if a carer such as a nanny regularly cares for the child in its own home, managing illnesses is generally easier. Where a parent had to take time off, two thirds of mothers (69%) said they would be the one to do so; 23% said they would divide the time with their partner and 8% said their partner would take the time off. Nearly all the mothers (90%) said that the carer would contact them if something was amiss with the child.

These replies from a sub-sample were consistent with replies from the full sample of mothers at Contact 4 about time actually taken off work in the 6 months preceding the interview for child-related reasons. Half the mothers (54%) had taken some time off in this period, twice as many as among the fathers (27%). Moreover, mothers who took time off had longer away from work than fathers; 61% (33% of the whole sample) had had 3 or more days off, compared with only 30% of fathers (8% of the sample). The most common cause for taking time off – reported for 40% of mothers and 12% of fathers – was a child's illness, while taking a child to a medical appointment and some problem with the carer (for instance, a childminder being ill) were reported for 18–19% of mothers and 7–8% of fathers.

Few mothers reported difficulties getting time off. Most frequently they, and fathers, took it as annual leave; 54% of mothers said they had taken some or all of their leave in this way. Discretionary leave from employers came next, some way behind, reported by 31% of mothers. Other methods included taking the time as personal sick leave (16%), receiving leave as an employment entitlement (13%) and taking unpaid leave (2%).

171

RESPONSIBILITY FOR
CHILDREN

The sub-set of mothers who received long interviews at Contact
4, and who had been continuously employed, were asked who had
the main responsibility for the child and his or her upbringing.
Over three quarters (77%) said that they had; the rest said that
responsibility was shared with their partners. On average, mothers
who said they were mainly responsible did more childcare work, as
measured by hours in sole charge, their total childcare score, taking
and collecting children from childcare arrangements or taking time
off if children were ill. Indeed, some women defined responsibility
in terms of the amount they did for their child or the time they set
aside to be with the child.

> I get her up in the morning, take her to the childminder,
> pick her up. I spend a lot more time with her . . . so in
> that sense I'm more responsible, in the sense I'm more
> responsible because I do more . . . Basically, we're both
> responsible for her . . . but obviously I'm more involved.
> I spend more time with her . . . like I said the simple thing
> is, if there's something on TV, he'll ignore her if she's talking
> to him. (Clerical worker; Contact 4)

Other mothers considered themselves mainly responsible for
their child and his or her upbringing because of their predominant
role in some other aspect of parenthood, in particular providing
comfort or discipline.

> Her father plays with her. But she comes to me with her
> tears. He can play with her much more because he can relax
> with her much more than I can, because I'm the mum, in
> the traditional sense of the word. I'm the one who makes
> her go to sleep. She'll never go to sleep with Daddy. I take
> responsibility for her discipline, mainly because he's so soft.
> He freely admits he can't smack her and I can. (Administrator;
> Contact 4)

> Me [mainly responsible]. Me and my husband will play and
> everything else, but I think about other things . . . although
> my husband does more for him, I believe it's me [who's
> mainly responsible]. *Why?* I don't know. I just believe it . . .
> my husband is good with him, but he doesn't really – I dis-
> cipline him more, I have to. Because if we were both soft on
> him, God knows – because my husband spoils him. I believe

if we were both like that, the children would have no sense of responsibility, no discipline, no respect for others. (Bank clerk; Contact 4)

Most often, though, responsibility was defined in terms of two functions: organization and decision-making. Many mothers felt that they had to ensure that their child's needs were met, whether or not they did the actual work involved in meeting these needs; they, rather than their partners or anyone else, were ultimately accountable. The terms 'down to me' and 'making sure' were frequently used in this context to describe this organizational function.

> Me . . . I like to make sure it's done . . . I just have that way. I can just make sure they're done. My husband might forget. I can tell him – but I also have to remember at the same time in case he forgets. (Bank clerk; Contact 4)

> I suppose me when it comes down to it. I kind of organize it I suppose . . . I still sort of feel I'm ultimately responsible. Things like the childcare arrangements are my responsibility when it comes down to it. *Even though you don't take and collect your Andrew?* I still feel it comes down to me actually . . . although I'm convinced we share out the jobs pretty equally, I'm the one who organises it, that's what it comes down to. (Teacher; Contact 4)

A few mothers regarded decision-making as shared, but that implementation of decisions, the organizational side, was their task.

> I suppose me [for main responsibility] . . . [though] I'd rather say it's our responsibility. I believe it's as much his responsibility as mine. But when it comes to organizing our responsibility, it's left to me. Like we're beginning to think of Sophie's schooling and I've done the necessaries for that . . . We discuss it and we know where we want to send her and what we want to do. It just seems for me to pick up the phone and do the letter writing. He thinks a lot about the future for us and for the children. I never take any decision about the children on my own. *You make the decisions together, but you implement them?* That's right. (Nurse; Contact 4)

More often, though, decision-making and organization were closely linked in how mothers defined themselves as being mainly responsible.

> I'd say I have [the main responsibility] because I'm the one

who picks his clothes, dresses him, does his washing, baths him. I don't think men would have the sense to stick him in the bath. *You see yourself as the person who decides things need doing?* Yes, in the baby's case. [I have] the main role. I think I'm the one who decides. In the morning, wrap him up. You see, he wouldn't do that unless I told him. I think of things like preventing him catching a cold, whereas my husband doesn't. (Traffic warden; Contact 4)

DOMESTIC WORK

A third major area that has to be managed by dual earner households, in addition to paid work and childcare, involves domestic work – the running and maintenance of the home. In examining this issue, we have focused on only some domestic work tasks – essentially, shopping, cooking and cleaning. These tasks need doing on a routine basis, at least weekly and some more often, and are also tasks in the running of the home that are associated with women. We have not covered a number of tasks commonly associated with men such as gardening, decoration and repairs; we cannot claim therefore to provide a comprehensive account and may have under-represented the total contribution to domestic work made by the fathers in our sample. To put this omission into perspective, a recent American study of dual earner households, which does include a wider range of domestic tasks, concludes that men do fewer undesirable household chores and have more control over when they make their contributions; even in households where men were rated as sharing domestic work, women still did most of the daily jobs. This replicates the pattern found in the sharing of childcare, where men spent more time on enjoyable activities, such as play, while women spent more time on routine 'maintenance' (Hochschild, 1989).

Material resources can be used to reduce the domestic work that parents have to do, for example through investing in labour-saving machinery. Among dual earner households at Contact 2, nearly all (96%) had washing machines, most (82%) had freezers and half (55%) had tumble driers; only a few (9%) had dishwashers; ownership levels, however, were not significantly different in single earner households. A second way to use resources to reduce the domestic workload of parents is to pay someone to do part of it. A small, but not insignificant, proportion of dual earner households employed 'domestic help', someone paid specifically to

174

do domestic work – 10% at Contact 2, rising to 14% at Contact 4. In households where the mother was not employed, the figure was not much less at Contact 4 (10%), but at each of the two previous contacts, only one of these households had 'domestic help'. A few households received domestic help from other external sources, mostly relatives, but occasionally from nannies; the number of households involved and the level of help were both small, and they are not considered separately in the next section.

The Division of Domestic Work
Between Mothers and Fathers

In assessing how domestic work, or at least those areas we chose to cover, was divided, we followed a similar method to that used for childcare tasks. At Contacts 2, 3 and 4, mothers indicated on a checklist of seven domestic tasks what proportion of each task they had done in the last week – all of the task (scored 4), most (3), half (2), some (1) and none (0). The tasks selected were preparing main meals, clearing away after meals, household shopping, washing clothes, ironing, vacuum cleaning and dusting. The scores for each of these tasks was then summed to give, for each mother, a 'total domestic work score', with a range from 0 to 28. As with childcare tasks, the difference between the mothers' total score and the maximum possible score of 28 is the result of two factors. In some cases, no-one had done the task in the last week; ironing was the main example. The rest was accounted for by the proportion done by others. Most of this would come from fathers, with the main exception being households which employed 'domestic help'; these have been considered separately in the analysis that follows.

We also asked mothers to indicate how often their partners did each domestic task, using the same five frequency options as for childcare tasks, ranging from 'every day' to 'never or only in emergencies'. In considering these data, it has to be remembered that while some tasks, notably preparing meals, need doing on a daily basis, others, such as shopping, usually need doing less frequently.

Table 10.3 shows the total domestic work score at Contact 2 and the frequency with which fathers did tasks in households where mothers were employed full-time or not employed. Mothers in households with 'domestic help' had the lowest total scores: 15 out of a maximum of 28. In other households, mothers scored well over half. Fathers were most likely to contribute to household

175

Table 10.3 *Division of domestic work in household at Contact 2*

			Mother's employment status	
			Not employed	*Employed FT*
Average total domestic work score	A		23.6	19.4
	B		23.5	20
	C		–	14.9
Frequency father				
Prepares main meals	E	(%)	37	21
	F	(%)	8	25
Does household shopping	E	(%)	31	18
	G	(%)	43	58
Clears meals away	E	(%)	13	11
	F	(%)	40	49
Irons	E	(%)	75	67
	G	(%)	3	17
Washes clothes	E	(%)	79	64
	G	(%)	8	19
Vacuum cleans	E	(%)	49	26
	G	(%)	16	41
Dusts and cleans house	E	(%)	49	35
	G	(%)	14	33

Key
A = all households, B = households without 'domestic help', C = households with 'domestic help', E = % of fathers who 'never' do task or only do it in emergencies, F = % of fathers who do task most or every day, G = % of fathers who do task at least weekly.

shopping and clearing away after meals; 40–60% did these tasks at least weekly (for shopping) or most days (for clearing away). Their contribution was lower on the other tasks, particularly preparing meals, ironing and washing clothes.

Non-employed mothers scored higher on the total domestic work score than mothers in dual earner households; this difference held when households with 'domestic help' were excluded, and in both cases was statistically significant. Fathers in dual earner households were also reported to do all tasks more frequently than fathers with non-employed partners; the difference was statistically significant for all items except clearing meals (done by many men in both groups) and ironing (done by few men). Both indicators – total domestic work score and frequency fathers did tasks – point to fathers in dual earner households doing more. As already noted, this was confirmed at Contact 2, when mothers in full-time employment were more likely to say their partner's help with the child and with housework had increased since the previous Contact.

FATHERS IN DUAL EARNER
AND SINGLE EARNER
HOUSEHOLDS

Numerous studies, mostly American, have examined the relationship between maternal employment and the participation of men in childcare and domestic work. The results have been somewhat contradictory. Pleck (1985) ascribes this to differences in methodology. 'Proportional' methods of assessing 'family work', which involve asking how each of a series of tasks is divided, have tended to show that when women are employed, their partners do proportionately more. Time use studies, by contrast, seek to assesss the time that men and women spend on various activities, and American studies from the mid-1960s and early 1970s 'consistently showed that husbands do not participate more in housework and childcare when their wives are employed' (ibid., p. 31). Pleck suggests that the reason for this apparent inconsistency is that 'wife-employed husbands do a higher proportion of the family work, but only because wives' absolute level goes down [because they spend less time on it], not because husbands' goes up' (ibid., p. 31).

Pleck also examines data from two large-scale American time-use studies from the mid-to-late 1970s. These again appear to show inconsistent results.

177

In the 1975–76 Study of Time Use (STU), consistent with earlier studies, husbands show no appreciable increment in family work when their wives are employed . . . by contrast the 1977 Quality of Employment Survey (QES) differs from earlier research in suggesting that husbands do more family work. However (unlike STU), these data confirm earlier research in finding that employed wives have substantially greater work loads than their husbands. (ibid., p.40)

Pleck, again, suggests that the key to this apparent inconsistency lies in different methodologies. The time study diaries used in the STU encourage a narrow definition of childcare work; the 'respondents' summary estimate' in QES takes a broader view, and tends to equate childcare work with the total time spent with children rather than with specific childcare tasks.

If this explanation is accepted, [the results] can be interpreted as follows . . . husbands do respond to their wives' employment, but primarily in their time availability to their children, not housework and more narrowly defined childcare . . . Husbands' increased time in more broadly-defined childcare is not enough, though, to lead to equality between husbands' and wives' total workloads in two-earner couples. When childcare is assessed more narrowly, however, then husbands do not appear to do more in the family when their wives are employed. (ibid., p. 51)

In an Australian study, using respondents' estimates of time allocated to 'family work', Russell (1983) provided 'qualified support for previous time-use studies of the impact of maternal employment on fathers' involvement in family work . . . when a simple analysis is conducted comparing maternal employment groups, no significant differences were found in the time spent by fathers in either child care, play or other interactions' (p. 59). However, the situation was somewhat different when the age of children was taken into account. In families with a child under 3, similar to those in our study, fathers spent more time on childcare tasks when mothers were employed; though the difference 'was not highly significant, the trend is of sufficiently substantial nature to warrant that it be investigated in a more systematic manner in further studies' (p. 59). There was also one marked difference irrespective of child age: maternal employment 'had a highly significant effect on the time spent by fathers taking sole responsibility for their children', 4.7 hours in the week, compared with 1 hour for fathers with non-employed partners.

In our study, using a proportional approach, fathers with employed partners took a greater share of domestic work than fathers whose partners were not employed. But unlike other studies using this approach there was no difference for childcare tasks. This may be due, in part, to adopting an assessment of childcare tasks that was limited to that part of the day when fathers were not at work and when both parents were likely to be available to their child at home. This approach removes the possibility of a father's share of childcare tasks being greater – even though the amount of work he does remains unchanged – simply because his partner is out at work for part of the day and therefore doing fewer childcare tasks herself.

We have also suggested that the categories used in our assessment of how tasks were shared may have been too broad to detect differences between fathers in single and dual earner households. That there might be some differences is suggested by other sources of data, in particular the diaries and the questions on the frequency with which men performed childcare tasks. The results from these sources are consistent with Russell's findings that where there were young children in the household, men with employed partners on average did more childcare tasks and had more sole charge of their children than men whose partners were not employed; our results from all sources also suggest that fathers in dual earner households did rather more domestic work.

Although our data show that men with employed partners did more 'family work' than those without, the most striking reality was that on every indicator studied, mothers with full-time jobs did the main part of this work. And although this balance might have been somewhat different for domestic work tasks if a wider range had been considered, the same cannot be said for childcare. To give a clearer indication of the full extent of this disparity, we have brought together four areas of 'family work' considered separately in previous sections of this chapter; for each two-parent household with both parents in full-time jobs, we have considered how many of these four areas were equally or nearly equally divided between the parents at Contact 4, and given a score of 1 to each area where this was the case. Households could therefore score from 0 (where no area was equally or nearly equally divided, and the mother did the main part of each) to 4 (where each area was equally or nearly equally divided, and the father could be said to be equally

179

participant in 'family work'). The four areas, and the criteria for defining an equal or near equal division, are:

1. Time in sole charge of the child. The time each parent was in sole charge of the child was the same or within 2 hours of the other parent.
2. Total domestic work score. The mother's score was no more than 14, out of a total possible of 24 (i.e. half, half+1, or half +2). Allowance was made for the use of paid domestic help.
3. Total childcare score. The mother's score was half, half+1, or half+2 of the maximum possible score. Allowance was made for variation in the number of tasks applicable to the child, so that the total score could vary from 20 (where five tasks were applicable) to 28 (seven tasks applicable).
4. Other childcare tasks. Four tasks were considered: taking and collecting the child from its childcare arrangement, taking time off work for childcare reasons, and taking the child to a health service. This area was rated equally or nearly equally divided where the father shared or did more of at least two of these four tasks.

These definitions are perhaps rather generous to fathers. Nearly equal sharing, rather than actually equal sharing, is sufficient for a score of 1 for each area. The results, therefore, somewhat exaggerate the overall contribution made by fathers. Even so, of the 74 dual earner households at Contact 4 for which there was information in all 4 areas, the great majority score 0 (36%), 1 (30%), or 2 (20%). Only 7% score 3 and the same small proportion score 4 (in addition, there are 12 households where there were scores for only 3 of the 4 areas; 7 score 0 and 5 score 1).

Households with Different Scores

To illustrate what these scores mean in practice, we have chosen five families, each with a different score.

Family A: Score 0. The mother was a senior librarian, aged 36, and the father was a general building worker in a local authority aged 32. The diary showed that the mother had been in sole charge of the child for 36 hours in the week, while the father had no sole charge. The total domestic work score was 18 (out of a total maximum possible of 28); the mother had done all the ironing, most of the cooking, clearing meals and washing clothes, half the shopping and some of the vacuum cleaning. The total childcare score was 15 out of 20; the mother saw to the child in the evening and at night, did most of getting the child up, putting him to bed and supervising meals and half the washing and bathing. The mother always took and collected the child from his nursery and had taken 4 days off because of the child in the last 6 months, compared with a $1/2$ day for the father. Each parent had been on one GP or clinic visit with the child.

Family B: Score 1. The mother, aged 31, was a senior superintendent in a government training school for clerical staff and the father was a self-employed hairdresser agd 41. The diary showed that the mother had had sole charge of the child for 33 hours in the week, while the father had had 16 hours (this relatively high amount of time was because the mother, having got the child up, set out for work at 6.40 a.m., leaving the father in sole charge until he left the child at its childminder at about 8.45). The total domestic work score was again 18; the mother had done all the ironing and clothes washing and most of the cooking and shopping, half the dusting and cleaning, and some of the vacuum cleaning and clearing away after meals. The total childcare score was 16 out of 24; the mother always got the child up, had done most of the bathing and washing and putting the child to bed, and had shared seeing to the child on the potty, supervising meals and seeing to the child in the evening and night. The score of 1 came from the father's always taking the child to the childminder and sharing the child's collection. In the last 6 months, the mother had had 4 days off work because of the child, the father none. The child had had 4 visits to a doctor or clinic in the last 3 months, being taken twice by the mother, once by the father and once by the childminder.

Family C: Score 2. Mother was aged 32 and a teacher, the father aged 32 and a social worker. The diary showed that the mother had sole charge of the child for 27 hours in the week, compared with 3 hours for the father. The score of 2 comes from total housework and childcare scores which in both cases were half the maximum + 1. The total domestic work score was 15; the mother had done all the clothes washing, most of the shopping, half the cooking, vacuum cleaning and ironing and some of the meal clearing. The total childcare score was 13 (out of 24), with the mother doing most of the bathing but half of all other tasks. The mother mostly took the child to her childminder and mostly collected her. In the last 6 months, the mother had had 3 days off for childcare reasons, compared with 7 for the father.

Family D: Score 3. The mother was aged 32 and a solicitor with a local authority. The father was a teacher, aged 33. The score of 3 came from the first three areas. The diary showed that the mother

181

had sole charge of the child for 4 hours in the week and the father 5. The total domestic work score was 16 (out of 28); the mother had done all the clothes washing and ironing, half the shopping, cooking and meal clearing and some of the vacuum and general cleaning. The childcare score was 15 out of 28; the mother had done most of seeing to the child at night, and half of all the other tasks. The mother always took the child to and from the relative who cared for him, while in the last 6 months the mother had had 3 days off work because of the child, compared with none for the father.

Family E: Score 4. The mother was deputy head of a home for disabled people and the father was a social worker; both were aged 31. The diary showed that the mother had had sole charge of the child for 15 hours in the week, compared with 21 hours for the father. The total domestic work score was 14 (out of 28); the mother had done most of the meal clearing and clothes washing, half the vacuum and general cleaning and ironing and some of the cooking and shopping. The total childcare score was 11 out of 24, with the mother doing half of all tasks except supervising meals, which her partner mostly did. The mother usually took the child to her childminder, but collecting was shared. In the last 6 months, the mother had had no time off work because of the child, but the father had taken a half day for a hospital appointment. Both parents had gone on the child's one visit to a doctor or clinic in the last 3 months.

OCCUPATIONAL STATUS, CHILDCARE AND DOMESTIC WORK

Little work has been done on whether the amount of childcare and domestic work done by women or their partners is related to the occupational status of the women. Some work, though, has been done on the relationship with men's occupational status. A few British studies (Newson and Newson, 1963; Oakley, 1974; Graham and McKee, 1979) have reported that men in higher status occupations generally do more childcare and domestic work. Other studies, in Britain and elsewhere (for example, Richards *et al.*, 1977; Entwistle and Doering, 1980; Beail, 1983; Russell, 1983; Moss, Bolland and Foxman, 1987) report no difference.

In our study, occupational status showed no relationship with the hours children spent in sole charge of mothers or fathers or in joint care at either Contacts 3 or 4. However, at both Contacts, children with mothers or fathers in low status occupations spent, on average, more time in non-parental care. While the difference was significant at Contact 3 for mother's occupational status (33.8 hours for children with mothers in high status jobs v. 41.2 hours for low status), but not for father's occupational status (34.2 v. 39.3), at Contact 4 the situation was reversed, with the difference significant for father's occupation (32.8 hours v. 41.2 hours), but not for mother's (36.5 hours v. 37.1 hours). One factor contributing to this difference was the inclusion of teachers in the 'high status' group. Teachers' 'hours at work' were shorter than other occupational groups, and their children, consequently, needed less time in non-parental care. Excluding teachers, the difference between 'high' and 'low status' reduces in each instance. At Contact 3, for instance, the difference based on mothers' occupational status falls from 7.4 to 2.3 hours, and is no longer statistically significant.

Total childcare scores were not related to women's or men's occupational status at Contact 2, 3 or 4, with the exception of single earner households at Contact 3, when mothers with partners in 'high status' jobs had a significantly lower score. For the total domestic work score there was no relationship with occupational status in single earner households; however, in households where the mother was employed full-time, there was a consistent relationship with parents' occupational status at Contacts 2, 3 and 4, except for fathers' occupational status at Contact 4: women in 'high status' jobs or with partners in 'high status' jobs had lower scores, in other words did less, the difference being statistically significant. This conclusion needs some qualification. At each Contact, the use of paid domestic help was closely related to men and women's occupational status; at Contact 2, for example, 17 of the 18 households with paid domestic help had a mother with a 'high status' job and 16 had a father in a similar status job. Excluding households with paid domestic help from the analysis, the relationship between total domestic work score and occupational status becomes somewhat weaker, and falls outside the 5% significance level for mother's occupational status at Contact 2.

Despite this, the evidence does suggest that mothers in 'high status' occupations or with partners in such jobs did rather less domestic work and that fathers, by implication, took a rather greater share – at least in dual earner households. It should be added that the difference in score between mothers who were employed full-time and not employed remains statistically significant even when occupational status is controlled for. The difference between dual earner and single earner households did not result from differences in the distribution of occupational status.

MANAGEMENT METHODS

So far in this chapter, we have dealt with how various types of work were divided between household members, and the use of resources to reduce the amount of childcare and domestic work done by household members. Within this division of labour, it is possible to distinguish different management or coping methods – the ways in which mothers and fathers manage their part of the dual earner lifestyle. We consider some of these methods under two broad headings – the organization of time and use of time.

Organization of Time

Employed mothers reorganized their time to cope with extra demands. On average, they got up earlier and went to bed earlier. Many women cut down on social life and leisure activities. Some changed their working hours, most frequently going in and coming home earlier, or else reduced their 'hours at work' while still working full-time. Reducing 'hours at work' mainly involved cutting down on lunch hours to get home earlier, or else reducing overtime by going in on time, rather than early, or not staying late or bringing work home.

> I don't go in as early as I used to. I never had to be in before a quarter to nine, but I always used to be in just after 8 simply because it was more convenient. I don't normally leave [now] till 8.30. I prefer to stay with [baby] an extra half hour. (Bank clerk; Contact 4)

> I take a shorter lunch break, and come in later and leave earlier. I slightly reduced my hours, from 37 to 35. The option exists [with flexitime system]. You can do a longer week and have a day off [a month], or do a 35 hour week and have no 'flexiday'. (Librarian; Contact 4)

While women might have some direct control of overtime working, reducing 'hours at work' in other ways depended on the existence of a flexitime system or doing an individual deal with employers or an immediate boss. In some cases women could cut their hours at work while doing the same amount of work as before; in other cases, reducing hours meant cutting back on the work that was done, producing new tensions and anxieties. Even where changes were made, the basic full-time week proved too much for some mothers, who left employment altogether or sought part-time hours, a process illustrated by this teacher.

> I used to do all these wonderful things and take the work [the children] had done and really check it in my own time. Now, I have to belt back, spend a good 4 hours at night with her, and by the time I've done that, there's no time for school work . . . I used to work at school till 5. But now I literally have to belt down and collect her from the nursery that shuts at 4.30 . . . I can't cope doing this job, that's why I'm going part-time.

Use of Time

Mothers also adopted methods that enabled them to make the best use of the time available to them. We did not ask mothers if they had reorganized the time they spent on housework, but many reported they had lowered standards or cut out certain jobs, both ways of coping with less time available for domestic work. Other approaches, mentioned by many mothers, were to work more efficiently through better planning, the application of a routine and working more intensively. Some mothers, as already noted, were very conscious of attempting to give their child 'high quality' time when with them, while others concentrated their efforts when working at their jobs, reporting that they 'wasted less time than they used to at work'.

> I work every minute I'm in there, there's less socializing and I do more in the day when I'm there. (Teacher; Contact 2)

This example illustrates clearly how, in practice, reorganizing time and use of time were often closely linked. Women might cut hours, but compensate to some extent by working more efficiently. At the same time, though, this might lead to a further erosion of time for non-work activities, such as socializing with work colleagues. Nor could greater efficiency always compensate for allocating less time to a task, and falling standards or a cutting back on certain activities might be the only way to manage.

Fathers' Coping Methods

We have focused on mothers, partly because the study provides less material on fathers, but also because the meaning and management of the dual earner lifestyle presented mothers with more complex

185

and greater demands. Some fathers, however, did reorganize their time at paid work between Contacts 1 and 2 (Chapter 9); in some cases this involved a reorganization or reduction in 'hours at work' for childcare reasons, and especially to enable fathers to contribute to taking or collecting children from non-parental childcare arrangements and to provide some care themselves while their partners were out at work. For example, one father, a 33 year old surveyor, reduced his hours after his wife resumed employment, leaving home later and finishing work more punctually to take and collect his son from nursery. A second father reorganized his hours but did not reduce them.

> I work flexitime, always have. I now go in as late as I can. He's just begun flexitime and goes in as early as he can so he can leave at 4 [and collect baby] . . . [this way the baby] is never at the childminder's longer than necessary. (Civil servant; Contact 2)

This family were unusual in that both parents made coordinated changes in 'hours at work', to increase the time the child spent in parental care; normally these changes involved one parent or the other.

Overall, fathers' hours at work were less likely than mothers' to reduce or change, and more likely to increase (Chapter 9). Moreover, while reduced or changed hours for mothers were mostly because of childcare or other domestic reasons, this accounted for only a minority of fathers with reduced or changed hours. In most cases, these changes were due to moving job or seasonal factors in their employment.

STRATEGIES AND TACTICS

We have discussed how certain aspects of dual earner lifestyle were managed. Our focus has been on the management of work, both paid and significant areas of unpaid 'household work'. In this concluding section we consider how the dual earner lifestyles we have described may have come about, in relation to the concepts of strategies and tactics. The concept of 'household strategies' has received considerable attention recently, especially in connection with work. Pahl (1984) has used the term household work strategies to refer to 'distinctive practices adopted by members of a household collectively or individually to get work done': a strategy is the household's 'particular mix of practices'.

186

In the case of our households, we find it useful to distinguish between strategy and tactics. By strategy, we mean the broad principles and priorities applied to the management of paid and unpaid work; by tactics we mean the detailed practices used in applying these principles and priorities. While tactics may be equated with Pahl's reference to practices, strategy is not best conceived as the sum of these practices. Rather practices/tactics develop within the framework set by strategy. Like Pahl, however, we view strategy and tactics as being collective or individual, and potentially involving conflict between household members.

The strategies in our households were the product of broad social and economic structures described in earlier chapters, which were reproduced at the micro-level. These structures provided an unsupportive context for employed parents and led many women and men to view women's employment as less important than men's and to define women as primarily responsible for the care of home and children. This in turn produced a strategy in most households based on men taking the lead role in paid work, while women took the lead role in important areas of unpaid work. While this strategy might be contested by women in some households, most seem to have broadly accepted it.

We did not examine household strategies before parenthood. Other research has shown that women's employment assumes a secondary role within the household context during the early years of marriage, and that employed married women take the lead role in housework well before having children. A study of newlywed couples concludes that:

> By the end of the first quarter of the first year of marriage, most newlyweds had established some routine for running their households, one which normally meant that the major portion of domestic chores was performed by the wives . . . in only a fifth of marriages did both husband and wife make more or less equal contributions to keeping house . . . the wives [are] the housekeepers with their husbands as the household aides. (Mansfield and Collard, 1988, p. 120 and p. 129)

This development is part of the broader 'emerging order of priorities concerning (paid) work and home' (ibid., p. 144), in which husbands' employment has priority, while wives assume primary responsibility for the home. This order of priorities is, in most cases, well established by the time women leave work for their first birth, with women doing most of the domestic work and

187

men working longer and more irregular hours in paid employment (Moss, Bolland and Foxman, 1987).

These studies suggest that 'decisions about priorities [have] already been made, either openly or tacitly, long even before a first child [is] conceived' (Mansfield and Collard, 1988, p. 150). Household strategies about work – both paid and unpaid – have emerged in most cases well before parenthood; subsequent changes to accommodate children are essentially tactical. Tactical changes include individual coping methods, such as reallocating time between different tasks and seeking to make better use of time; paying others to provide childcare and housework; investing in equipment, especially a second car; and limited redistribution of childcare and housework between partners, which does not however change the mother's lead role in these areas.

We asked at Contact 2 if couples had discussed and planned the division of childcare and domestic work prior to the mother's return to employment. About half of the women said there had been no discussion about the subject (40%) or that there had been a discussion that had reached no conclusion (6%). The remainder were divided between those who said there had been a discussion leading to an unspecific conclusion (26%), in particular that the husband would try and do more; and those who said that the discussion had led to some specific agreement (24%). These agreements invariably concerned how certain jobs were to be allocated (tactical redeployment), rather than addressing the overall workload (strategic review); the focus was on managing specific problem areas, and was more often about childcare than housework.

The absence of a comprehensive or strategic review partly reflects the fact that many women in our study saw returning to work after maternity leave as 'their' personal choice and decision, and not as part of a joint and strategic decision about the organization of household work (Chapter 4). As a personal decision, there seemed no justification for a joint a review of unpaid household work at this point; established priorities, and their implications for who does what, were not questioned. Nor was this response unique to the transition to parenthood. Mansfield and Collard (1988) observe, of their sample of newlywed couples, that 'while the young husbands and wives were aware of the issue of "who does what" in modern marriage, this did not result in a conscious appraisal of who did what in their marriages and few had ever discussed the arrangements' (p.121); divisions of work emerged tacitly, based on implicit assumptions and expectations.

We conclude with three cases which illustrate different strategies – the third case is unusual for the egalitarian division of all work, paid and unpaid, between the husband and wife – and tactical changes within basically unchanging strategies.

In the first household, the mother was 37 and the father 39; both were surveyors, working for the same employer. The father assumed the lead role in employment, which the mother recognized, accepting reluctantly at Contact 4, after her husband had been promoted, that his job was more important. The mother had always taken the lead role in housework and childcare; in this case there was evidence of an explicit division of work agreed well before parenthood. This was never revised and led to an increasingly unequal division of unpaid household work, especially with the birth of a second child, in whose care the father took no part. Among the tactics adopted by the mother to cope were reorganizing the times when she did domestic work, planning very carefully and tightly and paying for a nanny to come into the house to provide care and also for additional domestic help.

> He doesn't participate very much in the house, he never has. Primarily because we came to an agreement before we ever had children that I would look after the house and domestic chores and the garden, and he'd do the upkeep of the house mainly because we've always lived in wrecks. The first house was small and had a small garden. It wasn't terribly difficult for me to do it all and I also helped with the decoration – which was my choice because I enjoyed it and my husband tends to be a bit slow. With this house, it was in the same state. I've done very little in the way of decorating. I've had to do most of the garden and it's a huge great garden, and I've had to do all the stuff in the house. I don't object to this if my husband is doing something else I consider is towards the family benefit – if he's not then I get peeved . . . Before I used to do my jobs at the weekend because [child] slept. Now I have to do them in the week. I do the washing one night, the ironing another and Monday and Thursday I don't do anything except correspondence. I have all the bills and accounts, my husband does none of them. That's the only time I get to do that and catch up on it . . . This is purely to give me the weekends free with the children.

In the second family, the mother was 30 and a clerical worker in a bank, the father 32 and a postal worker. When the mother resumed work after maternity leave, the father changed his shifts to night work, so that he could care for the child for nearly half the time the mother was at work; for the rest of the time, a childminder was used. Yet despite this major rearrangement of the father's paid work, the change was essentially tactical, leaving the mother still with the main responsibility for childcare. At Contact 4, the mother was on maternity leave and had decided not to resume employment.

> When [she was younger and] I was here, he wouldn't do [anything for her] at all. When I was here, I was in charge. He'd rarely change a nappy or feed her. Now she's older, he's more into her. He'll bath her, give her breakfast even if I'm here. It's been a steady thing as she's got older. As she's got bigger, she's got easier to handle and she helps herself . . . It's the same with [the new baby]. Actually, all he's ever done with him, he's fed him more than he ever did with her for the simple reason I've got her. If he does the morning feed, he may get him dressed, it depends how he feels and if there's clothes out . . . At this stage [when they are young] he doesn't do so much for them. He's not frightened to handle him. It's too much bother, too hard . . . if [the baby] is crying, rather than sit and nurse him, he'd rather do without dinner and me sit and nurse him . . . even with her, all he could do was look after her. If I had worked the same shift as him, I'd have got up in the afternoon, I'd have her and I'd have had a dinner on the table. But he can't do that; he'd just have her and I'd come in and cook dinner.

In the final case, the mother was 33 and a course administrator at a polytechnic, the father 34 and a publicity assistant with a trade union. The couple had always had a strategy based on equal sharing of household work; the strategy of equality in all areas was well established and supported by both parents. As a result, it is clear that the father actually took equal responsibility for the child; it can also be seen how smoothly the couple made tactical changes in response to changed childcare arrangements.

> The person who takes and collects her from the nursery gets the supper ready, while the [other parent] clears the dishes and makes the bed. *How did that evolve?* It was just the easy way of doing things. That's why I'm embarrassed about this [the interview being with the mother only], my husband should be here also. He's a really 50% person, he's what every father should be. He did it without thinking 'I'm being really good

190

here' . . . When we thought about having a child, the first thing he said was 'That's great because I've got a nursery place at my work', so he used to do all the fetching and carrying [this involved a long and often fraught journey on public transport in the rush hour], so I tended to do more of the housework because he was travelling so much . . . [Then the child moved to another nursery and the parents changed to share taking and collecting] so I've done less [housework]. Now we do 50/50 [on the cooking] whereas before I did every night. [Mother does more house cleaning]. He has a higher tolerance factor and does different things. He normally does the rubbish and he's done more DIY . . . The responsibility for [the child] is split. *Down the middle?* I think so. If he picked her up [crying], she might want to come to me, there's still that bond there. It's changed over the last 6 months, she's more equally attracted to both of us . . . she sometimes says 'I don't want Daddy to take me to bed', but he still takes her. We don't want to let her tell us who is going to look after her.

The demands of managing the dual earner lifestyle fell mainly, if not exclusively, on mothers – as a recent American study of dual earner families concluded, 'most women still did most of the work' (Hochschild, 1989, p. 20). Fathers in these households might do rather more than in single earner households but, with a few exceptions, they assumed or continued in the role of assistant, helping out with children and other domestic work, rather than the role of equal participant. Unusual though it was in Britain in the mid-1980s, the dual earner lifestyle in early parenthood produced few examples of new household strategies, only the continuation with some adaptations of the predominant work strategy, emphasizing different priorities for men and women. Where adaptations, or tactical changes, occurred they mainly involved women responding actively to the pressures they faced both from a full-time job and from being mothers and housewives. In many cases they handled the demands arising from these different roles through increased efficiency and productivity. While this produced benefits – for children, employers, husbands, and, in some cases, the women themselves – there were also costs. Most of these costs were carried by the women – in employment, personal stress and tiredness and in reduced time for themselves.

11

Employed Mothers and Marriage

Women carry the major share of work and responsibility for childcare and other domestic work, even in dual earner households. The focus of this chapter is on the ways in which women respond to such household and marital inequality, including normative expectations of partners and the ways in which women present their households to the outside world. It also examines women's expressions of satisfaction and dissatisfaction with their husbands in relation to practical matters and emotional support, and pays particular attention to the methodology employed in the exploration of satisfaction within marriage.

Studies about services, which have employed questions about satisfaction, provide a relevant starting point. In general, these studies reveal an under-reporting of dissatisfaction. For example, research on medical services has indicated apparently high levels of satisfaction on the part of patients: studies of patients' satisfaction with general practitioners, which have generally painted a picture of stable and generalized satisfaction, are a case in point (Bevan and Draper 1967; Cartwright, 1967; Marsh and Kaim Caudle, 1976). One explanation for this is low expectations. Other explanations relate to methodological issues, for example the contexts in which these issues are explored. Surveys usually require respondents to answer direct questions which are rarely related to respondents' specific experiences of medical encounters. Such decontextualized responses frequently result in respondents' giving socially acceptable accounts.

To understand women's expressions of satisfaction with their husbands' contribution to childcare and other domestic work it is also necessary to contextualize their responses. As we shall show later, responses to general questions and to questions about specific events or experiences can produce different pictures. But women's responses also need to be placed in the context of women's expectations about husbands' support within the normative frameworks which guide action.

An examination of these expectations entails a number of problems. The first and more general problem arises when trying to derive underlying normative rules from people's accounts of their actions; this is not necessarily a valid way of proceeding since there may be other explanations for respondents' actions (Finch, 1989). The other and more specific problem arises because of the reproduction of dominant norms and ideologies concerning marriage. Because of a powerful ideological emphasis on marriage as an equal, intimate and harmonious partnership, and the widespread trend towards divorce when these expectations are not met, people in intact relationships are constrained to present their marriages to themselves and the world as relatively happy and harmonious – even in the face of behaviour which appears to contradict this picture (Burgoyne and Clark, 1984). Questioned about their own intact marriages in studies such as ours, respondents are under some pressure to make sense of them as ongoing relationships and hence to draw upon the dominant ideology. The raises a difficult question – should we assume dissatisfaction is absent when it is not expressed as such? As we shall show, it may only become apparent, and then only in a disguised or muted form, when certain kinds of research methods are employed.

NORMATIVE GENDER ROLES IN THE HOUSEHOLD

The term norm is used to refer to broad principles rather than to precise instructions for action (Finch, 1989). At a very general level the study examined norms and values to which respondents subscribed concerning the practice of the dual earner lifestyle and non-traditional gender roles. We asked single direct questions at Contact 1 while most women were still on maternity leave. Whether or not they intended to return to work, the great majority subscribed to a number of ideas about gender roles in the labour market, for example that women should have the same access as men to employment opportunities (88% returners; 69% non-returners) and to traditionally male jobs (88% returners; 73% non-returners). Employment intentions were a significant discriminator with respect to ideas as to whether women ought to be employed full-time in early motherhood (Chapter 7); non-returners were much less supportive of the idea than women intending to return to work. The great majority of both groups (returners 84%;

non-returners 94%), however, were in favour of equal sharing of childcare and housework in these circumstances.

There was much less support in both groups for the idea of non-traditional role models than there was for ideas about equal opportunities in the labour market and equality in the domestic division of labour. Only 38% of returners and 28% of non-returners were positive about role reversal – that is, the father looking after the child while the mother was at work. Only 25% of returners and 16% of non-returners favoured equality in breadwinner roles, with the rest either equivocal or favouring the man.

HOUSEHOLD IMAGES

The ways in which particular groups present themselves to the outside world are indicative, on the one hand, of the norms and values which prevail in the wider society concerning such groups and, on the other, of the ways in which such groups negotiate their relationships in practice. When people give public accounts of themselves to strangers there is a tendency for them to present themselves in a way least likely to offend. Public accounts are framed within 'a least common denominator morality' (Douglas, 1971).

Other studies of non-conventional family lifestyles show how, faced with the problem of how to present a family situation that deviates from the norm, parents commonly portray their families as 'just like' an ordinary or normal family (Voysey, 1975; Burgoyne and Clark, 1984). The household images which women in the dual earner households in our sample had constructed for themselves also retained elements of the 'public account'. Moreover, it is likely that the researchers constituted a key part of the audience for which these accounts were constructed.

In attempting to explore household image, a sub-sample (N=34) of women who had been continuously employed full-time were asked two kinds of questions at Contact 4. The first question simply asked respondents to describe 'the kind of family you are', the aim being to get immediate 'off the cuff' responses. The second question asked them to compare themselves with other families, in order to find out whether they attributed any differences to the dual earner lifestyle. Finally, unless it was already clear, respondents were asked whether they felt the same as or different from other households.

In the spontaneous definitions of household image, almost no one mentioned the dual earner lifestyle as a defining feature of their 'family life'. Instead, other themes emerged, the first and most common being an allusion to affective relations within the household – 'We're a close family', 'We're a happy family'. In some instances women's use of the term 'close' was clearly an allusion to the quality of relationships and interactions while, in other instances, the term conjured up the exclusive nature of the family circle. Typically, women described themselves as functioning as a 'family' rather than as a couple. Many respondents were at pains to emphasize that when they went out together they did so as a 'family' or as a 'unit'.

> *In your mind's eye what sort of family do you see yourselves as being?* We're a family. We're happy. We're very close. We do everything together. *You mean as a threesome?* Oh, definitely. My husband and I are planning our first weekend away without him [The child was aged 3 at the time]. Then we think why do we need to be alone? We can bring him along, no trouble. (Nurse; Contact 4)

A second theme centred on a pragmatic description of the management of 'ordinary family life' – 'We're well organized', 'flexible', 'a bit chaotic'. A third theme concerned the image, already referred to from other studies, of being a 'normal family' – 'just an ordinary working class family', 'just an ordinary family', 'pretty average', 'fairly normal', 'reasonably stable'. In the last instance, however, the woman queried the label she had just applied with the remark: 'Can we be normal if I go out to work and someone else looks after my child?'

The final theme directly confronted difference and deviation – 'odd', 'unique', 'single parent'. A mother who described the household as 'unique' said this was because 'my husband and I are more like grandparents than parents'. When pressed she attributed this to personality as much as to the fact that they were relatively elderly to be new parents. Only two comments in this group made any connection with the dual earner lifestyle: 'We've got more pressures than most', 'We're different because we don't have proper meal times'. When the interviewer probed these comments in the first case the mother explained: 'Because we've got a young child and we've got a mortgage and a house that's not livable in yet.' In the second, not having 'proper mealtimes' was attributed to the father's irregular working hours rather than to the wife's full-time employment.

In response to the question as to whether respondents felt their households were the same or different from others, half said they felt the same and a third felt different (the remainder were not sure). Asked to elaborate, some of the themes mentioned above were again suggested, together with some reference to the dual earner lifestyle. In many cases women compared their situations with those of friends; women who felt the same mentioned friends who were working while those who felt different mentioned friends who were at home. Even where women felt different only one suggested negative connotations to this. Significantly, she had just resigned her job. It is likely that having resigned from the labour market she no longer felt the need to defend herself against the potential stigma associated with being a working mother.

> *Did you think of your household as different?* Yes I felt I was missing out because I couldn't meet up with [other working mothers] . . . And [friends'] children all seemed to be doing things sooner than him. For example, potty training was the big thing . . . They didn't mean to be nasty but they'd say 'Still in nappies!'. Silly things. And they were all sleeping in beds and he'd still got his cot. Things that I thought had I been at home I'd have been able to sort out. (Teacher; Contact 4)

Overall, the images women projected of their households served to emphasize similarities rather than differences between them and other households. In their public presentation to the outside world women did not suggest that the dual earner lifestyle made them feel different or deviant. Images of deviance were reserved for other features of their lives, notably single parenthood. Indeed reference to the dual earner lifestyle was minimal. Women's silence on this subject can be seen as a way of defending themselves against stigma, and as a strategy to avoid confronting contradictions between ideology and practice.

Nor was the absence of a negative self image complemented by the presence of a positive one. Notions about what constitutes 'normal' or typical family life lay essentially undisturbed. Since resuming work, and creating a dual earner lifestyle, was regarded as an individual choice made by the mother (Chapter 4), women did not self-consciously construct a view of themselves as part of a wider collectivity of households in which employment and childcare were combined. Thus despite a high level of commitment to equality in the domestic sphere at a general normative level, there was little evidence that it had affected household image.

SATISFACTION WITH
HUSBANDS' ATTITUDES
TO WOMEN WORKING

Women's representation of their households as being little different from other households reflects the way they viewed their husbands – as little different from the prototype. The construction of the male breadwinner role was still pre-eminent among the returner group; in many cases women's jobs were regarded as secondary to those of their husband's and their earnings perceived as a surplus or peripheral source of household income (Chapter 6). Moreover, women still constructed motherhood as a full-time career and took on most of the responsibility for childcare and other domestic work. Before considering women's responses to this fact, and their evaluation of their husbands as providers of emotional support, it is relevant to consider husbands' attitudes towards, and their influence upon, women's decisions to return to work.

Given widespread normative disapproval in the wider society towards women's full-time employment when children are very young, husbands' attitudes were likely to be of some considerable significance. At Contact 1 the proportion of husbands thought to favour their wives working (41%) was almost equal to those thought to be opposed (44%); within these overall figures there were clear occupational differences; husbands of women in higher status jobs were more likely to be reported as being in favour (57%) than husbands of women in lower status occupations (27%). At one end of the spectrum of opinion were those husbands who felt that wives ought to be at home when children were young; in accordance with the dominant ideology these attitudes were generally applauded by women. At the other end of the spectrum, husbands were reported as wanting their wives to work but usually only for financial reasons; women's reactions to this view were dependent upon whether or not they themselves felt happy in employment. In between the two extremes a significant minority were quite unclear about their husbands' positions (13%).

A content analysis of the whole group reveals that few men had views which appeared to be clearcut, at least as reported by their wives. In many cases they were hedged in with qualifications. For instance, some were said to want their wives to work, but for shorter hours or in less demanding jobs. A characteristic response was: 'He leaves it entirely up to me' or 'He's never said I don't want you to go back'. Some husbands justified these non-committal attitudes on the grounds that they wanted their wives 'to be doing what they were most happy doing'. On the other hand, since finances were a major constraint upon women's decisions to return the matter was usually more complicated than the husbands seemed to pretend.

By their own accounts many women received mixed messages from their husbands; they rarely got unqualified or total approval. 'Sitting on the fence' was moreover a strategy which enabled husbands to hide their own ambivalence; by not expressing a clear, unequivocal view, men could abdicate responsibility, both from the decision and from its consequences. Even though most women did not dissent from the view that they should be the ones to decide, they were not necessarily happy with this view; almost no one reported the 'sitting on the fence' response to be useful. Overall, only a quarter of the women said their husbands were helpful over the decision to resume employment. Yet this did not mean that women criticized their husbands. When pressed with specific questions many gave a muted response, indicating an unwillingness to be overtly critical, a recurring theme in the chapter. In general, women did not have great expectations of their husbands' involvement in their decisions. For those who were highly committed to their jobs and very keen to go back to work it was sufficient that their husbands endorsed their decisions.

> And that is where I can say about my husband, he in particular, about my coming back to work. There has never been a shadow of doubt cross his mind. He has never ever said to me 'Well, you should be at home with the children'. Never once. I don't know if he actually thinks I should. But even if he did he's never said it. So that has obviously been great – that's the biggest thing he could ever do for me, to be honest with you. (Surveyor; Contact 4)

SATISFACTION WITH HUSBANDS' PRACTICAL SUPPORT

Just as women themselves made the decision to return, so too did they take the consequences of that decision upon themselves. Analyses of their responses to the unequal domestic division of labour come from two sets of data. The first set consists of responses to satisfaction questions put to the whole study group; women were asked how they felt about their husbands' involvement in certain areas – such as housework and childcare – or in certain processes, like making childcare arrangements, and their answers coded. Analysis of these coded replies suggests that women were relatively satisfied. To take several examples, only 15% of women were coded as being dissatisfied with their husbands' support over the decision to resume work, and only 13% over the making of the childcare arrangements. Dissatisfaction was somewhat greater for routine childcare and housework tasks, where over a third of the women (36%) were coded as dissatisfied with the amount their husbands did at Contact 2. An examination of what women had actually said in answer to these satisfaction questions indicates that they were often curt in their replies and that criticism was generally muted or qualified rather than outspoken and sweeping.

The second set of data comes from examination of the whole text of the main sub-sample interviewed in depth at Contact 4. It includes spontaneous comments about specific events which touched on the division of domestic labour. Some of these comments emerged in the more discursive parts of the interview in which the respondent could take the initiative, rather than in responses to the direct satisfaction questions. The text of these interviews was subjected to a content analysis which suggests four main ways in which women deal with the issue of husbands' inequitable contribution to the household: (a) they let them off the hook; (b) they adopted low expectations; (c) they made implied criticisms; (d) they praised them. These strategies served to sidestep or defuse criticism of husbands. Underpinning these themes was a concern by women to be 'fair' to husbands which amounted to presenting them in a favourable rather than unfavourable light and which served as a smokescreen for basic inequalities (Backett, 1982).

Letting Husbands off the Hook

Even where husbands made virtually no contribution at all to the running of the household, some women still appeared reluctant to criticize.

> *Since you went back to work does your husband do more of the housework?* He doesn't do any. *How do you feel about that?* I don't feel so bad about it now. But when I first went back to work I felt he should. But it's unfair to say that he doesn't do any. He does make a cup of tea. He doesn't do a great deal. He doesn't think to hoover – even if I asked him. It would be nice. (Receptionist; Contact 4)

This mother is on the verge of criticism at several points but decides against it, ending her remarks with a wistful 'It would

199

be nice'. In fact it turns out that they had earlier gone through a 'bad patch' in their marriage which was brought on by the wife's resentment of her husband's long hours and lack of involvement at home. Having decided to put the difficulties behind them she is reluctant to reopen the issue, going out of her way to be 'fair' to her husband, although making a cup of tea would appear to constitute a minimal amount of help. Later in the interview she legitimates his lack of involvement by invoking his commitment to his job and to breadwinning.

> It's not altogether his fault that he doesn't give anyway near what other husbands do. But it's because of his work. [Asked elsewhere about the respective importance of both their jobs, this mother played down the importance of her own earnings to the household and noted the considerable significance of her husband's job – he was a self-employed design engineer – to him.] But he never moans about it. He always says 'That's what I'm working for and eventually you'll be able to give up work'. *Does he really have to work so hard?* It's a bit of both. He has to do it if he wants to make a go of his company. Sometimes he doesn't want to go to a place but he has to. I feel a bit sorry for him.

The above is a striking example of a husband who appeared to be 'getting off scot free' from making any contribution to domestic work, even gaining some sympathy from his wife. Other husbands were also exempted on the grounds of the demands of their jobs, especially their working hours.

> Because he works nights I don't expect him to do a lot. [The child] is a handful anyway. He does more than most men. (Shop assistant; Contact 4)

Husbands gained exemption on other grounds, notably responsibility for other household tasks, for example car maintenance, DIY and gardening. For these tasks women were duly 'grateful'.

> I'm usually left with the slog work. He'll be doing things which I don't have so much knowledge of – power tools and various wonders he's got . . . plumbing and electrical work. I don't think he could help more than he does. He does an awful lot. (Television production assistant; Contact 4)

> *How do you feel about what he does?* I'm quite happy. I'd be pleased if he did more . . . Perhaps if he picked up his clothes off the floor and made the bed. But no, he's very good. He

does all the garden and everything . . . He is doing things – perhaps not my housework. But he is doing what I class as his jobs – he does the car and the gardening. He'd tidy up but I'd never ask him to do the dusting. (Secretary; Contact 4)

In this last example, criticism is again implied rather than overt. Moreover it is counterbalanced by the commendatory remark – 'But he's pretty good' – a genuflection to the fact that her husband does in fact make some contribution.

Men might also be exempted on the grounds of lack of skill. The mother quoted below says that her husband has a poor relationship with their son, but in any case believes men are less capable with young children.

When kids are very young there is a question in my mind as to whether a man could do exactly the same . . . Maybe some men could . . . But the majority of men – the way the society brings up men and women – the emotional side is different. There are very few men who have got enough insight and caring and instinct to really understand what's needed. I certainly think that it is possible that men can do it the same. But in most couples the woman is the better. (Nursery nurse; Contact 4)

Not surprisingly, some women justified the exemption of their husbands on the grounds that it was ultimately easier and sometimes more satisfying to take on the childcare oneself, especially where the mother performed the task better than the father.

He could do more. He's a bit lazy. But then I reckon he's probably tired too and the child is a bit of a handful . . . He hasn't got the patience like I have. It seems that the majority of men I know they only have eyes that go ahead of them. If the child is doing something they don't see it until it's done . . . Sometimes I leave my husband at home and Joe's at the nursery and I feel quite happy. At least I'm not going to come home to some disaster. (Nurse; Contact 4)

Children could also be quick to play on differences between their parents, behaving better with the more skilled and willing parent. If this happened to be the mother, as it often was, children could reinforce and justify the status quo by demanding that the mother did most of the caring. Fathers themselves were also often instrumental in perpetuating this state of affairs.

My husband doesn't feel he has the patience. He conveniently

201

says 'You do it so much better than I do', whereas in fact I'd love to have a break . . . He would never get his lunch ready or tea ready. I'm not so sure he'd ever know what to get ready for him. (Teacher; Contact 4)

Similarly with housework, husbands could be exempted by not acquiring the skills or claiming that they were not good at them.

He doesn't understand the nitty gritty of it. He says 'Oh well, what can I do to help you?' It's difficult to explain. Part of it is my fault that I don't say 'Get a cookery book and do this'. Because I'm quite good at it I'd rather do it myself which is wrong . . . better for him to learn how to do it. (Nursing officer; Contact 4)

Even where husbands were willing to 'help', women might be reluctant to put up with the drop in standards that this could entail. A woman might therefore choose to do the job herself. Other women might be reluctant to criticize for fear their husbands would cease helping altogether.

Finally, women might excuse their partners from crisis childcare – for example, looking after a sick child – on the grounds that it was easier for the woman to take time off work. It was not possible to judge whether this was in fact the case. Few women reported that they were entitled to take time off work for this reason, and most had to use annual leave or seek discretionary leave from their bosses. It is perhaps more likely that women felt compelled to take time off for a number of reasons – including their husband's unwillingness to do so, their belief that their husband's job was more important, or their feeling that their child needed them more – so that many men were never required to put their employers to the test.

Partners were therefore excused from not playing a greater part in childcare or domestic labour on a number of grounds. These grounds reflected stereotypical roles attributed to men and women on the basis of gender, principally men's roles as workers and main breadwinners which were assumed to preclude the acquisition of caring skills and to include the more 'expert' household skills – notably DIY and car maintainance.

Low Expectations

Exemptions to excuse men's low participation in domestic work were closely connected to low expectations held by women. These might be focused on some specific aspect of the partner's job or his perceived domestic competence, but more generally reflected a view about what men could reasonably be expected to do, given acceptance of their primary breadwinning role and the priority attached to their employment. Low expectations could make women grateful for even the most modest domestic contribution by a partner. They could also defuse or avert criticism. One strategy was to undermine the basis for criticism by suggesting that expectations of help were unrealistic. Moreover, in talking about particular instances or situations in which husbands were portrayed as deficient, women sometimes blamed themselves for 'expecting too much' of them, thereby taking the sting out of the criticism.

> He can't play with [our daughter]. He can't get down to her level . . . We've talked and talked and he does the same thing over and over again. I suppose it's the old old thing that you can't change somebody. So I'm just resigned to saying to myself – 'That's him'. So we'll have to get round it . . . Perhaps I want things too differently and too quickly. It's probably me expecting too much or wanting too much . . . But you've got to make compromises somewhere and make the best of what you've got sort of thing. (Clerical assistant; Contact 4)

Implied Criticism

Another related strategy was to imply criticism rather than to give full vent with a negative judgement. In a number of cases women did give vent at some point in the interview to frustration and anger at husbands' failure to contribute more – but when the interviewer put a general question designed to produce a global evaluation of satisfaction, respondents would avoid sweeping criticisms. The woman might retract the implied criticism: 'He's not so bad really'. Alternatively, she might balance out a criticism with a commendation: 'But he's very good in other ways' – a strategy also cited by Backett (1982) in her study of parenting. A third alternative was to limit the husband's shortcomings to a particular activity or context, a strategy which reduced the cause for complaint.

> I did feel annoyed on occasions. I did feel he should suddenly have to phone in and say 'I'll have the day off' and throw the place into chaos instead of me. (Teacher; Contact 4)

> I have moments when I think 'This isn't fair . . . I'm a

203

mother, a full time worker and you're just a worker'.
(Nursery nurse; Contact 4)

If complaints and requests for more help had no effect women
might say they had become resigned to the situation. Such
acceptance was reinforced by norms which sanction nagging or
whingeing, especially when done by women.

> He does think he's helping me but that might be just putting
> the clothes in the washing machine. He forgets there are lots
> of other things that have to be done . . . I would like him to do
> more but he feels he is doing his share . . . He'll always help
> if I ask but he doesn't think about things that need doing . . .
> He'll quite happily say 'Have I got a clean shirt?'. I might say
> 'I don't know – did you wash one?'. Well, it seems a bit mean
> to say that because he doesn't say it deliberately . . . But no,
> sometimes I have a little dig but on the whole I don't. (Fire
> brigade officer; Contact 4)

A further strategy was to dwell on the positive advantages
of carrying out domestic activities oneself. The mother quoted
below mentioned her husband as the most supportive person in
her life since having children, even though it was clear that he
contributed little in a practical way to the running of the household. The mother ultimately decided to do the chores herself
and to shoulder most of the responsibility. Although adopting a
generally positive approach, underlying frustration came through
at a number of points in the interview, especially when describing
specific experiences; she then qualified this implied criticism by
stressing the advantages of doing the work herself.

> He has no conception of the time pressures I'm under. His
> attitude is 'Leave it'. He says that about the ironing and the
> cooking. It irritates me to such a degree that I have to go out
> of the room or I would explode. The other night I was very
> tired and I said 'I've got to do the bloody ironing tonight'.
> He said 'Leave it – you can always do it tomorrow night'. I
> said 'Tomorrow night I have to do so and so'. He said 'Why is
> your life so planned?'. I said 'You wouldn't eat. The children
> wouldn't eat. You wouldn't have clothes clean if I didn't have
> a planned life'. *Have you ever tried to share the responsibilities?*
> No, I've decided in my mind that it isn't going to work or
> that he wouldn't do it on time . . . I would get irritated if
> he didn't do them when they should be done. (Surveyor;
> Contact 4)

Praise

The fourth set of strategies to avoid criticism was to praise partners for those activities which they did do. One cause for praise was fathers' increased involvement in playing with their children, as they got older and the fragility of babyhood passed. Given the central importance of play in the psychology of child development, and the fact that it could 'free' women to get on with other domestic tasks, this activity was appreciated by busy working mothers.

About a fifth of the mothers in the sub-sample said that they were completely satisfied with their husbands' practical contribution to housework and childcare because they shared the work. Although there were a few households where our quantitative measures pointed to this actually happening, this was not the case in most of the households where mothers said their husbands 'shared'. In practice, a number of the claimed 'shares' were qualified.

A fair split except in the football season. (Local government administrator; Contact 4)

Similarly, in the next instance the mother said that she and her husband shared; the mother, however, like most mothers in the study, does the ferrying of the child to and from the childminder's.

Everything is shared except of course taking Kim and picking him up . . . But I think I need to have the housework done more than he does . . . I can't expect him to do any more. I never ask, I usually tell him . . . It's always been shared. (Tax officer; Contact 4)

Praise was not however restricted to the minority of couples claiming to be equalitarian. As already indicated, women often balanced any negative or critical comment with an approving one. Characteristically, women drew upon notions of 'fairness', sometimes falling over backwards to acknowledge signs of help. Another approach was to be 'thankful for small mercies' – 'I can't expect him to do any more'. 'I think I'm very lucky.' Low expectations made women grateful for, and ready to praise, relatively small amounts of help, especially if they assumed and accepted the major responsibility.

Home, cooking and the child are my responsibility. He's helping out. And if he does I would say 'Thank you' to him whereas even if I got it I wouldn't expect it. I still feel it's my job – it's my work. I'm a mother and a wife. (Nurse; Contact 4)

A fairly typical commendation was 'He'll do anything I ask', a comment akin to praise. Such husbands not only attracted praise, they also drew sympathy for 'having' to help.

> Sometimes I think 'Poor thing!'. Having to do all these things when he gets in from work. Doesn't get a nice quiet sit down. But sometimes I think if he doesn't help me I'll never get it done. (Hospital pharmacy technician; Contact 4)

In this latter case there is clearly a conflict of interests between the woman and her husband. Yet instead of confronting this conflict by, for example, arguing that both have an equal right to 'a sit down', the woman adopts an altruistic stance, putting her husband's need first.

An examination of the ways in which women talked about their satisfaction with husbands' involvement has indicated a number of strategies for avoiding or defusing criticism. Except for the small number of couples who endeavoured to share the domestic workload equally, women excused their husbands from criticism or let them off lightly; an even more fortunate group were recipients of praise. The exemption of husbands from major criticism arose in the context of a variety of powerful normative assumptions concerning gender roles and marriage, and the ways these were negotiated in the interviews.

The first set of assumptions related to men's 'proper' role as breadwinners, which led to them being excused from sharing childcare and domestic chores. The second concerned ideologies of parenthood which emphasized maternal responsibility and exclusivity which led to women seeking investment in childcare. The third concerned norms governing the negotiation of the marital relationship: women were expected to be loyal to their partners and not to let them down by revealing their deficiencies outside marriage. Wives were also constrained by the normative emphasis upon happiness in marriage; admitting to deficiencies is uncomfortable and contradictory when an intact and hence 'happy' relationship is presented to the world. Sustained and overt conflict are normatively proscribed within an intact marriage and are reserved for situations of open warfare when the relationship is in jeopardy or has already broken down. Women's reluctance to criticize needs therefore to be understood in the context of a number of factors which together mitigated the practice of inequity. Yet, somewhat paradoxically, women invoked the equity principle by being 'fair' to their partners when they were invited to criticize them for inequitable behaviour.

SATISFACTION WITH
HUSBAND'S
EMOTIONAL SUPPORT

Husbands emerged as the main providers of emotional support. At the first contact, they were most frequently mentioned as confidants – persons to whom women 'would' turn in the event of a personal worry. They were also more likely to be consulted before any other confidant. When wives were asked who had been the most helpful during the three years of being a working mother, husbands emerged as the most significant figures (Chapter 12). There was moreover some connection between the distribution of childcare, and the degree to which husbands were felt to be supportive; the lower the proportion of childcare done by the mother, the more likely she was to perceive her husband as emotionally supportive, the relationship being statistically significant. The relative distribution of housework had no such effect.

A Sense of Understanding

At Contact 2, soon after returning to employment, women were asked whether their husbands were understanding of their experiences of being a working mother. Just under a half (47%) said, without qualification, that their husbands were able to appreciate their situations. The rest were felt to be understanding but with qualifications (36%) or not at all understanding (16%). A content analysis of their comments suggests that, in general, husbands were felt to have adopted understanding attitudes, without necessarily being able to put themselves in the position of the mother.

Sharing

Women drew upon the language of 'sharing' especially with respect to communication. They talked about being able to 'share things and talk them out' with their husbands – 'we share everything', 'we discuss any problems'. The result of these communicative acts was the achievement of psychological intimacy through the process of talk and the disclosure of confidences (Berger and Luckmann, 1966). These processes served an important function for these couples: they helped to override the gulf between their very different experiences as working parents.

207

'He's Always There'

Women also talked about husbands' emotional support in terms of being 'always there', or being there 'if I wanted him'. Women often talked about their mothers in a similar way. Husbands and mothers appear to be key figures in providing women with a sense of basic security – persons upon whom women felt they could rely in an emergency or crisis. Even in cases where it was evident that husbands' help had not been forthcoming, women still felt that they 'would' help in a real emergency. It was to this kind of support which a mother, a clerical officer, seems to refer when she said 'If it wasn't for him I couldn't cope'. In practice she relied on her husband for very little practical support nor was he reported as being particularly understanding or easy to confide in. In this and other similar instances support appeared more potential than real. Moreover, since expectations of practical support were low, as already suggested, and since women found ways of coping on their own or with the help of their immediate kin, husbands' ability to provide crisis support was infrequently put to the test. To that extent, such support was essentially symbolic, yet it was real in its consequences and many women felt heavily reliant upon it.

The Salience of Emotional Support
to the Marriage

Expectations of psychological and emotional support from husbands resonate with ideologies of love, sharing and togetherness, ideologies which constitute the cornerstone of modern marriage. According to this formulation of marriage, the marital relationship is negotiated on the basis of norms of altruism while notions of difference and inequity, power and self-interest do not figure. As Phyllis Rose (1985) notes in writing about Victorian marriage:

> Perhaps that is what love is – the momentary or prolonged refusal to think of another person in terms of power. Like an enzyme which momentarily blocks a normal biological process, what we call love may inhibit the process of power negotiation – from which inhibition comes, the illusion of equality so characteristic of lovers. (p. 16)

Not only are these ideologies of love, mutual support and togetherness central influences upon ideas about and the conduct of modern marriage, they also serve to obscure, or at least to deflect, attention from the continuing material inequalities which exist between husbands and wives. The strength of these ideologies is revealed when marriages run into serious trouble and break up. Under such circumstances wives complain not so much about a lack of practical support with housework and childcare, but about aspects of the psychological relationship – lack of love and affection, poor communication and so on (Thornes and Collard, 1979; Brannen and Collard, 1982). While the relationship is intact and presented to the outside world as a 'happy' one, women tend to play down complaints and criticism about husbands' failure to take responsibility for childcare and domestic work. Instead the 'rules' of marriage are only seriously contravened when husbands fail to fulfil the symbolic terms of the relationship as defined by the dominant marital ideology – namely, psychological togetherness and emotional support.

TWO CASE STUDIES

The chapter concludes with two cases which demonstrate the ways in which women evaluate and justify the unequal division of domestic and childcare responsibility and the context in which these occur. The two cases are arbitrarily chosen from two groups: those couples (the majority) where the husband made a less than equal contribution and those few whose contributions were roughly equal to one another.

In the first instance, the mother was a production assistant in television. She had worked for the same company for 13 years, but only recently had she tried to move on to the next rung on the career ladder. She was ambivalent about promotion because of the travel which it might entail, and felt that she had never been sufficiently single-minded in order to get on in the competitive media world. She had been married to her 39 year old engineer husband for 8 years when their first child was born. Although the pregnancy was unexpected, the mother had been pleased about it – 'a decision didn't have to be made; if you plan these things no time is right'. She always thought she would return to work: 'I feel I would be denying myself something if I didn't go back'.

She earned significantly less than her husband and for this reason had always considered him to be the main breadwinner; she described her earnings as only 'quite important', because 'we could manage without them'. Yet she was financially responsible for everyday household expenditure and for the costs of the dual earner lifestyle – the fees for the childminder and the cost of a car for taking the child to the childminder's and herself to work.

209

Moreover, her job was important to her. Interviewed when her daughter was three years old she had no regrets about having worked full-time. Despite three years of being a dual earner household, she saw her family as little different from other families except 'our lifestyle is more flexible' and they were less rigid about her daughter's mealtimes and bedtimes than other households. Parents and child went out as a threesome – 'We never go in for babysitters'.

Initially, her husband's views about his wife working were said to be 'neither one way nor another'. Later he is reported to be less enthusiastic, a change of position about which the mother did not comment – 'Unless I am going to get a great deal out of it his attitude is that I should leave . . . The implication is that I could be looking after her instead of someone else looking after her'.

In practice, her husband was a moderately participative father who did little housework. Despite subscribing to the view that housework and childcare ought to be shared when both parents work full-time, and despite having vaguely agreed (during maternity leave) that they divide the work, the mother still professed to be happy with her husband's contribution, a position based on her low expectations – 'I get as much as I could expect, I couldn't expect to get more really'. At Contact 4, this mother let her husband off the hook altogether; the touch of resentment, implied in her reference to 'slog work', was noticeably glossed over.

> *How do you feel about the amount of housework he does?* Fine. Because neither of us does very much. If ever I decide to do a bit of cleaning he will always be willing to do other things that I can't do or haven't got the knowledge to do . . . I'm usually left with the slog work.

Her only comment about her husband's role in childcare – in which she did most of the work and felt she took the main share of responsibility – referred to his lack of understanding about how long it took for her to get the child ready.

> I don't think he realizes that things take that much longer . . . Every time I've had the opportunity to get up, get ready and go out by myself – I find what a short time I can do it in.

Despite giving relatively little practical support, the father was rated by the mother as the second most helpful person in her three years as a working mother. The way in which she valued his support emerged when she was asked whether she depended on her husband.

> For emotional backup. If something horrible happens. In a practical way for things at home that I'm not sure how they work or if the car has broken down.

The second case involves a more egalitarian couple. The mother was 31 when she had her first child, and was head of department in a large comprehensive school. Her husband's employment history almost exactly mirrored her own, even though he qualified before she did. Aged 36, he taught the same subject in another school. They had been married for four years, though they had cohabited for several years before marriage.

The mother was very committed to her job and never seriously considered not returning to it, though she had periods of wondering if she had done the 'right thing'. Her main reason for staying in her job was personal satisfaction, together with the fact that they could not manage their financial commitments on one income. She considered herself to be equally the breadwinner, though she added that her husband might find it difficult if she started to earn more than he did. After the birth, employment continued to be an important feature of the mother's life, though at Contact 2 she said that if they had to choose between their two jobs 'I have a feeling it would have to be me [that stops] because I might find it easier to adapt to not having a job'.

Subscribing to an equal division of the domestic workload when both parents are in full-time employment, during maternity leave the couple made a vague agreement to share it. The husband was unusual in that he took paternity leave after the birth of the second child; he spent one month at home because of this leave and the timing of the school holidays – 'That was one of the nicest times we've had together'. Even after, when the mother had resumed work, the father proved to be highly participative, taking a rather larger share of the housework and having considerably involvement with childcare.

> I don't feel it's split down the middle, like we do exactly the same number of nappy changes and exactly the same number of dinners. But the amount of actual things we are doing to contribute to the general running of the house and to looking after Nicholas is equal.

At Contact 2, the mother was highly commendatory about her husband's involvement. Perhaps because he did so much she felt able to make further demands upon him. There were however hints that she took rather more responsibility.

211

I don't think you can escape from the fact that you play slightly different roles. Like last night, Nicholas was ill and he wants me. It's a different thing being a father than being a mother . . . I said 'It's not going to be me again tonight', but it was me who used to do it when he woke up in the night.

After the birth of the second baby, the mother depended even more on her husband for practical support; he was particularly helpful in taking the eldest child to the childminder while she took the baby to a different minder. But the responsibility for the care of the second child was much less equal than it was for the first. Asked at Contact 4 who has the main responsibility for the children, the mother answers

I still feel I'm ultimately responsible. Things like the childcare arrangements are ultimately my problem when it comes down to it . . . Although I'm convinced we share out the jobs equally I'm the one who organizes it – that is what it comes down to . . . I don't know if he understands really. I'm a bit confused myself. It's to do with role models you grow up with. I do every so often undergo a crisis when I think 'Am I being a good enough mother?' . . . It's sort of lurking in the depths of my consciousness . . . It's the whole idea that mothers should stay at home and look after the kids etc., etc. which is what we grew up with.

In her view children were, ultimately, the mother's responsibility and since her husband more than satisfied the normative criteria for being a 'good' father, she was very satisfied. But what the mother most valued was being able to talk to him. Her husband was considered by her to have been the most helpful person during her three years as a working mother; asked why, she commented that 'he's the one I would talk to first'. The couple's considerable ability to communicate with each other also facilitated the apportionment of domestic responsibilities, a subject of continual negotiation.

We've talked about it quite a lot. We've had to because both our individual parents – like presumably most people's parents – have more traditional roles. You literally have to work it out as you go along. We worked it out to some extent with the first child. We've got to work it out even more now we've got two . . . But we've worked it out by talking a lot between ourselves . . . So if I think I've been put upon or if I think I'm doing too much then I would tell my husband first. If he wasn't sympathetic – which has happened occasionally – then I would go and talk to [a close woman friend].

The second couple represent the equalitarian end of the spectrum, while the first couple are somewhere in the middle. In the first case, the husband does little housework and is not expected to; he does more with the child, but still does not share work or responsibility equally. Like most dual earner marriages, the wife has low expectations of and places little reliance upon her husband's practical support. She is unwilling to criticize him; he is most valued for psychological support, notably for what he 'would' do in the event of a crisis. In the second case, the husband is likewise most valued for psychological support, though he is also valued for his domestic contribution. Unlike the first case, this contribution is considerable and the negotiation of everyday domestic responsibilities is a continual process.

Dual earner lifestyles with both parents in full-time employment rarely result in an equalitarian division of the domestic workload even where beliefs are equalitarian. Women accommodate to this inequality by resorting to a number of strategies which enable them to minimize criticism. These strategies include excusing husbands on the grounds of other, mainly breadwinning, responsibilities; having low expectations of them; praising them for those activities they do do; and making implied criticisms which may be retracted or balanced out with commendations. These strategies are reinforced by ideologies concerning breadwinning, motherhood and marriage, and which legitimize the unequal division of domestic work. Ideals of married life emphasize the importance of emotional support and togetherness, and in their lived experience women give priority to the emotional rather than the practical support of husbands. Paying homage to emotional support deflects attention from the underlying inequalities in men's and women's material situations and serves to bridge their very different experiences.

12

Social Networks and
the Availability of
Informal Support

There is an abundance of literature which indicates that social support is critical to the prevention of ill health, protection from adversity – and to the successful negotiation of life course transitions (Gottlieb, 1981). Both groups of mothers in our study – those who were returning to work and those who were not – were accomplishing a significant social transition – namely, becoming a mother. As other studies have shown, first time motherhood entails losses as well as gains (Oakley, 1980). In addition, returners were experiencing a second transition – a return to work after maternity leave. While employment itself may constitute an important source of support for women with young children, protecting them from depression for example, employment can also be a source of stress (Chapter 8).

The return to full-time work after maternity leave was a relatively rare course of action in Britain at the time of our study and contravened the dominant norms of motherhood; there was little support from employers or government; and husbands' support was limited to 'helping out' and emotional support. Women with young babies who returned to work were therefore likely to be heavily reliant upon their own resources and informal sources of support drawn mainly from their social networks. In this chapter and the next, we examine this form of social support.

THE CONCEPT OF SOCIAL
SUPPORT AND SOCIAL
NETWORKS

The literature on social networks and support can be divided, roughly, into two traditions: the sociological and the social psychological. The focus of the approach within the sociological and

214

social anthropological traditions has been the structural features of networks – the web of social ties (Mitchell, 1969, 1986, 1987). The relationship of network members to one another, particularly their density and connectedness, has been of central concern (Barnes, 1969; Mitchell, 1969). In the empirical study of social networks the contrast has been drawn between highly interconnected networks, with a large proportion of cross-cutting linkages, and loosely connected networks, with few cross-cutting linkages (Bott, 1968). An association has been identified between particular types of network structure on the one hand, and the degree of normative consensus and the extent of mutual aid on the other (see, for example, studies by McKinlay, 1973; Horwitz, 1977; Laumann, 1973).

The concept is also claimed by social psychologists. The focus here is upon the individual's psychological and emotional state and the way in which this is affected by social ties (for reviews of the literature see, for example, Leavy, 1983; Berkman 1984; Cohen and Wills, 1985). Here social networks usually refer to core relationships, defined in terms of 'closeness', though the nature of these ties and the functions they fulfil are often treated as second order considerations. In this paradigm social networks are conceptualized as variables which mediate between the individual's internal psychological state and external factors (often termed provoking agents) which affect it. Provoking agents are characteristically conceptualized as life events and difficulties (Brown and Harris, 1978).

Much of this work is concerned with explanations of depression and other psychological distress. Whether or not the individual develops depressive symptoms, for example, is determined by whether or not social networks act as a buffer, either at the time or as an *a priori* protective factor. One of the principal aims of such work is to construct models of the various explanatory variables and to disentangle their temporal order; methods of analysis usually rely on predictive statistical models (Schaeffer, Coyne and Lazarus, 1981; Cohen and Wills, 1985; Brown *et al.*, 1986). Provoking agents such as life events and difficulties are treated heuristically, and hence theoretically, as separate entities from social ties and other protective factors. In other words social ties are treated as an independent factor, rather than as an intrinsic part of the social context which shapes all the variables in the model, including life events (Brown *et al.*, 1986; Schaeffer, Coyne and Lazarus, 1981).

There are important theoretical differences, therefore, between the sociological and psychological approaches to the notion of social network. Within the psychological paradigm, support is very largely conceptualized as a passive phenomenon; the sociological

215

approach, especially where it is concerned with the resource aspects of social networks, emphasizes the creative qualities of social relationships. On the other hand, a major drawback to the sociological approach is that it only concerns itself with beliefs and conscious action. It ignores the effects of the social ties on individuals' emotional and psychological states, seeming to take little account of the way in which feelings are structured by the social environment.

This study has largely drawn upon the sociological paradigm of social support, for several reasons. First, because it is concerned with the nature of support – the types of support which respondents found helpful or unhelpful in different crises and situations. Second, the study focuses on the practice of routine, everyday life. Third, because of its focus on the logistical processes through which support occurs in the lives of social actors, the study has less interest in the psychological paradigm – with, for example, the buffering effects of social ties on individuals' well-being – particularly since very few women developed symptoms of severe psychological distress during the study. Thus in so far as women newly returning to work needed social support, in most cases what was required was relatively mundane and routine. Finally, network analysis provides some insights into the social aspects of parents' choices of carers and their relations with them.

We also conceptualize networks as a resource, using the concept in two ways. First of all, social networks are an ideological or normative resource in the sense that they encompass the beliefs of significant others about the issue of mothers' returning to work when children are small. These beliefs influence how mothers feel about the issue and the experience, as well as their decisions and actions. Depending upon their nature, they may act as a constraining or as a facilitative force. Moreover, the effects of these sets of beliefs, as they exert influence over the individual, are not necessarily additive or cumulative; these effects are likely to depend upon the structure of relationships between those who comprise the networks. For example, networks with a close knit structure are likely to exert greater power and influence over the focal individual than are loose knit networks. Social networks constitute, therefore, a key arena in which normative guidelines concerning the conduct of 'family' and working lives are promulgated and reinforced.

Second, social networks are a potential resource which may provide material and inter-personal support. They may provide financial help, goods and services, especially help with childcare, and less tangible sources of support such as moral and emotional support.

Finally, we make the conceptual and methodological distinction between potential or available support and its utilization or the experience of being supported. This chapter focuses on availability, the next on utilization.

DESCRIBING
SOCIAL NETWORKS

This chapter describes women's social networks, first using quantitative measures, notably size and composition. This quantitative approach was applied to all women in the sample, both employed and non-employed, at two points in time: Contact 1 when children were 4–5 months old (before most women's return to work) and Contact 2 when they were 10–11 months (after women's return to work). We examine whether the expectation of returning to work (or not) made any difference to the availability of network resources – in terms of size and composition – at Contact 1 and, similarly, the actual effect of returning (or not) upon networks at Contact 2.

In order to gain a structural and qualitative understanding of networks, a typology of networks was developed based on the linkages between network members, their personnel and the nature of the relationships to the focal respondent. This analysis was confined to a subset of respondents (N=66) who remained continuously employed until their children were three years old. The chapter describes the extent of structural change in this group, drawing upon two contrasting cases which indicate the logistics of change over time and their implications for social support.

Network membership, for all women at Contacts 1 and 2 and for the sub-set at Contact 4, was calculated on the basis of frequency of contact; people contacted at least once a month were included, with weekly contact distinguished from monthly contact. Telephone contact was treated as equivalent to face to face contact. Spouses and respondents' children were not included. Respondents' mothers and fathers were included as separate links whilst all other couples, together with dependent children (under 16), were regarded as single linkages. Other information was also collected: the first names of friends; whether network members met independently of the respondent; whether the relationship was mainly with the respondent or a couple relationship; whether the network members had children and the age of the youngest child; and limited information about context and origin of relationships.

Some Caveats

Using this approach excluded people who might have been available to provide support in certain circumstances, but with whom women were not in regular contact. It also excluded contacts made at work, unless respondents saw them outside working hours. Although work contacts are unlikely to provide certain kinds of support, such as childcare, they may provide other kinds, especially moral and emotional support. Little evidence was found which indicated practical support from bosses and work colleagues, though respondents were exceedingly grateful for understanding and sympathetic attitudes (Chapter 3).

Even if network members were in frequent contact there are still problems about assuming that they were available to give support; this problem is insurmountable unless network members are also part of the investigation. People's circumstances change, affecting their own resources and availability, for reasons often quite unconnected with the person requiring support. At any one moment their support potential may vary; they may be able to give one type of support but not another. Moreover, if there is considerable change over time in network personnel, as was the case for friends in our study, 'replacement' acquaintances may not necessarily have the same support potential. Newness in acquaintance may be a significant factor constraining respondents from seeking certain kinds of support.

A final caveat concerns a central tenet of the argument – namely, that the 'take up' of support is dependent only upon its availability. In addition to the issue of what constitutes available support there is the question of the social and psychological constraints upon the individual in seeking or taking up potential support resources – for example, attitudes towards seeking or accepting support. We return to this issue later.

NETWORKS AFTER THE BIRTH AND BEFORE THE RETURN TO WORK

Four months after birth, mothers were in regular (at least monthly) contact with, on average, 10.5 persons. At this point there were differences in the size of networks between women who intended to return to work and those who did not; returners had smaller networks – that is, based on monthly contact. The differences however were only statistically significant between non-returners

218

and those women in the returners group who had already gone back to work (11.4 v. 9.6), which suggests that the actual return to work had more effect than the intention.

Intention to return, however, had more effect on network composition. While on maternity leave non-returners were significantly more likely to have contact with other mothers of young children – that is, in contrast to both groups of returners (those already returned to work at Contact 1 and those who had not yet done so). Such contact is likely to provide a pool of supportive and reciprocal relationships, especially with respect to knowledge about young children and childcare. There were no statistical differences in contact with parents of older children nor with childless people; indeed, first-time mothers, whatever their work intentions and employment status, had notably little contact with families with older children. By contrast, non-returners were less likely to know working mothers; returners knew more women who had worked full-time with a child under four years, with those who had already returned knowing the most. Moreover, women's accounts suggest that they had made these acquaintances, which were not restricted to the workplace, in anticipation of their resumption of employment.

In contrast to the findings of other studies (see, for example, a cross-national study by Cochran and his colleagues, 1984) there were no differences in network size at Contact 1 between women who had been in high or low status jobs before childbirth. This is probably because our study under-represents women in less skilled manual occupations. There were however differences in network composition; women in higher status jobs had more friends than relatives in their networks (6 v. 4.5) whereas for women in lower status jobs the situation was reversed (4.5 v. 5.6). Lower status women also had more frequent contact with kin than higher status women. This may be partly explained because women in lower status jobs lived nearer their relatives, being significantly less likely to have moved out of the areas where they had been born than women in higher status jobs. On the other hand, the impact of such proximity was lessened since telephone contact was treated as equivalent to face to face contact; nearly everyone in the study had a telephone, although not necessarily the same income to spend on its use.

SOCIAL NETWORKS AFTER
THE RETURN TO WORK

Ten months after birth there were clear differences in women's networks according to whether or not they had returned to work. Women who had resumed employment had significantly smaller networks (8.9 v. 11), fewer weekly contacts, fewer network linkages (16.3 v. 21.9), knew fewer people with children, both young (1.7 v. 3.6) and older dependent children (0.9 v. 1.2). They also saw fewer friends alone and had more couple-based relationships than non-returners, a finding which is probably explained by the fact that women at home had more social contact with other mothers at home with young children. This pattern of difference occurred in both of the two main occupational groups.

There was an increase in network contact between Contacts 1 and 2 among non-returners, a trend similar to that reported in an American study where there were significant increases in contact with relatives and with parents with young children between 3 and 9 months after birth (Belsky and Rovine, 1984). More significant, however, is the decrease in network contact among women in employment at Contact 2; comparing the situation at Contact 2 with that at Contact 1, there were statistically significant differences between returners and non-returners for network size, both monthly and weekly contacts, network linkages, contact with mothers of young children and contact with friends seen singly (i.e. seen without the respondent's partner). Average scores for returners fell for each of these variables between Contacts 1 and 2, with those who had returned to work before Contact 1 experiencing smaller reductions (having begun to experience a decrease in contacts before Contact 1). By contrast, non-returners show an increase, on average, for each variable.

The pattern of differences in quantitative measures of social networks between returners and non-returners was consistent over a range of variables. These findings are not particularly surprising. It seems likely that returners invested less effort during maternity leave in building up acquaintances made with other pregnant women and mothers (for example, at childbirth classes) because they knew they would have difficulty sustaining relationships once they were back at work. More generally, according to women's accounts it was generally they and not their husbands who maintained contact with kin and friends (see also Wallman, 1985). Mothers in full-time employment had limited time and energy for such activities. In the evening they were too busy and too tired; at the weekend they were preoccupied with 'family' and household activities and, if

220

they went out, they tended to do so 'as a family' rather than as a couple or by themselves. Cutting down on 'social activity' was one of the main strategies returners adopted in order to conserve personal resources (Brannen and Moss, 1988).

A TYPOLOGY OF NETWORK
STRUCTURE

The quantitative measures of social contact do not take account of the structure and density of social networks created by the ties between network members. Other studies have shown that network structure is highly related to behaviour, especially the provision or take-up of support. Bott's generative study showed a strong association between network structure – defined in terms of interconnectedness – and the degree of conjugal role segregation (Bott, 1968); close knit networks, in contrast to loose knit networks, were related to traditional (i.e. segregated) marital roles. A study of the utilization of ante-natal services by working-class women found 'take-up' of these services was higher for women with differentiated network structures. McKinlay (1973) suggested that differentiated structures provided more latitude in decision-making than undifferentiated networks; they enabled the individual to pick and choose between the different sets of advice provided by the networks' distinctive unconnected segments. By contrast those with undifferentiated networks were more likely to be constrained by the network as a whole because of its cross-cutting structure. A study of troubled marriages found an association between very small networks (termed truncated) and lack of disclosure, in particular a failure to discuss marital problems within the marriage or to disclose them outside it (Brannen and Collard, 1982).

We have drawn upon these three studies in the creation of a four-fold typology which has been applied to the networks of the sub-set of women in continuous employment up to Contact 4.

1. Truncated networks, derived from Brannen and Collard (1982), contain few members (in practice five or less) and few linkages between members. Membership is usually restricted to members of the families of origin of the respondent and her spouse (parents and parents-in-law). They contain few or no friends.
2. Family of origin networks are largely confined to the families of origin of the respondent and the respondent's spouse, together with a maximum of three non-kin. They contain

rather more persons than truncated networks.

3. Differentiated networks, derived from McKinlay (1973), have a star-shaped or segmented structure, with few or no links between segments. Segments are composed mainly of single friends or clusters of friends who do not know one another. They tend to be larger than family of origin networks, and a rule was imposed that they should contain not less than four non-kin.

4. Close knit networks, derived from Bott (1967), are defined by their interconnected structure of cross-cutting ties, both between members and segments. Most of these ties are defined by kinship – of blood and/or marriage. They tend to be large and to contain few friends.

It needs to be emphasized that this classification consists of ideal types, and at the boundaries respondents' networks are allocated somewhat arbitrarily. To some extent the types fall along a size continuum (with some overlap at the margins). Truncated networks are the smallest followed by family of origin, differentiated and close knit.

Table 12.1 shows the distribution of network types for the subset of women at Contacts 1, 2 and 4, using this classification. The most common structure at each contact was the differentiated network. These were typically segmented, containing discrete sets of relatives and friends between which there were few or no cross-cutting ties. Because of this structure, these networks provided the individual with some latitude in decision-making. They minimized the risk of group censure and gossip between network segments and so enabled the individual to pick and choose between different possible sources of support. This also meant that respondents were subject to different sets of unconnected ideological influences which might constrain or facilitate the experience of being a working mother.

Differentiated networks were followed in frequency by the family of origin network type and next by the truncated network type. The close knit type was least common and only found among respondents with large families of origin and/or extended families; this included the few households in the study where one or both parents were of Asian, Italian or Turkish origin.

Over the course of the study, there was considerable movement between network types. Like the quantitative network data discussed earlier, the direction was more likely to be from larger to smaller types of networks than the other way round. Between Contacts 1 and 2 (before and after the return to work in most cases), 31% changed their structure; in two thirds of these cases,

Table 12.1 *Social network types at Contacts 1, 2 and 4 for women in sub-sample (N = 66)*

		Social network type			
		Truncated	*Family of origin*	*Differentiated*	*Close knit*
Contact 1	(%)	15	26	51	8
Contact 2	(%)	18	33	44	4
Contact 4	(%)	24	29	40	6

movement was from larger to smaller networks. Between Contacts 1 and 4, 40% changed their type of network, and again two thirds moved to smaller types.

There was little movement either into or out of the close knit group; these were the most stable networks (and also the least common). This is not surprising since such networks are usually based on ascribed ties of kinship rather than achieved ties of friendship. Moreover, because close knit networks tend to be bound by local ties, they are not subject to piecemeal change unless of course the respondent moves away and severs all ties at one go.

Although the return to work clearly resulted in the atrophy of social networks, in general the changes appear to have been relatively gradual and piecemeal. Most women did not experience a dramatic change, and the majority moved from one type to an adjacent type defined in terms of size. Between Contacts 1 and 2, 65% of the 31% of networks that changed type moved to an adjacent type; similarly, between Contacts 1 and 4, 63% of the 40% that changed moved to an adjacent type.

Detailed comparisons of the persons in respondents' networks at different contacts also reveal considerable change. As might be expected, kin relationships were more static than non-kin. Just over a half of network members mentioned at Contact 1 were not mentioned at Contact 4, and these losses were largely due to attrition among friends; 75% of friends mentioned at Contact 1 were not mentioned at Contact 4. As we cautioned earlier, this is not to say that these friends were not replaced nor that they were lost altogether. In some cases it was clear that there was less frequent contact because of some routine event – for example, the respondent or the friend moving house. In a few cases, though, events in the women's lives had brought about a major change in structure and/or composition of their networks; however, few of these events appeared to follow from the women's employment, although they may be affected by it.

CONSTRAINTS UPON SEEKING/ACCEPTING SUPPORT

In the next chapter we consider whether there was an association between network structure and the support women received. But factors other than availability can affect support. Here we consider one of these – the attitude or orientation of individual women to turn to others for support irrespective of its availability.

Orientations towards the use of networks may be explored from both sociological and psychological perspectives. The psychological explanation suggests that orientations derive from the individual's deep-seated disposition to disclose (or not), considered as a facet of personality (Andrews and Brown, 1988). In this literature it is somewhat unclear as to whether or not disclosure is considered to be a 'healthy' behaviour. Failure to disclose may be interpreted negatively as indicative of a lack of trust; alternatively, it may be regarded positively as an indicator of considerable personal resources. On the other hand, a ready disposition to disclose may be interpreted as a too easy reliance on 'inappropriate' sources of support (Andrews and Brown, 1988). By contrast sociological explanations focus either upon the social norms governing the appropriateness of such behaviour or they suggest that orientations are conditioned by opportunities for exchange. In this study a sociological approach was adopted although it was only possible to cover some constraints and not others and then only superficially.

At Contact 1 we explored women's attitudes to turning to other people with any personal worries or problems. In general the great majority was positively disposed (90%); only 8% were definitely against. However, most said that they had no personal experience of confiding in others, since they had never had a problem of sufficient magnitude, or expressed reservations about the importance of finding the right person and the right conditions.

At Contact 2 women were asked whether they would find it difficult or easy to seek or accept help from others. Considerably more said they found it difficult (33%) than had said, at Contact 1, that they were against turning to other people. The question asked at Contact 2 seems more likely than the question at Contact 1 to have elicited responses which were grounded in the reality of women's lives; women may have had in mind specific problems to do with managing childcare and work responsibilities. Furthermore, in view of the generally hostile climate to mothers' employment and because the decision to embark on the dual earner lifestyle was a private individualistic 'choice', women's attitudes were likely to reflect values concerning the social unacceptability of seeking help outside the household and the importance of couples, and of mothers themselves to some extent, being self-sufficient and autonomous.

This emphasis on self-reliance and autonomy can however be seen as an increasing and general trend in British 'family life'. To take a quite different example from a study of families experiencing unemployment, goods and services (though not money) were transferred to these families from their kin networks. These transactions, however, were sanctioned and constrained by strong normative assumptions emphasizing the desirability of being a self-sufficient and autonomous nuclear family (McKee, 1987). Adherence to such normative guidelines within a society is likely to inhibit individuals from asking for help, especially from non-kin who, even more than kin, are likely to be bound by rules of reciprocity.

Negative orientations towards using social networks as a source of support could also be influenced by women's anxiety about being able to reciprocate and the practical limitations of being able to do so arising from limited time and energy. Having a full-time job as well as bringing up a young child may make a working mother feel she cannot enter into many ties of obligation for fear she may not be able to fulfil them. This interpretation gains support from other evidence about reciprocity. This suggests that households in which two earners are employed full-time are less likely to engage in informal transactions with other households than are households in which the husband is employed and the woman is at home or works part-time; conversely, dual earner households in which both partners work full-time are more likely to buy in services through the formal economy and to be self-provisioning (Pahl, 1984).

TWO CASE STUDIES

The chapter concludes with two cases which highlight the process of network change over the course of the study. The first is an atypical case where dramatic change takes places in the respondent's social network, from a differentiated to a truncated structure; this change has little to do with the return to work and follows major life events. The second case involves lesser and more gradual change.

The mother in the first case had been continuously employed since giving birth to her daughter relatively late in life. A caretaker in the block of flats where she and her husband lived, she returned to her job soon after the birth very much against her will, not wanting to 'leave' her child; her feelings on this point did not alter over the course of the study. However, she was under considerable financial pressure to return to work, which was compounded by the fact that the family lived in accommodation tied to the mother's job. The husband worked in a local factory.

At Contact 1, by which time she had been back at work for a couple of months, she had a differentiated network consisting of her own parents, a cousin, two brothers, her mother-in-law and six friends and neighbours, including the childminder who lived upstairs. Three of her friends had young children. Most members of her network lived in the locality. At Contact 2 her network was still classified as differentiated but it had increased in size, unlike those of most returners, to include another cousin, her husband's brothers, and some more friends. Potentially at least her network appeared to offer considerable support.

But by Contact 4, this mother's network had shrunk dramatically and was classified as truncated: she reported being in regular contact with only her parents and one neighbour. In the preceding few months a number of adverse events had befallen the couple: her husband's father and brother had both died suddenly within a short time of one another and this had led to her husband becoming depressed. Shortly before the last interview he took an overdose. The mother also hinted at serious financial problems and showed signs of being depressed herself.

226

Because of its dramatic contraction, we may conclude that her network offered little potential support at Contact 4. Alternatively, it could be argued that this mother simply reported fewer contacts because of being depressed, although it seems more likely that the couple's difficulties and depression had resulted in an avoidance of social contact.

There are also grounds for thinking this mother an unlikely candidate for drawing upon the resources of her network even were they available. First, it seems probable that her network members were low in material resources themselves; even if the network contained considerable resources, the couple may have felt unable to draw on them because of an inability to reciprocate. Second, at Contact 1 she described herself as being ill-disposed towards turning to others with personal problems. Asked a similar question at the last contact, her attitude was the same – 'I don't like burdening other people with my problems really, and I don't like everyone knowing my business'. Nonetheless whatever the reason for this woman's lack of disclosure it seems likely that the truncated structure of her network at the time of her troubles made her feel alone and unsupported and so contributed to her depressed feelings. At Contact 4 the only persons she mentioned as having been helpful over the three years of being a working mother were her husband (now with major problems of his own) and her mother to whom she said she did not turn because 'she's not very well'.

The second case is a much less dramatic example of change. The mother, a pharmacy technician aged 29 at the start of the study, began with a differentiated network which consisted of eight persons – including her parents, an aunt, a long time bachelor friend, a former colleague with a young baby (who did not return to work) and three other women whom she had met at ante-natal classes. By Contact 2, back at work 6 months, her network had shrunk to a truncated structure – her parents, an aunt and the bachelor friend. 'Well, there's a few people I don't see now [Laughs]; I'd like to see them more but I don't really have the time'. Interviewed shortly after the second birth she is seeing more people regularly, and the network is reclassified as family of origin. The increase in contact is with kin; she has not re-established contact with the women she came to know during her first pregnancy, though she had recently made a new friend with a young baby.

This mother intended to return to her job after her second maternity leave; she felt she had little choice since her husband was on a low income as a hospital porter and they had a heavy mortgage. At Contact 4 she was looking forward to returning to work and to her elder daughter's resuming her place at the hospital creche. The daughter had been extremely difficult since the birth of her sister; but for the help of her mother, who regularly looked after the older child and did bits of housework, the mother felt she would have had difficulty coping, especially since her husband had not been particularly helpful following the birth of the second child. Although she saw no problem in turning to others for help, she regarded her reliance on her mother as back-up support rather than as a permanent feature of her life. She had little time, energy or incentive to invest in other relationships at this point in her life.

Networks underwent considerable changes in size, personnel and structure during the 3 year period of the study. While non-returners increased in size, at least initially, the networks of women who remained in full-time employment underwent shrinkage, mainly due to loss of friends. The contraction was in general gradual and piecemeal; sudden transformations were more likely to be the result of some major life events. However the size and structure of a network is no sure guide to its use as a means of support. Other factors mediated, including the individual's ability to reciprocate and her orientation to seeking help which was shaped by norms guiding the conduct of 'family life' which have increasingly emphasized privacy and self-reliance. These norms were probably experienced even more acutely by women in full-time employment, who find themselves undertaking a course of action which was the subject of widespread social disapproval and which was perceived to be an individual and personal choice of the mother (who, by implication, should be expected to manage the ensuing tensions and difficulties).

Networks are a significant constituent of the moral and normative context which impinges upon the individual. They also provide a potential resource of informal support, able to offer various types of practical help. The notion of social network as a resource therefore encompasses both aspects of the divide within sociological theory – both the facilitative as well as the constraining elements of social structure. The extent to which, in practice, networks provided women with social support in the experience of being a working mother – either negatively or positively – will be considered in the following chapter.

228

13

The Experience of
Social Network Support

Having considered the availability of social network support in the previous chapter, the main focus in this chapter is whether women used their social networks as a means of support to them as working mothers and how far they felt supported. The issue needs breaking down into a number of questions. How do network members view mothers' employment? Do social networks provide support for working mothers? If so, are particular types of network likely to offer more or less support than others? Are networks likely to affect women's feelings of being supported or unsupported when they decide to return to work?

Before turning to these questions it is first useful to examine some of the dimensions of support (Selye, 1956; Weiss, 1969; Caplan, 1974; Berkman, 1984). According to Berkman (1984), support fulfils seven main functions for the individual.

1. Intimacy – the creation of an emotional climate in which individuals may express themselves unreservedly without fear of rejection. An intimate relationship is built on the premise that the other person has a complete and (paradoxically) 'perfect' understanding of the other. In our culture intimacy is often sexual as well as emotional.
2. Social integration – this feeling is transmitted through a sense of community or belonging which arises out of shared experiences, norms and values. Social integration is commonly provided by friends, neighbours, work colleagues and, in some cases, by kinship.
3. Opportunity for nurturant behaviour – this usually involves caring activity and is carried out through a sense of obligation often to a dependant, for example a child or elderly sick parent. It frequently combines a sense of caring for as well as caring about, thereby entailing work as well as nurturant behaviour (Stacey, 1981; Graham, 1987).

229

4. Reassurance of worth – refers to the way in which the individual feels valued as a person. It may also involve a feeling of competence in a role which in turn contributes to the individual's self-esteem. Relationships with family members or work colleagues typically provide such reassurance.
5. Practical assistance – social ties may provide money, goods and services. It is mainly kin who make such provision over an extended period of time.
6. Information, guidance and advice – such feedback may be provided by formal as well as informal sources.
7. Access to other persons who may fulfil any of the above. For example, a study of the social networks of women seeking abortion showed that particular kinds of social network were more able to provide access to information about abortion than others (Lee, 1969).

In practice respondents in our study were not always able to articulate clearly the ways in which social ties were helpful to them. Moreover, they frequently only 'had a feeling' that a person 'would' be supportive in a crisis. Such presumptions were typically reserved for people felt to be 'very close' and confidants. Until tested such support may be more symbolic than real.

THE DECISION TO RETURN
TO WORK

At Contact 1, women were asked with whom they had discussed their employment decisions. They were encouraged to talk about each person in turn – what was said and how they themselves felt about it. Many had mentioned or discussed the decision with relatively few other people – the median being four persons, the mode three persons and the range 1–6 persons. Almost all had talked to their partners (95%) and 80% had discussed it with at least one member of their social network. Only 22% turned to any formal agency; often this involved discussion in a personal rather than a professional capacity – for example, with health visitors, or in one case a woman doctor, who had returned to work themselves when their children were small. A qualitative analysis of 61 cases showed that under half had talked to any friends; given the predominance of the differentiated network type among the study group, this seemed a low proportion.

At least a half of those people with whom respondents had discussed the matter were said to be disapproving: 50% of parents, 51% of friends, 58% of other relatives, 56% of work colleagues. Since an expectation of disapproval may have deterred women from entering into discussion about their decisions, disapproval was probably even more widespread among social network members with whom the matter was not discussed.

Several other pieces of evidence suggested that women felt they had not enough sources of support for discussing their employment decisions. First, as mentioned in the last chapter, returners were more likely than non-returners to know other mothers who had worked when their children were small. In many cases these women were not members of respondents' social networks since they were not regular or close acquaintances; respondents sought them out because of their specialized knowledge and experience (the role of the lay specialist in providing social support has been noted elsewhere, for example by Caplan (1974) and Brannen and Collard (1982)). Women wanted to know how other working mothers coped; they needed reassurance that they too could manage; and they also sought the seal of moral legitimacy – that it was 'all right' to work with a young child.

> What I really did was to seek out friends who had worked with children. I wanted to hear their story and to find out how they managed to achieve it. *Was that helpful?* Yes . . . What I tended to do was to seek out the ones I thought had been good at it. The ones I've hoped I'll get a good response . . . and I've tended to seek out the ones who'll reinforce the rightness of it. (Director of publishing firm; Contact 1)

Second, at Contact 1 the researchers became very aware of women's need to express their anxieties and doubts about going back to work, without fear of disapproval. After the interviews had ended, women often continued to talk about their worries and many said spontaneously that they had found the interviews useful in this respect; the researchers were often asked how other women in the study were faring. Thirdly, on the questionnaire which respondents were asked to complete at Contact 2 about methods of coping with the return to work, 80% of women agreed with the statement that they would like 'the opportunity to talk to women in the same boat' as themselves.

Despite a substantial amount of disapproval and the fact that

231

returners had relatively few relatives or close friends who had worked when their children were small, most women did not express dissatisfaction with the support they did receive, in response to a general and direct question; over two thirds of returners (69%) said that support overall had been adequate. However, when responses to detailed questions about the ways in which named individuals were supportive (or not) are considered, respondents appeared less satisfied with support. A qualitative analysis of 61 interviews reveals that, in the case of respondents' own mothers, of those consulted (one half) well under 50% were regarded as helpful (12/32), together with a similar low proportion of friends (12/32) and just under half of work colleagues (10/21).

Turning to the types of support distinguished earlier, it is obvious that some of these are more relevant than others to the decision to return. Intimacy and the opportunity for nurturant behaviour are not particularly relevant, but a sense of belonging and shared experience clearly are. For example, in seeking out other working mothers, women were in part looking for role models with which they could identify – persons who would make them feel that what they were doing was not deviant or socially unacceptable. In fact few women had close friends who had returned or intended to return to work full-time, and only 14% of their own mothers had worked full-time when they had a child under school age. Women were therefore lacking in this type of support and had to search beyond their networks for such persons.

In practice many experienced the very antithesis of a sense of inclusion or belonging; some were made to feel different, even deviant by other people, thereby reinforcing their own underlying guilt about working. This mother was fortunate in at least one of her work colleagues.

> You tend to feel you're the only mother who has let your child down. I feel quite an affinity to her because she's going through those feelings as well. (Clerical worker; Contact 1)

In making the decision to return, women needed to feel reassured and valued, both in a moral sense – that what they were doing was right – and in a practical sense – that they were coping adequately with their babies, their jobs and their homes. They also wanted and welcomed guidance and advice, as long as it was constructive. Although some women did receive advice from their network members, the feedback many received was on the whole much less directive than the term 'advice' implies – more empathy and a 'listening ear'. In some cases older work colleagues who had themselves worked when their children were small provided reassurance.

> Maureen [a work colleague] is a sympathetic listener and is quite encouraging. She had to go back to work when her child was very young. She had to because she was the only one supporting the child. She sort of listened and gave moral support. (Hospital manager; Contact 1)

In many instances sympathy was offered but in the context of a negative construction of the return to work. Work colleagues and friends were said to be 'understanding' or 'sympathetic' if the women 'had to go back for financial reasons'. Women varied in their response to such sympathy: some discounted it while others accepted it, whether or not they held the same view.

FINDING CHILDCARE

Just as the decision to return to work was the mother's own, so too was she responsible for finding childcare (Chapter 10). At the time of the study, relatives were the principal source of childcare outside the home in Britain (Martin and Roberts, 1984). Relatives as carers were under-represented in our sample, for reasons discussed in Chapter 2. Most of the relatives providing care, in our study and nationally, were grandmothers, the majority maternal. Apart from relatives, 19% of childminders were known to the mothers before they began to use them as carers. Most mothers, however, relied on childcare purchased from the private market or on workplace nurseries.

As might be expected, women with family of origin and close knit networks were more likely to use relatives as carers (7/20 and 3/6, respectively) compared with women with truncated and differentiated networks (1/24 and 0/6). The reverse was true for use of nurseries, which were also most likely to be used by women in the sample who were older, better qualified, earned more and had partners who had higher status jobs (Moss, 1986). In so far as women in lower status jobs had less financial resources, together with more frequent contact with kin, it is not surprising that they drew upon kin networks for the care of their children.

Although most mothers did not rely on their network to provide childcare, they drew considerably on the knowledge, advice and contacts of network members to make childcare arrangements. Sixty-two per cent consulted at least one network member. By

233

comparison, 90% discussed the issue with husbands, and only 40% with formal agencies (predominantly Social Services Departments, but also some health visitors). Overall, women consulted a range of 0–8 persons, with a median of 3 persons and a mode of 2.

Those who used relatives as the main form of care very largely only contacted relatives; indeed, a third did not even have to make the approach, because a relative made an offer to provide care without being asked (this occurred usually early on in the women's pregnancies). Among those who eventually arranged for a childminder as carer, 36% started their search for childcare by approaching a relative or friend, and half eventually found a childminder via their social network or a work colleague. In contrast, of those who ended up eventually using nurseries, only a small proportion first contacted members of their networks (9%), while more discussed the matter first with a work colleague (18%) (most of this group used workplace nurseries which they already knew about; for most of this group, the first move was to go direct to the nursery).

Many mothers involved more than one person in their search for childcare.

> I asked my mother if she would have him . . . She's nearest, she was the initial thought. But I think she found the idea a little daunting, getting up early in the morning, having a young child on her hands all day. I didn't think she could cope both physically and emotionally. A friend asked me what I was doing and it was her offer. Mother had not said yea or nay at the time . . . I said [to my friend] if my mother says no – yes! (Audiology technician; Contact 1)

Informal support with childcare was often obtained in complex ways, with the mother putting out feelers through her social network and the offer coming back via an intermediary. A differentiated type of network was likely to prove helpful in this respect since the various discrete segments were likely to tap different information sources.

> I used to visit a friend quite often and her childminder would be there. Quite often we went home together for a cup of tea so I got to know her. She eventually told my friend that if I was considering going back to work that she'd like to look after the baby. (Secretary; Contact 1)

It would be wrong, though, to give the impression that there existed a great pool of knowledge about sources of childcare within respondents' social networks and beyond. Women did not always strike as lucky as the following instance.

> I went up to her [neighbour] and said 'Do you know anyone?' because she knows the whole road. And she said 'Oh no, dear, apart from me', which was exactly what I was hoping she would say. (Bank clerk; Contact 1)

Not surprisingly, in many instances women did not confine their informal approaches to their immediate social networks. For example, in their search for childminders, some teachers asked around in school and among mothers at the school gates. In one instance the services of the school caretaker were secured, in another a pupil's mother offered. An example of an even more wide-ranging search is that of the husband who, even before his daughter's conception, approached the local tennis club members for information about childminders in the area.

Women were a little more vociferous about lack of support with respect to finding childcare than they were over the decision to return to work. Forty per cent were dissatisfied over the search for childcare, compared with 31% over the decision to return. Most of their criticism was directed towards formal agencies, however, Social Services in particular. Those women whose relatives had agreed to provide childcare, and were least likely to have approached any formal agency, were least dissatisfied – just 18%, compared with 44% for minders and 59% for nurseries. Moreover, if the minder group is reduced by excluding cases where there was an unsolicited offer of childcare, the dissatisfaction level in the two non-relative groups was very similar, at rather over 50% (Moss, 1986).

CONSTRAINTS UPON USING INFORMAL SUPPORT

The first constraint arose from low expectations concerning the need for support. At Contact 1, before the return to work in most cases, most women knew little about either the general or specific childcare situation. They did not know about the unavailability of public sector provision nor did they find out a great deal about their local situations since on average they only visited one potential placement and, indeed, only 19% visited more than one. But they did assume that formal agencies had some responsibility for information and advice about how to find childcare and indeed for the provision of services, which may explain the higher levels of dissatisfaction with these agencies. By contrast the qualitative material suggests that mothers did not appear to expect their relatives or other network members to provide a great deal of help in these respects. If relatives offered, women were 'extremely grateful'. They may have harboured the hope of an offer from relatives but they did not expect their services to be forthcoming.

Over half the children (59%) who went to relatives when their mothers initially resumed work were no longer cared for in this way by Contact 4; by then either their mothers were no longer working or some other form of care was being used. The proportions were lower for children who initially began with childminders or at nursery (41% and 31%). This differential was partly due to some women's using relatives on a temporary basis, either because they only intended resuming work on a short-term basis or until a permanent childcare placement in some other form of care became available. Others moved their children when the arrangement did not work out.

It seems likely, therefore, that there are constraints upon using informal networks, particularly relatives, as a sustained source of childcare. One is that full-time, as opposed to part-time, employment may deter women from relying too heavily upon them – even those in lower status jobs who were most likely to do so. As other studies have found, many grandparents do not want to be overburdened especially by the long hours necessitated by parents' full-time employment. Preference is for the care to be limited in time and scope (Albrecht, 1954; Hill, 1987). Many users of relatives did not give them any payment (29%) or they paid a much lower fee (an average of £15 a week) than was charged by nurseries or childminders (the average in each case at Contact 2 being £30 and £28, respectively). Women therefore became considerably indebted to relatives who looked after their children. Moreover, since those using relatives earned less than those using other forms of care they were less able to repay them in cash and had to find other ways of reciprocating their services.

One indicator of the weight of indebtedness to relatives was the tension reported by some women in their relationships with carers, though this tension was often managed and did not necessarily lead to the ending of the arrangement. A recent study in Scotland also found a number of grounds for tension: potential rivalry for the child's affection, together with tension around the normative right of grandparents to 'spoil' their grandchildren (Hill, 1987). Indeed, reasons given for ending these arrangements rarely focused on the problem of reciprocity, with women referring instead to particular events which had precipitated the change – a disagreement with the relative, or the relative's becoming too ill to look after the child. The veracity of these reasons is not in doubt, but it also seems very likely that the build-up of unreciprocated obligations may have underlaid some of the tensions. In the following example, the relationship with the carer – a sister-in-law – was described as increasingly marked by tension which in turn seemed to originate, in part at least, in problems of reciprocity and indebtedness.

The mother was 37 years old and worked as an executive officer for the Inland Revenue, where her husband also had worked. By Contact 4, he had moved to become a consultant for a private firm of accountants and was earning a great deal more than he formerly did at the Inland Revenue. During the study the couple purchased and moved into the council house of the husband's parents, having bought them another house outside London. The mother's network was differentiated in structure, including close and frequent links with her husband's working-class family; her own parents were both dead.

Her sister-in-law, who lived across the road from the paternal grandparents' house, had looked after the child since the mother returned to work after maternity leave. The sister-in-law was a widow with three dependent children. The couple felt under considerable obligation to her, especially because their income was so much higher. They went to considerable lengths to repay her – by giving her much more than the 'going rate' for childcare, together with expensive gifts for herself and covenants of money for her children. At the final interview there was considerable tension in the relationship, which appeared to have been fuelled by the economic disparity between them and, most recently, by gifts of money. The parents had become even more dependent on the sister-in-law for childcare since moving-in across the road from her and the departure of the father's parents from London.

> I think she feels on the receiving end too much. And I've always felt guilty that the two of us have good well-paid jobs and she's trying to live on next to nothing with three children.

Significantly, the mother was considering whether to give up work or go part-time.

Thus even though informal sources (mostly relatives) provide the bulk of care for children of working parents (in Britain) it is possible to see how full-time employment may inhibit their sustained use. Further analysis of the childcare histories suggests that when mothers worked part-time, especially very short hours, they relied mainly on their partners, their parents or parents-in-law or they took care of the children themselves while they were working. In contrast, households in which both parents worked full-time were more likely to buy in childcare and when back-up care was needed – when the child was ill for example – they tended to manage it within the couple (which usually meant in practice the mother taking the time off work). The findings therefore lend some support to Pahl's thesis that two full-time worker households are less likely to engage in informal transactions for household services than are households in which the woman is not employed or employed part-time (Pahl, 1984).

SUPPORT FOR WORKING MOTHERHOOD

Supportive Persons

At the final Contact, women were asked to review the support they had received during the course of the three years of being a working mother. With this aim respondents were asked to select three persons who, they felt, had been most supportive to them over the three years. The following analysis focuses on the sub-set of women (N=62) who had worked continuously full-time since maternity leave and who were intensively interviewed at Contact 4.

Twenty-seven per cent were unable to mention three persons. Predictably, those with smaller networks (truncated and family of origin networks) were less likely to do so – 38% and 40%, respectively – compared with those with larger networks – differentiated (29%) and close knit (none); differences and cell size are however too small to draw inferences. Five types of people were mentioned:

1. Husbands – 85%; in 66% of cases husbands were mentioned first.
2. Mothers/parents/mothers-in-law/other female relatives – 67%.
3. Children's carers – 50%.
4. Friends – 24%.
5. Work colleagues – 15%.

There are a number of points to be made about this list. Not only did the great majority mention husbands, but women had a great deal more to say about them than they did about other people. Second, there is some overlap between categories 2 and 3 – 'children's carers' included 10 mothers or mothers-in-law and 2 sisters-in-law who had also been counted under category 2; if they are excluded from the carers category, then the relatives category assumes even greater importance. Grandparents were particularly significant people, though, unlike Hill's study (1987), paternal grandparents were almost as often mentioned as maternal ones. It is notable that friends and work colleagues were not often mentioned and that professionals were not mentioned at all – that is, apart from the carers (childminders, nannies and nursery workers).

The degree of overlap between supportive persons at Contact 4 and confidants mentioned at Contact 1 was examined (confidants were defined as persons in whom respondents said they 'would' confide, with respect to personal problems and problems to do with the child). There was in fact considerable overlap in that most 'supportive persons' were also confidants; however, most confidants (62%) were not mentioned as supportive persons at Contact 4. One reason for this is that supportive persons were more likely to have provided practical help than the opportunity to confide.

Only 3 of the 66 women interviewed about supportive persons at Contact 4 mentioned a friend as a supportive person who had also been mentioned as a confidant at Contact 1; none mentioned a professional as a supportive person and a confidant. Although it is possible that respondents had not experienced a sufficiently serious problem requiring the services of friends or professionals, it seems more likely in practice that they were reluctant to turn to either of these groups. Moreover, there was a considerable turnover of friends in respondents' networks during the course of the study (Chapter 12). In practice, therefore, it seems that respondents' consulting behaviour is a more conservative phenomenon than the hypothetical confiding questions, asked at Contact 1, would lead one to expect.

An examination of the association between network type and category of supportive person suggests some differences, though these were small and not statistically significant. Women with truncated networks were more likely to mention support from carers who were not relatives or friends (6/6 v. 6/12 family of origin, 8/12 differentiated and 1/5 close knit). Also, and rather predictably since family of origin and close knit networks were mainly composed of kin, women with these networks were more likely to mention relatives (nearly always mothers or mothers-in-law) as supportive. There was little difference between network types in the frequency with which husbands were mentioned.

Women's comments about the ways in which the selected persons were helpful included a number of specific types of support – practical help with childcare, access to information and advice concerning children and childcare, and emotional/moral support. Others provided what we have termed 'symbolic' support, while some in effect appeared to have given no support at all. We consider these last two categories first, before looking at the more specific types of support mentioned.

Unsupportiveness

Unsupportiveness is likely to be under-reported since women avoided people who were disapproving or unhelpful. In some instances it was clear that people nominated at Contact 4 as 'most supportive' during the 3 years since childbirth were not so in practice, since only unhelpful aspects of behaviour or attitudes were mentioned. This clinical tutor, for example, named her mother and sister as supportive persons but then mentioned nothing positive about them:

> My mother and sister have always been available but I just don't see them. They have been when I've contacted them but not on a day to day basis. I'm the only one in the family who's ever done this [gone back to work]. Everyone else has stayed at home . . . My sister doesn't say anything and my mother was very upset. (Truncated network)

Relatives, especially respondents' mothers, were frequently reported as initially disapproving of women's return to work but 'coming round' in due course. Moreover, given the evidence of the shrinkage in networks after the return and the loss of friends from women's networks, it is not unlikely that unsympathetic friends may have been 'dropped'.

In talking about supportive persons, women sometimes recalled the unsupportive ones, indicating the support they would have liked to have had. Women work colleagues were amongst those mentioned as being particularly unhelpful, undermining women's self-esteem and making them feel the exception rather than the rule.

> [Work colleagues] used to try and say I shouldn't come back

240

to work, that I should stay at home . . . older women. There's one in particular who seems to stir it. (Insurance clerk; differentiated network)

They've said you're an absolute fool to come back to work, you'll miss the first smile, first step, first word. (Nurse; differentiated network)

I don't think they are aware of how much tougher it was for me to cope with the same job . . . The girls, most were young, they hadn't children, they didn't particularly enjoy the work and their idea was when they had children to stop working. (Bank clerk; family of origin network)

Symbolic Support

In some cases support turned out to be more symbolic than real. This was often the case with husbands, while some parents were referred to in this way, especially if they did not live nearby or if, for some other reason, they were precluded from proffering practical or emotional help. In these instances women presumed that they would be supportive in a crisis but the need for support had not arisen – it had yet to be tested. Such persons had not therefore provided any everyday or routine practical help, but they seemed to be central to the individual's basic sense of security; support in its imagined sense was important to the individual. This bank telephonist mentioned her parents second in her list of supportive persons; even though they did not appear to have given any actual support, she still felt that they were 'there' if she really needed them.

Although they haven't done as much as I thought they would do they're always – I've always felt that if I was really desperate, I could always count on them. They've always been in the background. (Truncated network)

TYPES OF SUPPORT

Practical Support

Supportive persons seem to have been most valued for their practical help, especially with the child; this was the type of help most frequently mentioned. Women were most appreciative of having someone who cared about, as well as cared for, their children. At times of major difficulty supportive childminders were particularly helpful. This insurance clerk with two children was recently separated at Contact 4. Her family of origin lived in Liverpool. Her differentiated network provided her with a number of friends, one of whom offered her and her children accommodation when she was forced to leave home following marital violence. Most important, however, was her childminder, whom she described as a 'lifeline' and the first of only two supportive persons.

> The childminder definitely. 100%, 200%. It's only because of her I've managed to get through the last year, in fact the last two years . . . Even through all her adversities she's been there for the kids.

In this second example, the mother had also separated from her husband during the study. Again, the childminder was nominated most supportive person by the mother, describing her as 'the mainstay' of her life, and as supportive to her as a friend as well as taking care of her child:

> She is very reliable . . . and she's a very good friend. She's always been my biggest stop-gap and always been there. I wouldn't have been able to do it without her. Even before [she became the childminder] she was like a back up childminder . . . If I didn't know he was safe and happy I wouldn't have peace of mind at work. I couldn't do my work. (Senior progress officer; differentiated network)

In some cases network members gave limited or occasional childcare help – babysitting – or the very occasional back-up support if, for example, the child was ill. Mainly it was the grandmothers – maternal and paternal – and the occasional grandfather who provided this kind of help. As Hill (1988) also found, friends and neighbours were used only on rare occasions or for the occasional hour or so when relatives were not available, probably in part at least because of working mothers' inability to reciprocate – 'I do find it a bit embarrassing to have to take up their offers, because I can't reciprocate'.

On the whole, such practical support was confined to childcare. In a rare instance a woman's mother took over the running of the house as well as the care of the child.

> I've been very fortunate because my mother has been looking after her and she's been a tower of strength. She's been there all the time running the household for me . . . She's been terrific . . . My Mum's always been a terrific pal to me. (Teacher; family of origin network)

242

Information and Advice

Information and advice were also provided by supportive persons; this was mainly confined to the bringing-up of children, rather than non-parental childcare or the dual earner lifestyle. Mothers, mothers-in-law and female relatives were the main repository of 'good tips' and 'hints' about childrearing.

> I suppose my mother. When I've been het up about something she says 'Oh! They grow out of that'. I know everyone says those phrases but I believe my Mum. She's often got some very practical suggestions when Jo won't use the potty – useful in that respect. (Teacher; differentiated network)

> My mother. Just being there I suppose and knowing about children and being prepared to give advice. And to tell you it does get better which my husband couldn't say because he doesn't know. (Surveyor; close knit network)

In a few cases paid carers – childminders and a nanny – were also a source of information and advice about bringing up children. The mother just quoted provides an example.

> The nanny, because she's always been there and she's been trained and you can find out things from her and get the professionals' point of view.

One woman who worked in a hospital got some helpful advice about children from some of the doctors:

> The fact that I work with people who have children at the creche – doctors who know about children [is helpful]. If I have any problems I tend to discuss them in the work situation and get professional help. It's a supportive situation. (Medical laboratory scientific officer; differentiated network)

Moral and Emotional Support

Friends and occasionally a work colleague were the main providers of moral and emotional support rather than other types of support. They did not provide a great deal. That friends' support did not figure more, given that the differentiated network structure (which by definition included a significant proportion of friends) was the most common, may seem, at first sight, surprising. It should be recalled, however, that returners had less contact in their networks with women with young children compared with mothers at home

(Chapter 12). It seems likely therefore (and there was some qualitative evidence for this) that many returners' friends were 'old
friends', rather than women they had got to know through pre- and
post-natal contact.

As already discussed, emotional support covers a number of
themes. A few women commented on the importance of having
'someone to talk to' by which they usually meant a friend –
'someone who seems to know the right things to say not to
make things worse'. Differentiated networks offered women the
opportunity of turning to friends but also prevented the spread of
gossip. A nursing officer with such a network described the value
of friends.

> They empathize and understand what it's like. I think that's
> it really. It's what they say – they make helpful comments.
> Or a good laugh. If we go out to the pub [a friend] will
> moan about her husband and I'll moan about mine . . . I
> think women are very lucky really because they can talk
> to other women. Men don't talk to men in the same way.
> Certainly I know a tremendous amount about my girlfriends'
> marriages and they know plenty about mine. And I think
> it's very supportive when you can unburden yourself about
> various illnesses and know it won't go any further. That's
> really what it boils down to.

Women rarely found that simply talking to other people was
particularly helpful unless it was a two-way process. As mentioned earlier, returners sought out other women with similar
experiences to themselves, but only a minority had close friends
who were working mothers. This mother, a teacher, was one of
this minority. She had a differentiated network and two friends
(not actually in her network according to the study criteria) who
had similar experiences to her own. She described both as helpful.
It is clear from her account that a search for women in a similar
position affected the construction of her network.

> I think I'm fortunate I can turn to Ann and Shirley . . . friends
> who have been through it. The more you turn to people the
> more confused you get. I'm lucky to have the people with
> the experience . . . I'm lucky in that I found people who've
> gone back to work that I've become friendly with and made
> friends with. I think you feel very isolated in a group if you're
> the only one who's gone back to work. *Do you think you got
> friendly with certain people because you and they were going back*

to work? I think it must have done. The friends I talk to on a more or less same level are the ones who've gone back to work. I met them all when they were on maternity leave and we've kept contact ever since.

This mother, a hospital manager with a family of origin network, was not so fortunate in the women she met:

When I was expecting the first child I went to NCT classes. I thought 'This is a great way to meet people and talk to people about going back to work' but it was like a closed book. They were horrified and the teacher just didn't want to talk about it at all. She just said 'Have a word with so and so – she's done it', in hushed tones. I was amazed . . . incredibly narrow.

A third example, a teacher with a differentiated network, was fortunate in having a very close friend and confidant with whom she exchanged emotional and moral support over any difficulties with their respective partners.

I suppose the situation is that I try and talk to my husband. But if there is a real row about something then I would go and discuss it with her and vice versa . . . Throughout the whole of this thing [working motherhood] we've been feeling our way. Just things like how much of this and that we're each supposed to be doing . . . If I think I'm being put upon or if I think I'm doing too much then if he isn't sympathetic, which has happened occasionally, then I would go and talk to her.

Reassurance of personal value or worth was an important dimension of emotional and moral support – giving the individual a sense of value in what she does and what she is. Being an employed mother in this sense is not only a work role, but also central to the woman's identity. Mothers in paid employment were judged in terms of their whole personae and they were especially at risk of being stigmatized. One way of defending themselves against the label of being 'a bad mother' was for a relative to look after the child. This was often mentioned by respondents as 'the next best thing' to mothers' care and, at Contact 1, the main legitimation for preferring relatives.

Nor surprisingly, therefore, women felt very reassured if childminders treated their children 'as if they were their own'. For example, an executive officer in the Civil Service found her childminder reassuring in a number of ways and put her top of her list of supportive persons. Undoubtedly her childminder was exceptionally capable, having brought up several children of her own. But this mother's feelings of reassurance need to be understood in the context of her truncated network which consisted of her elderly parents, who provided no practical help with childcare, and one neighbour; this network provided little possibility of support. As well as lacking support, she was subject to other stresses: she was a magistrate as well as having a demanding full-time job, while her husband had in effect two demanding jobs and was very little involved with their son. She described being reassured by the childminder's experience with children and particularly by the fact that she gave her son what she felt unable to give him herself – a 'proper family life'.

> I think she can provide things that I can't. *In what way?* A family. A husband who, unlike my own, is quite happy to get down on the floor and wrestle. Some things there that he would have missed out on. Your child comes home and says 'I'm doing exercises, Mum' or 'I'm doing breakdancing'. You realize he's getting a lot out of life!

In remaining in paid employment with a very young child women risked being and feeling excluded from the community of 'normal mothers'. Their self-esteem was likely to be raised if what they were doing was treated as unremarkable and acceptable. Though some work colleagues were particularly unsupportive, support of this type was more forthcoming from women's work environment than from their relatives or friends outside work.

> [At school] I talk to people and find they have the same problems as me, the fact that they are tired, have been up all night, deadlines to pick children up . . . It makes you feel you are not isolated, that you are not only doing it for the money. (Teacher; differentiated network)

TWO CASE STUDIES

The analysis of the experience of support concludes with two contrasting cases – in terms of availability of support, attitudes towards seeking support and experiences of support. The cases, selected somewhat arbitrarily from both ends of the support spectrum, demonstrate the interplay of these different factors.

The first case is a clerical worker in a bank, aged 20 when she had her first child. Her husband ran a small car repairs business and spent his weekends doing up the house they were buying. The mother continued in her former job after maternity leave 'because of finances . . . everything happened at once – my husband was in the process of getting a business together, then we were getting married and then we had David the same year'. She had a large network which, at Contacts 1 and 2, was classified as differentiated since it included a lot of friends and rather fewer relatives. At Contact 4 the network included rather more kin – her own family and her husband's large family of Asian origin – and was classified as close knit.

Her mother-in-law provided a lot of childcare support, looking after her grandson not only while his parents were at work but also at other times, even taking him to the doctor's when necessary. Comments about her husband's family give a 'feel' of the quality of the ties in this mother's network.

> Even if he'd gone to a nursery he would still have that relationship but not as intense. It would still be there because they are a family group. Asians stick together and seeing it's their first grandchild as well. So even if he hadn't been there everyday he would have been there a couple of evenings a week and weekends.

Her own mother was also supportive and often looked after the child for a day or a night:

> If like my mother-in-law went into hospital my mother's been there to pick up the pieces. Although she works part-time she always says 'If you need help, I'm there'. If he's been in need – clothes and things or if I mention he needs a new jumper. She's great that way, always willing to help.

Not surprisingly, this woman mentioned her mother and mother-in-law in her list of most supportive people over the three years. However she put her husband first on the list. His support turns out to be more symbolic than real – 'he's always there' – though he is the person in whom she confides.

> If I've got any domestic problem he's always there. I can talk to him about almost anything, anything really. Whether he can do anything is not the point. But he's always there.

Despite her large network, this mother relied on only a few members for support. This does not mean though that the cohesiveness

247

of her network was irrelevant. It seems likely that the close knit structure, particularly that of her in-laws, was a major factor in reinforcing childcare values and obligations. She did not fully subscribe to these values and was initially very worried about what amounted to an assumption on her mother-in-law's part, as soon as the child was born, that she would take care of her grandchild; she was concerned about cultural influences upon the child and this anxiety was exacerbated by the powerful impact of the close knit kinship group. But by Contact 4, this concern had lessened.

> I was worried that she might influence him on their culture. She's Asian but he's cockney . . . If anything it has done him good – given him two languages. She speaks Urdu to him and he replies in English. The kids [her husband's young brothers and sisters] are very English as well as being Asian. They eat both foods – you know fish and chips and pizzas.

In terms of subscribing to values about seeking or accepting help from others and turning to others with personal problems, this mother was generally in favour. However, she qualified this by emphasizing the importance of finding suitable confidants, bearing in mind perhaps the risk of gossip in the sort of close knit network to which she herself belonged.

> I feel it's a good idea to get things off your chest and unhealthy to keep them bottled up. I feel that sometimes I need to talk – it's nice to have someone to talk to. Although some things you can't say to other people.

In the second case, the mother was also a clerical worker in a bank; her husband initially worked as a technician in a business developing photographs but, by Contact 4, was trying to establish his own business as a motor mechanic. At Contact 1 she had a family of origin network, but at Contacts 2 and 4 it had shrunk to a truncated type consisting of her father, brother, sister and her mother-in-law (her mother was dead). At Contact 1 there appeared to be little support from any source, not even from her husband, especially over her decision to return to work. At Contact 4 her close friends, sister-in-law and some work colleagues were said to disapprove of her being a working mother and she did not discuss the matter with them. She found the childminder herself and did nearly all the childcare work at home – 'I think in all his three years of life my husband's had only one day with him on his own'. If her son was ill she took the time off; there was no back-up support and no one she could rely on to have her son for a day, night or even an hour or so.

In the interview at Contact 1, the mother made some critical remarks about her husband for leaving most of the responsibility for their son to her. Yet overall, her attitude continued to be one of acceptance and resignation. The fact that childcare and household responsibilities were not more equitably distributed was 'put down' by her to innate 'character', her own greater organizational skills, and the historical fact that she has always done it; she also 'excused' her husband on work grounds.

> I suppose my husband is like that. He loves [his son] but I think his life revolves around cars . . . I think he thinks more about his work than his home . . . I suppose it's just our characters. Maybe I'm a better organizer. A lot of things he's left to me and I've always done them. At least I have the peace of mind that they are being done.

Neither does she express dissatisfaction about the lack of support from other quarters. Asked who has been most supportive over the past three years she says:

> Very hard to say. I can't really think of anybody. I suppose I should say my husband. Only the childminder really.

The absence of criticism and acceptance of lack of support in this mother's case were reinforced, perhaps even shaped by, a strong belief in self-sufficiency. Asked at Contact 2 about seeking or accepting help from others, she said: 'I don't tend to ask people for help'. While at Contact 1, asked about the value of turning to someone with a personal worry, she commented:

> The way I look at it is – if you listen to a person saying 'You're doing this wrong or this right' – when it comes down to it it has to be your own decision. In my view it doesn't really help.

Social networks of whatever size or structure did not provide much support over the decision to return to work, but informal sources of support, mostly within networks, were far more important for finding childcare. Apart from husbands and, in a few cases, the child's carer, the persons regarded as most supportive over the three years comprised a relatively small segment of women's social networks – female relatives largely drawn from the women's own and their partners' nuclear families of origin. Other segments of women's

249

networks featured little as sources of support. Because the support provided by non-kin and extended kin was in practice so limited, network structure had few effects on the experience of support.

In some instances it was possible to see the ways in which particular types of network were relevant to particular experiences of support. A truncated network might lead a mother to depend on a childminder. A differentiated network, if composed of women also with experience of motherhood and employment, might lead to mutually supportive exchanges between women. The historical context of friendship decided, in part at least, similarities of life stage and lifestyles; it may therefore constitute an important determining feature of support in some cases. Similarly, the extent to which networks were based on the workplace or the local community were also important determinants; in practice, mothers of young children were likely to be particularly reliant on local networks, even those in paid employment.

One of the main factors preventing social networks from proffering more support was the absence among members of a great deal of knowledge about and experience of being a mother with a young child and in full-time employment. Women were also inhibited from seeking more informal support because of low expectations reinforced by adherence to norms of household self-sufficiency, together with the fact that, in the main, they managed to cope by relying upon their own resources. Nor were women very dissatisfied with a lack of network support, for too great a reliance would have posed problems of reciprocity and called into question the rationale for the dual earner lifestyle – the ideology of 'individual choice'. Where a lifestyle is chosen people are expected to provide themselves for the consequences of such decisions.

Overall, then, social network resources and structure did not make a great deal of difference to women's experience of combining full-time employment with new motherhood. More critical was the existence of supportive members – in most cases only one or two – in the women's nuclear families of origin or those of their partners, especially mothers and mothers-in-law. This situation may change with time as increasingly more women return to work after maternity leave. For the group in our study, however, the negotiation of careers as mothers in full-time employment was a somewhat lonely and unsupportive experience, though women had no great expectations that it would be any different.

14

Conclusions

A central theme of our study has been the way in which dominant ideologies shaped women's experience as mothers in full-time employment, as well as how they interpreted that experience. Dominant ideologies about motherhood emphazise women's primary responsibility for children and remain highly ambivalent about women with very young children having full-time jobs. Over time the area of primary responsibility for mothers has expanded – from physical health and well-being to all aspects of children's development – and these increasing demands have offset a decrease in other demands resulting from women's having fewer children. In contrast, ideologies of fatherhood continue to emphasize the importance of male breadwinning, and therefore employment. While men are now expected to give rather higher prominence to household responsibilities – for instance, to be present at the birth of their child and help out with children – their primary responsibility continues to be working and earning. Ideologies of marriage emphasize the importance of love, companionship and emotional support, downplaying more material values such as equitable divisions of labour, money and power. Finally, ideologies of 'family life' emphasize self-sufficiency, autonomy and privacy, reflected at a political level by government assertions that childcare is a private, family responsibility. This brings us back full circle, since within two-parent families, mothers are regarded as primarily responsible for children.

These ideologies influenced the support available to, and experienced by, the women in our study. Public support (for instance, childcare and parental leave) was virtually non–existent. Fathers did not equally share childcare or other domestic tasks, nor did they accept equal responsibility for these areas. Support from social networks was important in some ways and for some women, but generally inadequate. Many women who returned to work experienced hostile attitudes from relatives, friends and work colleagues, while limited time and energy reduced their ability to reciprocate services with other women, especially those with young children. Relatives, and especially mothers and mothers-in-law, were the main source of practical help, but their availability to do this on a regular basis varied considerably.

Irrespective of what they thought, women were forced by circumstances to rely largely on personal solutions to the demands and tensions of managing the dual earner lifestyle, which fell largely upon them. They adopted a variety of personal coping methods, for example in their use of time, and bore most of the financial costs of the dual earner lifestyle, some such as childcare that occurred in most families, others such as paid domestic help which were confined to higher income families. In a substantial number of cases, solutions involved women's employment – they changed jobs, cut their hours, postponed seeking promotion, to create more space in their lives for children and domestic work. One of the most striking features of the study was the proliferation of employment histories within a short period – and the close relationship between these histories and occupational mobility.

Dominant ideologies legitimized the low level of support and the heavy load carried by women. Women in dual earner households constructed the initial decision to return to work very much in personal terms rather than as a joint or household strategy. Not only was their employment optional, it was also viewed as less important than their partner's, while many women thought of their earnings as peripheral rather than core income. This perception was reinforced by men as well as women who set the costs of the dual earner lifestyle against women's income rather than the joint household income. Women's employment and earnings therefore became marginalized in the thinking of both parents, with an expectation in many cases that the mother would give up work at some point. For many women and their partners the dual earner household was seen as a temporary phase, until a second child was born or certain material targets had been achieved, not as a permanent state requiring permanent adjustments, both of behaviour and attitudes. In such a context, it was easy and natural for women to assume and accept that the consequences of their 'individual choice' to return to work (for example, childcare arrangements) were essentially down to them to deal with; and for women to have low expectations for support and to be grateful for low levels of support.

Dominant ideologies helped women handle some potential conflict areas or to avoid facing the possible negative consequences of their actions. Women played down criticism of their partners' unequal contribution to domestic labour, praising them for the help they did give and excusing them for not doing more. At the same time, they emphasized and valued the emotional support that their partners provided and their potential supportiveness in the event of a crisis.

Just as women did not in general take long-term considerations into account when making their decision to return, so too they rarely confronted the potentially serious long-term consequences of subsequently leaving employment or leaving their full-time job for another part-time one. Not only could these actions affect future career prospects, pensions and long-term household income, but they left women (and their children) economically vulnerable to the future loss of their partner's financial support because of marital breakdown or for some other long-term reason. At one level this short-term employment perspective was because women were highly oriented to the lives of their children and focused long-term planning on them rather than employment careers. However, ideologies of marriage discouraged addressing issues about the allocation of resources and power within households and confronting in advance the consequences of what has become a 'high risk' event, with one in three marriages likely to end in divorce.

Ideologies, though powerful influences, do not completely determine experiences. Nor do they avert all conflicts. Some dissatisfaction with the support of husbands and others was voiced. Women expressed conflicting views about their children; they might believe that as a 'good' mother they should give as much time as possible to their children yet doubt that this was actually necessary to their child's well-being, not least because their children might appear to show no ill effects from not receiving full-time maternal care. They might express powerful, pervasive feelings of anxiety, guilt and loss about leaving their children, yet also see clear benefits to themselves and their children. In such cases of conflict and contradiction – between ideas about what it means to be a 'good' mother and the reality of the dual earner lifestyle – women often adopted a strategy of keeping two closely linked features of their lives, motherhood and employment, separate and unconnected.

While women were constrained by dominant ideologies and lack of support, they were not simply passive subjects reacting to external forces. They deployed personal resources to develop a range of methods for coping with the double workload of paid employment and domestic labour. Most found benefits in full-time work; and in emphasizing positive aspects for the child and the mother–child relationship, they were beginning to create a new discourse around maternal employment. They worked to reconcile the implications of dominant ideologies about motherhood with what they felt and observed in practice. They achieved a great deal – for their children, their employers, their partners and themselves – in often difficult and unpromising circumstances.

Yet while it is right and necessary to emphasize the positive side of women's experience, the negative side remains. Employment changes, especially to part-time jobs, often led to occupational downgrading, with losses of earnings, pensions and other benefits. Managing a full-time job and the greater part of domestic labour increased tiredness and imposed other strains. In order to cope, women had to give up time for themselves and social relationships. Choices, in childcare or the organization of working time, were very limited. Conflicting demands and ideologies created feelings of anxiety, guilt and stress, exacerbated for many women by a sense of isolation in the course they were following. So, while our study reveals much that is positive, it also emphasizes a continuing darker, negative side.

MOVING ON FROM THE
MID-1980s

We have emphasized throughout this book the particular time and place in which our study was set. While this matters for any research, it is particularly important given the subject of our study. Since our fieldwork finished, important and relevant changes have occurred in the labour market. In particular, a large reduction in the number of school leavers and a sustained period of economic expansion (at least up to 1989) have created a developing labour shortage, especially in areas such as the south-east of England. Employers are having to seek new sources of recruitment, with one consequence being a rapid growth in women's employment – 'two thirds of the labour force growth between 1983 and 1987 was made up of married women and by 1995 the projected increase in the size of the female labour force is some three quarters of a million, over 80% of the total [increase]' (Department of Employment, 1988, p. 8). Given the low rates of employment among women with children under 5, in absolute terms and compared with other women, this group forms one of the most accessible reserves of labour.

Employers' needs, together with longer-term factors which have led to a steady if slow growth of employment, are producing a rapid increase in employment among women with young children. Early signs of this were apparent during the period of our study; employment rates among women with children under 5 grew from 24% in 1983 to 35% in 1987 (OPCS, 1989, Table 9.11). While there was a substantial rise in part-time work (from 18% to 24%), which still accounted for over two thirds of employed mothers, full-time employment increased even faster, from 5% in 1983 to 11% in 1987.

This growing demand for women workers has produced other changes. Between 1985 and 1988, the number of private nurseries grew by 44%, while the number of places at childminders grew by 29%. Employers have shown increasing interest in providing support to working mothers (or parents, since most schemes are, in theory, available to men and women employees). Career breaks, job sharing and other part-time working and more flexible hours have all become more common. Employers are also increasingly involved in providing some childcare support – through workplace nurseries, sponsoring places in outside services, or providing some form of subsidy to employees' childcare costs. A 1989 survey of 106 leading companies revealed that 60% were offering extra help with childcare or were reviewing their policy – 'the specific childcare option most often mentioned in the course of our survey was a workplace nursery [but] two other forms of provision, childcare allowances and career break schemes, have also generated some interest' (Working for Childcare, 1990, p. 8).

Since our study finished, therefore, there have been some significant developments affecting the position of working mothers. This has stimulated more interest in the subject of 'working mothers' and more initiatives by employers and private childcare providers than at any time since the War. Overall, the situation of working mothers in 1990 has improved over what it was in 1985.

This does however need to be put into perspective. Private nurseries, which in London cost over £100 a week for full-time care for children under 2, will remain too expensive for many families (for example, many lone parents, families with two children under 5 and lower earning parents), while their numbers remain relatively small (they still provide places for less than 2% of the under fives population) and their distribution uneven. While there is clearly a lot of employer activity occurring, the statistics are lacking to actually quantify the extent of change and improvement, or indeed to know whether improvements are

255

occurring generally and evenly, are benefiting particular areas (for example, where labour shortages are greatest) or groups (for example, those with skills in greatest demand). A recent survey of major employers suggests that workplace nurseries are heavily concentrated in the south of England and in medium-sized towns and concludes that there are limits on 'employers' ability to provide the comprehensive childcare service Britain desperately needs' (Working for Childcare, 1990, p. 22). In practice, the market-led developments which are occurring will be partial and uneven in coverage, and of most benefit to higher income and higher skilled workers in areas with the most acute labour shortages.

Similarly, while the number of women with young children in employment is growing, there is inadequate information to judge what is happening in terms of the quality of their employment. How far, if at all, is the quality of part-time jobs improving? What proportion of the growth of part-time employment results from extending opportunities for part-time work into higher skilled and better paid jobs and how much is the result of an increased supply of low skilled and low paid jobs? Are women with young children in full-time work in a better position to benefit from promotion opportunities?

There may have been some improvement in the position of some employed mothers since the mid-1980s, largely because of increased employment opportunities and greater responsiveness by some employers to their needs. There has however been little change in a number of the key factors constraining working mothers. There is no reason to think there has been a major shift in men's participation in domestic labour; the dual earner lifestyle continues to rely mainly on the hard work, organizational skills and sacrifices of women.

Continuing inequality in the division of domestic labour as more women enter the labour market is likely to have increasingly serious consequences. Some of these can be seen in the USA where employment rates among women with young children have been increasing rapidly over the last 15 years or so. By 1987, over half of all women with a child under 1 were in the labour force and if current trends continue, over two thirds of pre-school children will have an employed mother by 1995; moreover, most mothers in the USA have full-time jobs (Phillips, 1990).

Despite these employment changes, in her study of dual earner parents in the USA Arlie Hochschild (1989) found that domestic work was shared in only 18% of households, and in nearly two thirds of households men still did little. Moreover, three quarters of men did not believe that they should share the responsibility and work of domestic labour. What has changed however has been women's ideas. Most women (60%) did believe that domestic labour should be shared.

This created potentially serious conflict. Forty per cent of marriages had a clash of 'gender ideology', mostly between women who sought equality both in the home and at work ('equalitarian ideology') and men who accepted their partners' working but expected them to remain primarily responsible for domestic work ('transitional ideology'); this reflected a growing social tension between 'faster-changing women and slower-changing men' (p. 205). Over 50% of mothers had tried to change how their domestic workload was shared, most unsuccessfully. Such domestic situations not only place additional stresses on women (and also, Hochschild argues, on men) but also on marriages – 'people who conclude that it is women's work that causes divorce look only at what women are doing (when) what contributed to happiness was the husband's willingness to do work at home' (p. 212).

The American experience suggests that the failure of men to assume greater responsibility for domestic work is likely to create increasing tensions in Britain as more women with young children enter employment and in particular as more take full-time jobs (or longer part-time work). Women's ideologies and therefore their expectations are likely to change, leading to increased demands for men to share responsibility for children and housework – and growing dissatisfaction and marital tension if they do not do so. Women are also likely to reassess the importance of their work and its long-term significance, both in terms of career and the financial risks of divorce. In the USA 'more women now work not simply to "help their husbands" financially or to "use their talents" but because they fear for their marriages . . . [for] over the last century, the economic footing which marriage has provided women and their children has become less secure' (Hochschild, 1989, p. 140).

Government's position has also not changed. There has been no active public involvement in the development of policies and services which could provide support to all working parents – no development of publicly funded childcare services, no improvement in maternity leave, no initiative to introduce statutory parental leave or leave to care for sick children. Faced by a major economic and social change, the official position has been to re-emphasize the private nature of childcare and parental employment, and the primacy of market forces working through private provision of services or through employers' making provisions where their labour force needs require such initiatives.

Government's role in the changed circumstances has been confined to drawing the situation to the attention of employers and others (for example, by suggesting to school governors that they consider the possibilities of using school premises for after-school care) and making a few marginal initiatives to encourage private and employer provision (for example, encouraging the establishment of a voluntary accreditation scheme for private childcare services). While the Ministerial Group on Women's Issues has considered childcare, their conclusions have been limited to a few short press releases; there has been no policy review either on childcare provision or the wider issues raised by growth in parental employment.

There is also very little sign of change in dominant ideologies, nor indeed of any serious examination of them. While overt hostility to working mothers has abated, the assumption that working women remain primarily responsible for their children has remained intact. The position of fathers, and the need for change in their roles, has received little serious or sustained attention; men's role as primary breadwinners and secondary carers remains unchallenged. Government policies have drawn on and reinforced notions about private responsibility for children and their care and the need for family self-sufficiency. In short, at best, adjustments are being made within existing ideological frameworks; new and more supportive frameworks are not emerging.

The dilemma faced by women entering motherhood in the mid-1980s remains for women making this transition in the early 1990s. To stop work for a period or to leave full-time employment and take a part-time job ('the updated model of the traditional division of labor' (Moen, 1989, p. 148)) can have serious and adverse short-term and long-term effects on employment opportunities and earnings; the consequences may be particularly serious and adverse both for a mother and her children in the event of losing the financial support of a partner in full-time employment. It may create frustration and dissatisfaction, either with being at home full-time or doing a low quality part-time job.

But to attempt to continue in full-time employment is likely to involve a heavy workload, made up of disparate demands from home and employment, with accompanying stresses, conflicts and tensions that reduce well-being and quality of life, and make it difficult to take full advantage of the employment opportunities available to full-time workers. Women may appear, on the surface, to be able to compete equally with men: yet they carry the dual disadvantage of domestic work and having little of the 'backstage support' which most married men get from their wives at home.

One apparent solution to this is to spend increasing sums of money on paying others to do domestic work. Women shed their domestic workload by paying other women to do it. One response to the changes in women's employment in the late 1980s has been a growth of nannies, mothers' helps, domestic cleaners and so on. Yet this strategy has severe limitations. The costs involved limit its applicability to high income households. Most of the work is poorly paid and women are only willing to do it because of inadequate alternative employment opportunities. As these alternatives become more available, domestic labour becomes more expensive, harder to find and increasingly difficult to retain; this process continues to the point where, in countries such as Denmark and Sweden where nearly all women are in the labour market, virtually no domestic help is available. As an option, therefore, paying others to do domestic work is transitory in nature, available to a small minority at a certain stage of labour market history before better alternative employment creates yet another 'servant problem' (a recurrent event as labour market changes price different types of servant systems out of reach of all but the super-rich).

The strategy raises another problem. It often involves the assimilation of highly paid women workers into traditional male work culture – 'couples capitulate to "workaholism à deux"' (Hochschild, 1989, p. 254). In the American context, Hochschild also argues that this strategy, based on 'an ever broadening lower tier of women doing bits and pieces of the housewife's role for pay' continues the process of devaluing caring work and homemaking, a process begun by men but being continued by women who seek equality with men on traditional male terms.

A CHALLENGE TO BE FACED

The UK faces a formidable challenge concerning two fundamental national requirements: economic production and social reproduction. It must find ways:

1. to provide children with conditions that ensure them a good quality of life now and the best opportunities for full and healthy development in all its many facets;

259

2.   to ensure that the experience of parenthood, for women and men, is satisfying and rewarding, and that parents have the best 'working' conditions for undertaking their role;

3.   to facilitate genuine equality of opportunity between men and women in paid work and other areas of life;

4.   to provide an adequate supply of labour and to make full use of the potential and actual skills and experience in the labour force.

Tackling all of these objectives, rather than one or two, and reconciling them and the interests involved, is a major undertaking. It needs little short of a revolution – in behaviour, attitudes and ideas, and involving government, employees, trades unions, women and men. Such a revolution is difficult to start and even harder to maintain. In the USA, where employment rates among women with young children have risen rapidly in recent years, the revolution has stalled – 'women have gone to work, but the workplace, the culture and most of all the men have not adjusted themselves to this new reality' (Hochschild, 1989, p. 235). Hochschild emphasizes the importance of change in men's involvement in domestic labour. Women, she argues, are already doing all they can – 'it is men who can do more . . . it is time for a whole generation of men to take a second historic shift [the first being women entering the economy] – into work at home' (p. 238).

Another major structural change must be in the workplace and in particular in how work is organized; this must involve developing and extending much more flexible ways of working, both at any one time and over the life course, so that employment careers can be successfully pursued following different pathways rather than following the traditional, male-careerist pathway of continuous, full-time work. There are already many examples of new employment rights for parents – building on maternity leave, to include paternity leave, parental leave and leave to care for sick children and for other family reasons. There are also an increasing number of examples of employers introducing new 'family-friendly' working practices. The main challenge, however, remains to be tackled. Does the traditional masculine model of employment continue to be the norm, with alternatives available to a minority at the price of career advancement and other disadvantages? Or is work restructured on the basis that all employees, men and women, have childcare responsibilities – and indeed other social responsibilities and relationships (to elderly or disabled relatives, to partners, friends, local communities) – that require long-term recognition? At the heart of the issue is the place of paid work in the lives of people and the wider society, and the balance that needs to be struck to produce a healthy as well as a prosperous society.

The revolution needs changes elsewhere. Good quality services are needed for children to attend while parents are at work – or engaged in other activities. These must be equally available to all children, and not depend on the lottery of what job parents do, how much they earn or where they and their children live. They must also be concerned not just with the provision of secure care for children, but with providing experience that will supplement the home and enhance children's development. They need to be part of the fabric of all communities and to be part of a process of re-creating communities that are child-friendly. What is needed, in short, is equal access by all children (irrespective of where they live or their parents' income or job) to good quality, stable and local care and education services; such services should be a general right, not an employment benefit available to certain favoured workers.

Finally, change is needed in what Hochschild (1989) calls 'the culture' and what we have called ideologies. New ideas about work, childhood, parenthood, marriage and family need to be explored, ideas that support the economic and social changes under way and become a genuine resource for working mothers (and fathers) rather than a constraint. The starting point must be recognition of existing dominant ideologies and of their inappropriateness and potential for damage.

To bring about such a revolution is a very tall order. It requires a broad approach with an emphasis on discussion, explanation and persuasion. Attention needs to be paid to identifying resist-ances and blockages – in beliefs, feelings and behaviour – and to working at many levels and in many places (in school, in other services, in the workplace, in the media) to erode these obstacles. Government has to play a central role, laying out the issues, encouraging debate, offering some sort of vision and also more specific objectives, helping others to set up provision but also making its own contribution – through developing and funding a policy to ensure equal access for all children to good quality care and education while their parents are at work and by ensuring that all parents have certain basic employment rights.

In this respect, Sweden sets standards which we believe to be desirable and feasible. A programme of public support for the development of high quality care and education services is closely integrated with a programme of employment rights which include flexible parental leave, paternity leave, leave to care for sick children and the right to work part-time in an existing job, all except the latter paid at 90% of earnings. Sweden also offers another important model, being the only country where policy explicitly recognizes the importance of gender equity, and sets as an objective increased participation by fathers in the care of their children.

Government – both central and local – has a crucial strategic role because the issues involved affect the social and economic well-being of society. It must ensure that the interests of economically and politically weaker groups – children and women – are recognized and balanced adequately against those of more powerful interests. But government must work in partnership. Employers will have to implement statutory rights, but they must build on these to introduce more wide-ranging and imaginative ways of restructuring the way work is organized, encouraging and supporting the participation of men, as well as women, in these new ways of working. A focal point for this change will be the workplace. Trades unions can also play a key role in stimulating, prioritizing and facilitating change, working both with employers and with their own members (a Swedish trades union, for example, has run education programmes for members to increase take-up by men of parental leave). Finally, there is a whole network of services and community resources that can contribute to the revolution – discussing the issues, introducing new ideas, providing support to parents.

It is only through such an undertaking in the public sphere that the 'stalled revolution' can move ahead. At the same time it has to be recognized that such radical change requires a change in cultural goals with respect to gender roles in the workplace and in that most conservative of spheres – 'family life'. Only when society attaches importance to women being able to provide adequately for themselves and for their children throughout the course of their working lives, and only when husbands and fathers internalize a sense of day to day responsibility for children, will mothers, living with or without partners, no longer be forced into an inequitable position, trading motherhood against employment.

References

Ainsworth, M.D.S. (1962), 'The effects of maternal deprivation', *Deprivation of Maternal Care: A Reassessment of its Effects* (Geneva: World Health Organization).

Albrecht, R. (1954), 'The parental responsibilities of grandparents', *Marriage and Family Living*, pp. 201–14.

Althauser, R.P. and Kalleberg, A.L. (1981), 'Firms, occupations and the structure of labour markets: a conceptual analysis', in I. Berg (ed.), *Sociological Perspectives in Labor Markets* (London/San Francisco: Academic Press).

Andrews, B. and Brown, G.W. (1988), 'Social support, onset of depression and personality' *Social Psychiatry and Psychiatric Epidemiology*, vol. 23, pp. 99–108.

Arber, S., Gilbert, N. and Dale, A. (1985), 'Paid employment and women's health: a benefit or a source of role strain', *Sociology of Health and Illness*, vol. 7, no. 3, pp. 345–97.

Ashford, S. (1987), 'Family matters', in R. Jowell, S. Witherspoon and L. Brook (eds), *British Social Attitudes: the 1987 Report* (Aldershot: Gower).

Ashton, D. (1986), *Unemployment under Capitalism: The Sociology of British and American Labour Markets* (Brighton: Harvester Press).

Backett, K.C. (1982), *Mothers and Fathers: A Study of the Development and Negotiation of Parental Behaviour* (London: Macmillan).

Barnes, J.A. (1969), 'Networks and political process', in J.C. Mitchell (ed.), *Social Networks in Urban Situations* (Manchester: Manchester University Press).

Barrett, M. and McIntosh, M. (1982), *The Anti-Social Family* (London: Verso).

Barron, R.D. and Norris, G.M. (1976), 'Sexual divisions and dual labour markets', in D.L. Barker and S. Allen (eds) *Dependence and Exploitation in Work and Marriage* (London: Longman).

Beail, N. (1983), 'Father involvement in pregnancy, birth and early parenthood', PhD Thesis, London University Institute of Education.

Becker, J. (1963), *Outsiders: Studies in the Sociology of Deviance* (New York: Free Press).

Beechey, V. (1978), 'Women and production: a critical analysis of some sociological theories of women's work', in A. Kuhn and A.M. Wolpe (eds), *Feminism and Materialism: Women and Modes of Production* (London: Routledge and Kegan Paul).

Beechey V. (1987), *Unequal Work* (London: Verso).

Beechey, V. and Perkins T. (1987), *A Matter of Hours* (Cambridge: Polity Press).

Bell, C., McKee, L. and Priestley, K. (1983), *Fathers, Childbirth and Work: A Report of a Study* (London: Equal Opportunities Commission).

Belsky, J. and Rovine, M. (1984), 'Social network contact, family support, and the transition to parenthood', *Journal of Marriage and the Family*, vol. 46, no. 2, pp. 455–62.

Berger, P.R.L. and Luckmann, T. (1966), *The Social Construction of Reality* (New York: Doubleday).

Berkman, L.F. (1984), 'Assessing the physical health effects of social networks and social support', *Ann. Rev. Public Health*, vol. 5, pp. 413–32.

Bevan, J.M. and Draper, G.J. (1967), *Appointments Systems in General Practice* (London: Oxford University Press for Nuffield Provincial Hospital Trust).

Blumer, H.S. (1969), *Symbolic Interactionism: Perspective and Method* (Englewood Cliffs, New Jersey: Prentice-Hall).

Bonney, N. (1988), 'Dual earning couples: trends of change in Great Britain', *Work, Employment and Society*, vol. 2, no. 1, pp. 89–103.

Bott, E. (1968), *Family and Social Network* (London: Tavistock Publications).

Boulton, M. (1983), *On Being a Mother: A Study of Women with Pre-School Children* (London: Tavistock Publications).

Bowlby, J. (1951), 'Maternal care and mental health', *Bulletin of the World Health Organization*, vol. 3, pp. 355–534.

Bowlby, J. (1958), 'The nature of the child's tie to his mother', *Journal of Psychoanalysis*, vol. 39, pp. 350–73.

Bowlby, J. (1965), *Child Care and the Growth of Love* (Harmondsworth: Penguin, 2nd edn).

Brannen, J. (1987), 'Taking maternity leave: the employment decisions of women with young children', TCRU Working and Occasional Paper No. 7 (London: Thomas Coram Research Unit).

Brannen, J. (1988), 'Research note: The study of sensitive subjects: notes on interviewing', *Sociological Review*, vol. 36, pp. 552–63.

Brannen, J. (1989), 'Childbirth and occupational mobility', *Work, Employment and Society*, vol. 3, no. 2, pp. 179–201.

Brannen, J. (forthcoming), 'Combining qualitative and quantitative approaches'.

Brannen, J. and Collard J. (1982), *Marriage in Trouble: The Process of Seeking Help* (London: Tavistock Publications).

Brannen, J. and Moss P. (1987a), 'Dual earner households: women's financial contributions after the birth of the first child', in J. Brannen and G. Wilson (eds), *Give and Take in Families: Studies in Resource*

Distribution (London: Unwin Hyman).

Brannen, J. and Moss, P. (1987b), 'Fathers in dual earner households: through mothers' eyes', in C. Lewis and M. O'Brien (eds), *Reassessing Fatherhood: New Observations on Fathers and the Modern Family* (London: Sage).

Brannen, J. and Moss, P. (1988), *New Mothers at Work: Employment and Childcare* (London: Unwin Hyman).

Brannen, J. and Wilson, G. (1987), *Give and Take in Families: Studies in Resource Distribution* (London: Unwin Hyman).

Broberg, A. and Hwang, C.P. (1990), 'Daycare for young children in Sweden', in E. Melhuish and P. Moss (eds), *Day Care for Young Children: International Perspectives* (London: Routledge, Chapman and Hall).

Brodersen, A. (1964) (ed.), *Alfred Schutz: Collected Papers Vol. 11* (The Hague: Martinus Nijhoff).

Bronfenbrenner, U. and Crouter, A. (1982), 'Work and family through time and space', in S.B. Kamerman and C.D. Hayes (eds) *Families That Work: Children in a Changing World* (Washington, DC: National Academy Press).

Brown, G.W. and Harris, T. (1978), *The Social Origins of Depression* (London: Tavistock).

Brown, G.W., Andrews, B., Harris, T., Adler, Z. and Bridge, L. (1986) 'Social support, self-esteem and depression', *Psychological Medicine*, vol. 16, pp. 813–31.

Brown, R. (1986), 'Occupational identity and career change', Paper given at the Annual Conference of the British Sociological Associaton, The Sociology of the Life Cycle, Loughborough, March.

Brown, R., Curran, M. and Cousins, J. (1983), *Changing Attitudes to Employment*, Department of Employment Research Paper No. 40 (London: HMSO).

Bryman, A. (1988), *Quantity and Quality in Social Research* (London: Unwin Hyman).

Bryson, R., Bryson, J.B. and Johnson, M.F. (1978), 'Family size, satisfaction and productivity in two earner couples', *Psychology of Women Quarterly*, vol. 31, no. 1, pp. 67–77.

Burgoyne, J. and Clark, D. (1984), *Making a Go of it: A Study of Stepfamilies in Sheffield* (London: Routledge and Kegan Paul).

Cain, M. and Finch, J. (1981), 'Towards a rehabilitation of data', in P. Abrams, R. Deem, J. Finch and P. Rock (eds), *Practice and Progress: British Sociology 1950–1980* (London: George Allen and Unwin).

Caplan, G. (1974), *Support Systems and Community Mental Health* (New York: Behavioral Publications).

Cartwright, A. (1967), *Patients and their Doctors: A Study of General Practice* (London: Routledge and Kegan Paul).

Cavendish, R. (1982), *Women on the Line* (London: Routledge and Kegan Paul).

Central Office of Information (1987), *Policies for the Advancement of Women in Britain* (London: COI).

Central Statistical Office (1989), *Social Trends 19* (London: HMSO).

Chaney, J. (1981), *Social Networks and Job Information: the Situation of Women who Return to Work* (Manchester: Equal Opportunities Commission).

Chodorow, N. (1978), *The Reproduction of Mothering: Psychoanalysis and the Sociology of Gender* (Berkeley: University of California Press).

Clarke-Stewart, A. (1982), *Day Care* (Glasgow: Fontana).

Cochran, M., Gunnarsson, L., Grobe, S. and Lewis, J. (1984), *The Social Support Networks of Mothers with Young Children: A Cross National Comparison*, Department Educational Research, University of Gothenburg, Research Bulletin, No.25.

Cohen, B. (1988), *Caring for Children: Services and Policies for Child Care and Equal Opportunities in the United Kingdom*, Report for European Commission's Childcare Network (London: Commission of the European Communities).

Cohen, S. and Wills, T.A. (1985), 'Stress, social support and the buffering hypothesis', *Psychological Bulletin*, vol. 98, no. 2, pp. 310–57.

Colletta, N. (1983), 'At risk of depression: a study of young mothers', *Journal of Genetic Psychology*, vol. 142, pp. 301–10.

Cornwell, J. (1984), *Hard-earned Lives; Accounts of Health and Illness from East London* (London: Tavistock Publications).

Cragg, A. and Dawson, T. (1984), *Unemployed Women: A Study of Attitudes and Experiences*, Department of Employment Research Paper No. 47 (London: HMSO).

Craig, C., Garnsey, E. and Rubery, J. (1984), *Payment Structures and Smaller Firms: Women's Employment in Segmented Labour Markets*, Department of Employment Research Paper No. 48 (London: HMSO).

Dale, A. (1987), 'Occupational inequality, gender and the life cycle', *Work, Employment and Society*, vol. 1, no. 3, pp. 326–51.

Daniel, W.W. (1980), *Maternity Rights: The Experience of Women* (London: Policy Studies Institute).

Denzin, N. (1970), *The Research Act in Sociology* (London: Butterworth).

Department of Employment (1988), *Employment for the 1990's* (London: HMSO).

Dex, S. (1984), *The Sexual Division of Work: Conceptual Revolutions in the Social Sciences* (Brighton, Sussex: Wheatsheaf Books).

Dex, S. (1987), *Women's Occupational Mobility: A Lifetime Perspective* (London: Macmillan).

Dex, S. and Shaw, L.B. (1988), 'Women's working lives: a comparison of women in the United States and Great Britain', in A. Hunt (ed.), *Women and Paid Work: Issues of Equality* (Basingstoke: The Macmillan Press).

Doeringer, P. and Piore, M. (1971), *Internal Labour Markets and Manpower Analysis* (Lexington, Mass: D.C. Heath).

Douglas J. (1971), *American Social Order: Social Rules in a Pluralistic Society* (New York: Free Press).

References

Elias, P. (1988), 'Family formation, occupational mobility and part-time work', in A. Hunt (ed.), *Women and Paid Work: Issues of Equality* (Basingstoke: The Macmillan Press). ⁓

Elias, P. and Main, B. (1982), *Women's Working Lives*: evidence from the National Training Survey, Institute for Employment Research, University of Warwick.

Entwistle, D.R. and Doering, S.G. (1980), *The First Birth* (Baltimore; Johns Hopkins University Press).

Evetts, J. (1988), 'Managing childcare and work responsibilities', *Sociological Review*, vol. 36, no. 3, pp. 501–31.

Fielding, N. and Fielding, J. (1986), *Linking Data*: Qualitative Research Network Series 4 (London: Sage).

Finch, J. (1983), *Married to the Job: Wives' Incorporation in Men's Work* (London: Unwin Hyman).

Finch, J. (1989), *Family Obligations and Social Change* (Cambridge: Polity Press).

Frazer, E. (1988), 'Teenage girls talking about class', *Sociology*, vol. 22, no. 3, pp. 343–58.

Gerson, K. (1987), 'How women choose between employment and family: a developmental perspective', in N. Gerstel and H.E. Gross (eds), *Families and Work* (Philadelphia: Temple University Press).

Giddens, A. (1973), *The Class Structure of Advanced Societies* (London: Hutchinson).

Giddens, A. (1976), *New Rules of Sociological Method* (London: Hutchinson).

Giddens, A. (1979), *Central Problems in Social Theory* (London: Macmillan).

Giddens, A. (1987), *Social Theory and Modern Sociology* (Cambridge: Polity Press).

Gilligan, C. (1982), *In a Different Voice: Psychological Theory and Women's Development* (Cambridge, Mass: Harvard University Press).

Gold, D. and Andres, D. (1978a), 'Developmental comparisons between adolescent children with employed and nonemployed mothers', *Merrill-Palmer Quarterly*, vol. 24, pp. 243–54.

Gold, D. and Andres, D. (1978b), 'Developmental comparisons between ten year old children with employed and nonemployed mothers', *Child Development*, vol. 49, pp. 75–84.

Gold, D. and Andres, D. (1978c), 'Relations between maternal employment and development of nursery school children', *Canadian Journal of Behavioral Science*, vol. 10, pp. ‡16–19.

Goldberg, D. and Hillier, V. (1979), 'A scaled version of the General Health Questionnaire', *Psychological Medicine*, vol. 9, pp. 139–45.

Goldthorpe, J., Lockwood, D., Beckhofer, F. and Platt, J. (1968), *The Affluent Worker: Industrial Attitudes and Behaviour* (Cambridge: Cambridge University Press).

Gottfried, A.E. and Gottfried, A.W. (eds) (1988), *Maternal Employment and Children's Development: Longitudinal Research* (New York: Plenum).

Gottlieb, B.H. (ed.) (1981), *Social Networks and Social Support* (Beverley Hills: Sage).

Graham, H. (1987), 'Being poor: perceptions and coping strategies of lone mothers', in J. Brannen and G. Wilson (eds), *Give and Take in Families: Studies in Resource Distribution* (London: Unwin Hyman).

Graham, H. and McKee, I. (1979), *The First Months of Motherhood*, Report on a Health Education Council Project concerned with women's experience of pregnancy, childbirth and the first six months after birth, Mimeographed report: University of York.

Hakim, C. (1979), *Occupational Segregation*, Department of Employment Research Paper No. 9 (London: HMSO).

Halfpenny, P. (1979), 'The analysis of qualitative data', *Sociological Review* vol. 27, no. 4, pp. 799–825.

Hallden, G. (1988), *Parental Belief Systems and Time: Parents' Reflections on Development and Childrearing*, Research Bulletin No. 13, The Institute of Education, University of Stockholm.

Hammersley, M. and Atkinson, P. (1983), *Ethnography: Principles in Practice* (London: Tavistock Publications).

Hardyment, C. (1983), *Dream Babies* (London: Jonathan Cape).

Hertz, R. (1986), *More Equal than Others: Women and Men in Dual-Career Marriages* (Berkeley and Los Angeles: University of California Press).

Hill, M. (1987), *Sharing Child Care in Early Parenthood* (London: Routledge and Kegan Paul).

Hochschild, A. (1989), *The Second Shift: Working Parents and the Revolution at Home* (New York: Viking Penguin).

Hoffman, L. (1961), 'Effects of maternal employment on the child', *Child Development*, vol. 32, pp. 187–97.

Hoffman, L. (1980), 'The effects of maternal employment on the academic attitudes and performance of school-aged childen', *School Psychology Review*, vol. 9, pp. 319–36.

Hoffman, L. (1984), 'Maternal employment and the young child', in M. Perlmutter (ed.), *Minnesota Symposium on Child Psychology* (Hillsdale, N.J: Erlbaum).

Hoffman, L. (1987), 'The effects on children of maternal and paternal employment', in N. Gerstel and H.E. Gross (eds), *Families and Work* (Philadelphia: Temple University Press).

Hoffman, L. (1989), 'The effects of maternal employment on the two-parent family', *American Psychologist*, vol. 44, pp. 283–92.

Hoffman, L. and Nye, F. (eds) (1974), *Working Mothers* (San Francisco: Jossey-Bass).

Horwitz, A. (1977), 'The pathways into psychiatric treatment: differences between men and women', *Journal of Health and Social Behaviour*, vol. 18, pp. 169–78.

Hurstfield, J. (1987), *Part-timers Under Pressure* (London: Low Pay Unit).

Hymes, D. (1971), 'On communication competence', in J. Pride and J. Homes (eds), *Sociolinguistics* (Harmondsworth: Allen Lane).

IDS (Income Data Services) (1985), *Maternity and Paternity Leave (Study 351)* (London: IDS).

Jephcott, P., with Seear, N. and Smith J. (1962), *Married Women Working* (London: Allen and Unwin).

Joshi, H. (1984), 'Women's participation in paid work: further analysis of the women and employment survey', Department of Employment Research Paper No. 45 (London: HMSO).

Joshi, H. (1987), 'The cost of caring', in C. Glendinning and J. Miller (eds), *Women and Poverty in Britain* (Brighton, Sussex: Harvester Press).

Jowell, R., Witherspoon, S. and Brook, L. (eds) (1988), *British Social Attitudes: The 5th Report* (Aldershot: Gower).

Kappel, B.E. and Lambert, R.D. (1972), 'Self worth among the children of working mothers', University of Waterloo, Ontario.

Kessler, R.C. and McRae, J.A. (1981), 'Trends in the relationship between sex and psychological distress: 1957–1976', *American Sociological Review*, vol. 46, pp. 443–52.

Kliger, D. (1954), 'The effects of employment of married women on husband and wife roles: a study of cultural change', PhD dissertation, Yale University.

Laumann, E.O. (1973), *Bonds of Pluralism: The Form and Substance of Urban Social Networks* (New York: Wiley).

Leavy, R.L. (1983), 'Social support and psychological disorder: a review', *Journal of Community Psychology* vol. 11, pp. 3–21.

Lee, N.H. (1969), *The Search for an Abortionist* (Chicago: University of Chicago Press).

Lewis, S. and Cooper, C. (1988), 'Stress in dual-earner families', in B. Gutek, A. Stromberg and Larwood (eds), *Women and Work: An Annual Review*, Vol. 3 (London: Sage).

Lilestrom, R. (1981), 'The public child, the commercial child, and our child', in F.S. Kessel and A.W. Siegel (eds), *The Child and Other Cultural Inventions* (New York: Praeger).

Lindesmith, A.R. (1968), *Additives and Opiates* (Chicago: Aldine).

Mansfield, P. and Collard, J. (1988), *The Beginning of the Rest of your Life: A Portrait of Newly Wed Marriage* (London: Macmillan).

Marsh, G. and Kaim-Caudle, P. (1976), *Team Care in General Practice* (London: Croom Helm).

Martin, J. and Roberts, C. (1984), *Women and Employment: A Lifetime Perspective*, The Report of the 1980 DE/OPCS Women and Employment Survey (London: HMSO).

Mayall, B. and Petrie, P. (1983), *Childminding and Day Nurseries: What Kind of Care?* (London: Heinemann Educational).

McCartney, K. and Phillips, D. (1988), 'Mother and Childcare' in B. Burns and D. Hay (eds), *Different Faces of Motherhood* (New York: Plenum).

McGee, R., Williams, S., Kashani, J. and Silva, P.A. (1983), 'Prevalence of self-reported depressive symptoms and associated social factors in

269

mothers in Dunedin', *Psychological Medicine*, vol. 7, pp. 641–52.

McKee, L. (1987), 'Households during unemployment: the resourcefulness of the unemployed' in J. Brannen and G. Wilson (eds), *Give and Take in Families: Studies in Resource Distribution* (London: Unwin Hyman).

McKinlay, J.B. (1973), 'Social networks, lay consultations and help seeking behaviour', *Social Forces*, vol. 51, pp. 275–91.

Melhuish, E. and Moss P. (eds) (1990), *Day Care for Young Children; International Perspectives* (London: Routledge, Chapman and Hall).

Melhuish, E. (1990), 'Research on day care for young children', in E. Melhuish and P. Moss (eds), *Day Care for Young Children: International Perspectives* (London: Routledge, Chapman and Hall).

Miller, L. (1988), *Violent Families and the Rhetoric of Harmony* (Calgary: University of Calgary).

Mitchell, J.C. (ed.) (1969), *Social Networks in Urban Situations* (Manchester: Manchester University Press).

Mitchell, J.C. (1986), *The Quality of Urban Life* (Berlin: Walter de Gruyter).

Mitchell, J.C. (1987), 'The components of strong ties among homeless women', *Social Networks*, vol. 9, pp. 37–47.

Moen, P. (1989), *Working Parents: Transformations in Gender Roles and Public Policies in Sweden* (London: Adamantine Press).

Morgan, D.H.J. (1975), *Social Theory and the Family* (London: Routledge and Kegan Paul).

Morgan, D.H.J. (1985), *The Family, Politics and Social Theory* (London: Routledge and Kegan Paul).

Morris, L. (1984), 'Redundancy and patterns of household finance', *Sociological Review*, vol. 32, no. 3, pp. 492–523.

Morris, L. with Ruane, S. (1989), *Household Financial Management and the Labour Market* (Aldershot: Gower).

Moss P. (1986), *Child Care in the Early Months: How Child Care Arrangements are Made for Babies*, TCRU Occasional Paper No. 6 (London: Thomas Coram Research Unit).

Moss, P. (1987), *A Review of Childminding Research*, TCRU Working and Occasional Paper No. 6 (London: Thomas Coram Research Unit).

Moss. P. (1988), *Childcare and Equality of Opportunity: Consolidated Report to the European Commission* (Commission of the European Communities).

Moss, P. (1990), 'Daycare for young children in the United Kingdom', in E. Melhuish and P. Moss (eds), *Day Care for Young Children: International Perspectives* (London: Routledge, Chapman and Hall).

Moss, P. and Brannen, J. (1987), 'Fathers' employment', in C. Lewis and M. O'Brien (eds), *Reassessing Fatherhood: New Observations on Fathers and the Modern Family* (London: Sage).

Moss, P. and Fonda, N. (1980), *Work and Family* (London: Temple Smith).

Moss, P., Bolland, G. and Foxman, R. (1980), *Transition to Parenthood,*

Report on a DHSS-funded project, Mimeographed report, Thomas Coram Research Unit.

Moss, P., Bolland, G. and Foxman, R. (1987), 'The division of household work during the transition to parenthood', *Journal of Reproductive and Infant Psychology* vol. 5, pp. 71–86.

Myrdal, A. and Klein, V. (1970), *Women's Two Roles* (London: Routledge and Kegan Paul).

Newson, J. and Newson, E. (1963), *Infant Care in the Urban Community* (London: Allen & Unwin).

Oakley, A. (1974), *The Sociology of Housework* (Oxford: Martin Robertson).

Oakley, A. (1980), *Women Confined; Towards a Sociology of Childbirth* (Oxford: Martin Robertson).

Oakley, A. (1986), 'Feminism, motherhood and medicine – who cares?' in J. Mitchell and A. Oakley (eds), *What is Feminism?* (Oxford: Blackwell).

Oakley, A. and Rajan, L. (forthcoming), 'Social class and social support: the same or different?'.

OPCS (Office of Population Censuses and Surveys) (1985), *General Household Survey 1983* (London: HMSO).

OPCS (Office of Population Censuses and Surveys) (1987), *General Household Survey 1985* (London: HMSO).

OPCS (Office of Population Censuses and Surveys) (1989), *General Household Survey 1987* (London: HMSO).

Pahl, J. (1980), 'Patterns of money management within marriage', *Journal of Social Policy*, vol. 9, no. 3, pp. 313–35.

Pahl. J. (1983), 'The allocation of money and the structuring of inequality within marriage', *Sociological Review*, vol. 31, no. 2, pp. 237–62.

Pahl. R. (1984), *Divisions of Labour* (Oxford: Basil Blackwell).

Parnes, H.S. (1970), *Dual Careers: A Longitudinal Study of the Labour Market Experience of Women*, Manpower Research Monograph. 1 (Washington, DC: Government Printing Office).

Parry, G. (1986), 'Paid employment, life events, social support and mental health in working-class mothers', *Journal of Health and Social Behaviour*, vol. 27, pp. 193–208.

Parsons, T. and Bales, R.F. (1956), *Family Socialization and Interaction Process* (London: Routledge and Kegan Paul).

Pearlin, L.I. and Johnson, J.S. (1977), 'Marital status, life strains and depression', *American Journal of Sociology*, vol. 42, pp. 704–15.

Pearlin, L. and Schooler, C. (1978), 'The structure of coping', *Journal of Health and Social Behaviour*, vol. 19, pp. 2–21.

Pendleton, B.F., Paloma, M.M. and Garland, T.N. (1982), 'An approach to quantifying the needs of dual career families', *Human Relations*, vol. 35, no. 1, pp. 69–82.

Phillips, A. and Taylor, B. (1980), 'Sex and skill: notes towards a feminist economics', *Feminist Review*, vol. 6, pp. 79–88.

Phillips, D. (1990), 'Day care for young children in the United States',

271

in E. Melhuish and P. Moss (eds), *Day Care for Young Children: International Perspectives* (London: Routledge, Chapman and Hall).

Platt, J. (1988), 'What can case studies do?' in R.G. Burgess (ed.), *Studies in Qualitative Methodology* (London: Jai Press).

Pleck, J. (1985), *Working Wives/Working Husbands* (Beverly Hills: Sage).

Plewis, I. (1985), *Analysing Change: Measurement and Explanation using Longitudinal Data* (London: Wiley).

Rapoport, R. and Rapoport, R.N. (1969), 'The dual earner family: a variant pattern and social change', *Human Relations*, vol. 22, no. 4, pp. 3–30.

Rapoport, R. and Rapoport R.N. (1971), *Dual Career Families* (Harmondsworth: Penguin).

Rapoport, R. and Rapoport R.N. (eds) (1976), *Working Couples* (London: Routledge and Kegan Paul).

Rapoport, R.N., Fogarty, M.P. and Rapoport, R. (eds) (1982), *Families in Britain* (London: Routledge and Kegan Paul).

Richards, M.P., Dunn, J.F. and Antonis, B. (1977), 'Caretaking in the first year of life', *Child: Care, Health and Development*, vol. 3, pp. 23–6.

Rimmer, L. (1980), 'The distribution of income within the family', Paper prepared for SSRC Social Security Workshop, September.

Rose, P. (1985), *Parallel Lives: Five Victorian Marriages* (Harmondsworth: Penguin).

Rosenberg, M. (1965), *Society and Adolescent Self Image* (Princeton: Princeton University Press).

Russell, G. (1983), *The Changing Role of Fathers* (St Lucia, Queensland: University of Queensland Press).

Schaeffer, S., Coyne, J.C. Lazarus, R.S. (1981), 'The health-related functions of social support', *Journal of Behavioural Medicine*, vol. 4, no. 4, pp. 381–405.

Schmidt, D. (1987), 'Daycare services in Denmark', unpublished National Report for the European Commission Childcare Network, European Commission, Brussels.

Schutze, Y. (1988), 'The good mother: the history of the normative model "mother love"', in *Growing up in a Modern World*, Proceedings of an International Disciplinary Conference on the Life and Development of Children in Modern Society, Vol. 1, Trondheim, Norway.

Select Committee of the European Communities (1985), *Parental Leave and Leave for Family Reasons* (London, HMSO).

Selye, H. (1956), *The Stress of Life* (New York: McGraw-Hill).

Sharpe, S. (1984), *Double Identity*: The lives of working mothers (Harmondsworth: Penguin).

Stacey, M. (1981), 'The division of labour revisited or overcoming the two Adams', in P. Abrams, R. Deem, J. Finch, and P. Rock (eds), *Practice and Progress: British Sociology 1950–80* (London: George Allen and Unwin).

Stamp, P. (1985), 'Research note: balance of financial power in marriage:

an exploratory study of breadwinning wives', *Sociological Review*, vol. 33, pp. 546–66.

Thornes, B. and Collard, C. (1979), *Who Divorces?* (London: Routledge and Kegan Paul).

Tivers, J. (1985), *Women Attached: The Daily Lives of Women with Young Children* (London: Croom Helm).

Tizard, B. (1986), *The Care of Young Children*, Thomas Coram Research Unit Occasional Paper No. 1 (London: Thomas Coram Research Unit).

Urwin, C. (1985), 'Constructing motherhood: the persuasion of normal development', in C. Steedman, C. Urwin and V. Walkerdine (eds), *Language, Gender and Childhood* (London: Routledge and Kegan Paul).

Vedel-Petersen, J. (1988), 'Childcare policies and programs in Denmark', Paper given to 'Workshop on Child Care policies and Programs: International Perspectives', organized for the National Academy of Sciences' Panel on Child Care Policy, August 1988, Woods Hole, Mass.

Voysey, M. (1975), *A Constant Burden* (London: Routledge and Kegan Paul).

Weiss, R.S. (1969), The Fund of Sociability, *Transaction*, vol. 6, pp. 36–43.

Wallman, S. (1985), *Eight London Households* (London: Tavistock).

White, M. (1983), *Long-term Unemployment and Labour Markets* (London: Policy Studies Institute).

Wilson, G. (1987), 'Money: patterns of responsibility and irresponsibility in marriage', in J. Brannen and G. Wilson (eds), *Give and Take in Families: Studies in Resource Distribution* (London: Unwin Hyman).

Wilson, G. (1987), *Women and Money: The Distribution of Resources and Responsibilities in the Family* (Aldershot: Gower).

Winnicott, P.M. (1962), *The Child and the Outside World* (London: Tavistock).

Working for Childcare (1990), *Meeting the Childcare Challenge: Can the Market Provide?* (London: Working for Childcare).

Yeandle, S. (1984), *Women's Working Lives: Patterns and Strategies* (London: Tavistock).

Yudkin, S. and Holme, A. (1963), *Working Mothers and Their Children* (London: Michael Joseph).

273

Index

For Product Safety Concerns and Information please contact our EU
representative GPSR@taylorandfrancis.com
Taylor & Francis Verlag GmbH, Kaufingerstraße 24, 80331 München, Germany

www.ingramcontent.com/pod-product-compliance
Lightning Source LLC
Chambersburg PA
CBHW071843270326
41929CB00013B/2088